DOG CREEK

A PLACE IN THE CARIBOO

HILARY PLACE

Heritage House

Copyright © 1999 Hilary Place

Canadian Cataloguing in Publication Data

Place, Hilary, 1920-
    Dog Creek

    Includes index.
    ISBN 1-895811-70-8

    1. Place, Hilary, 1920-   2. Cariboo Region (B.C.)—
Biography. 3. Frontier and pioneer life—British Columbia—
Cariboo Region. 4. Dog Creek (B.C.)—History. I. Title.
FC3845.C3Z48 1999   971.1'7503'092   C99-910164-1
F1089.C3P52 1999

First edition 1999

Heritage House wishes to acknowledge the support of Heritage Canada
through the Book Publishing Industry Development Program, the
British Columbia Arts Council, the Canada Council for the Arts, and
the British Columbia Archives and Records Services (BCARS).

Cover and book design: Darlene Nickull
Editors: Audrey McClellan, Janine Sutherland

HERITAGE HOUSE PUBLISHING COMPANY LTD.
Unit #8 - 17921 55th Ave., Surrey, BC V3S 6C4

Printed in Canada

Dedication

I dedicate this book to my wife, Rita, who has been with me through thick and thin since 1942; and to my three sons, Adrian, Martin, and Carmen, who have always been a pride and joy; and to my grandchildren, Raylene, Renelle, Rylea, Sara, Cecilia, and Logan.

Acknowledgements

I would like to acknowledge the help I have received from the following people in the writing of this book. Again Rita must be remembered for being the sounding board and prompter. Thanks to my friend Dr. Jack Mills, whose red pencil did remarkable things for clarity and presentation. Thanks to my son Martin, who produced the copies of the photographs by some magic computer shenanigans and also got me a computer to work on. I must mention the patience and consideration that was accorded to me by Rodger Touchie of Heritage House Publishing Co. and by the editors, Audrey McClellan and Janine Sutherland. All the people at Heritage House have been most helpful and kind.

Most of all I would like to acknowledge the people of the Cariboo and particularly the people of Dog Creek, who shared their lives with me in that small and remote valley so many years ago. I hope this book reflects the love and appreciation I have for you all.

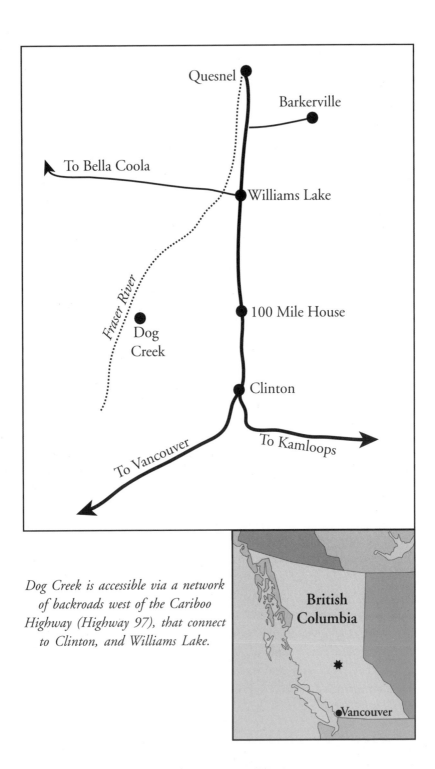

Quesnel

Barkerville

To Bella Coola

Williams Lake

Fraser River

Dog Creek

100 Mile House

Clinton

To Vancouver

To Kamloops

Dog Creek is accessible via a network of backroads west of the Cariboo Highway (Highway 97), that connect to Clinton, and Williams Lake.

British Columbia

Vancouver

Contents

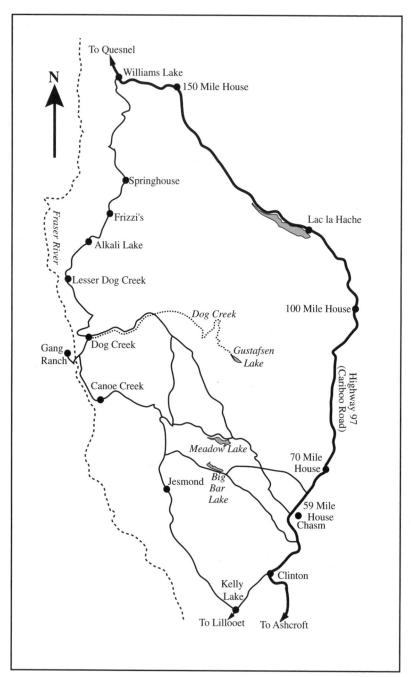

The southern Cariboo showing backroad access to Dog Creek.

PROLOGUE

There were two things that prompted me to sit down and write these scribblings. The first was when one of my granddaughters asked me, "What did you watch on television when you were young, Grandpa?" The other was when I filled in for a guest speaker at a real estate company meeting in Vancouver by giving a short talk on business in the Cariboo. A young salesman came up to me afterwards and said, "Do you expect me to believe you bought fur for the Hudson's Bay Company? Who do you think you are, Daniel Boone or something?"

It stuck in my mind that they simply did not understand the difference that a few years and a few miles can make in lifestyles.

My granddaughter was very young at the time and didn't realize that television had not been invented when I was her age and would not be available for many years to come. The same availability applied to telephones, radios, automobiles, refrigerators, indoor plumbing, electricity, and so many other things that we take for granted today.

There was little communication outside of our home area and consequently we got to know the few people around us very well. They were like all people. There were good and bad sides to them all and that is the way I have tried to present them, as the saying goes "With warts and all." Some were heroic almost beyond belief and some were not. We often find ourselves loving the ones that were not more than we do the worthy, but that is human nature.

I made up my mind that I would try to give an honest portrayal of these people so that my grandchildren and the readers of this book will have some idea of the conditions under which we lived in those days and the type of people that were there.

There were all kinds of people that came to Dog Creek and all were welcome in our home. Some were world famous and some, during the 1930s, were hoboes with packs on their backs. I will always remember one young fellow who arrived at our table at suppertime. My brother Geoff wanted to quit school and was arguing about it at the table. My Mother turned to the young guest and asked him what he thought. His reply was, "An education is a lot easier to pack around than that roll of blankets. See that packsack? Well it's got everything I own in the world in it and it ain't very heavy."

Nobody passed our door hungry. During the 1930s that was quite an accomplishment, for which my Dad received scant praise. I salute him here for his efforts and also my Mother, who treated all guests alike and well.

A storyteller must start somewhere and the Cariboo started in Barkerville, so we will start there.

CHAPTER 1

EARLY DAYS

When Barkerville got established in the 1860s with its sizeable population, it presented a considerable challenge to the packers who supplied it with everything a bustling young city required. There were literally armies of men and animals transporting everything imaginable, from staples like flour, rice, sugar, and beans, to such items as French champagne and grand pianos. Stories are still told of the ways the packers overcame the weather, mud, ice, snow, mosquitoes,

Old Robbins with pack horses at Dog Creek (right). You can see how the packs were set up on the horse in the foreground. Below, Jean Caux's mule pack train is seen at W.B. Bailey's warehouse in Ashcroft.

and God knows what else during these trips back and forth from Yale to Barkerville. Winter would eventually close in and the pack trains would have to stop until spring.

It is interesting to note that the route the packers took was not the same as the Cariboo Road, especially from Clinton north. Most people believe that the route went past the roadhouses of 70 Mile, 83 Mile, 100 Mile, 150 Mile, and on to Soda Creek where the road goes today, but that was not so. One of the considerations that the packers had to deal with was feed for their pack animals. The route past the roadhouses was heavily timbered and did not have good grass for the horses to eat, so although it was relatively level and easy travelling, it was not suitable. The route used by the majority of packers stayed close to the Fraser River. It was a more arduous journey as they had to climb in and out of the various valleys, but it had the advantage over the other route because it had some of the finest bunch grass flats in the country.

Naturally the packers would keep going as long as they could in the fall, fighting their way out of Barkerville at the last minute before they were snowed in, with their horses in belly-high snow. They would head downriver to the "dry belt," where their horses could paw through the snow and get enough feed for the winter. There is a great climatic variation in the Cariboo, almost as if there were a line drawn through Soda Creek. Everything north of Soda Creek is in the wet belt and receives three or four times the amount of precipitation the area south of Soda Creek does. The packers found ideal wintering conditions at Soda Creek, Williams Lake, Chimney Creek, Alkali Lake, Dog Creek, Canoe Creek, Big Bar, and so on downriver towards Lillooet.

You will notice that all the places mentioned are on the east side of the river. There is good reason for this. The Shuswap people who occupied the east side of the river were a friendly group that welcomed the white man and in fact helped the whites cope with the exigencies of the country. The Chilcotins, who occupied the west side of the river, were decidedly unfriendly and did not want the white man on that side of the river at all. (With considerable justification, I might add.) Consequently, each packer would come down the east side of the river from Barkerville until he found suitable pasture for his stock and settled there for the winter. He would build a cabin to keep out the elements and more often than not would find an Indian girl to keep him company. It wasn't long before she was building a home and a family for her man. He would make his summer trips back and forth from Yale to Barkerville and she would stay and look after the cabin and the children. Soon she would be growing a garden and a bit of hay for their saddle horses, and before you knew it, a small ranch had started. As the packer grew older, the trips with the pack horses became more arduous and the temptation to stay home and cater to the other packers' needs became more attractive. Often he would settle down and start a small store or stopping house or blacksmithing business rather than fight the elements on the trail. Usually these endeavours were accompanied by a small ranch-type operation that sustained the family.

This is how a great number of the famous pioneering Cariboo ranches started. It is an ironic fact that quite a number of the men who started the ranches in the manner that I have described, when they had reached such a degree of prosperity that they could afford to travel back to their home country, would make the trip. Often they brought back a white wife, and the Indian woman and the children from that association would be unceremoniously booted out, back to the reserve, while the new wife took over the domain that the Native wife had helped build. That is why even to this day we often find two families of the same name, one on the ranch and one on the reserve. Of course there were some men who did not perform this rather immoral and unethical deed and did stay with their Indian wife and raised their families well. Such men were not honoured in those times but were chastised for being "Indian lovers" and looked down upon by the rest of the society.

Dog Creek was one of the areas where there was good winter feed for pack animals. It was therefore one of the communities that started in the manner that I have described. During the 1860s, 1870s, and 1880s there were a great number of packers using the area as a wintering place for their pack trains. The old pack trail went right through Dog Creek, so it was convenient and accessible.

My grandfather, Joseph Smith Place, a carpenter and storekeeper, arrived at Dog Creek in the early 1880s. When he got there he found a thriving settlement of several hundred people. There were three large stores, four hotels, a dance hall, two houses of ill repute, and cabins all over the place from the River Ranch to Rabbit Park. Remember that at this time there was not much at Vancouver, which did not exist until 1885. Some of the old-timers of the Dog Creek community were Nels Gustafsen, Twentymen, Bill Wright, Pierre Colin, Raphael Valenzuela, Jean Caux (known as "Cataline," his province of birth), Magnus Meason, and Gaspar de Versepeuch. They were great old tough characters, each with a story to tell. Also there was a large Chinese population, about 100 people, that mined the banks of the Fraser River and built an incredible ditch that ran several miles

Jean Caux, one of the early packers, always took half of his drink of whisky and rubbed it into his scalp. "Growa da hair," he said, and it looks like he was right.

up the west side of the river from Gaspard Creek. Chinese miners directed water from the ditch into sluice boxes, where they washed the gravel of the bench lands for gold. The ditch is clearly visible to this day.

J.S. Place was born in Bury, Lancashire, England, on January 24, 1854. Nobody around today seems to know what motivated this individual to come to North America and eventually to Canada. I know that he had a sound grade school education, probably until he was fourteen. My parents told me he was an apprentice carpenter. After coming to this country he married Alice Coxon, the daughter of the stopping house owner at Nicomen, but she died after two children were born, a boy named George and a girl named Alice. After J.S.'s wife's death, her mother took the two children and raised them, first

Nicomen House in the 1870s when it was owned by John Clapperton (above). He sold it to George Coxon later in the decade.

taking them to England and then to San Francisco. J.S. Place apparently inherited the Nicomen house from his father-in-law, George Coxon, in about 1884 and sold it shortly after. It appears that there was some bad feeling involved here, for to my knowledge my Grandfather never had contact with the Coxon family again on a personal basis. I do have a copy of a letter that he wrote to his lawyer, telling the lawyer how to make sure that George and Alice were properly treated in the distribution of some funds, but that is the only record we have that they exist. No member of his later family ever contacted the first Place progeny.

My parents said that J.S. Place once had a store in Nicomen and they believed he also had one later in Yale. I have no idea how he got to Dog Creek except that Dog Creek was on the regular pack trail and it would be natural for him to follow it. In any event, he got there and bought a store formerly owned by a Chinese man. J.S., as everyone called him, was five foot nine, a solid man, physically quite strong. He was pleasant by nature and "one of the boys." He was a better than average singer and enjoyed the impromptu concerts that were in vogue in that day. He was a fine-looking man, always neatly dressed, with blondish hair, piercing blue eyes, full beard. Under all this exterior affability was a hard-driving businessman and manager.

He wasn't long at Dog Creek before he started to buy out the interests of those around him, first one and then another of the Chinese-owned stores, then a few acres of property, then one of the hotels. About this time he felt he was well enough established as a merchant to take a wife. He found her on one of his many trips to Victoria to buy supplies for his store. She was Jane Ann Beaumont, not long out from England and the governess for Sir James Douglas's grandchildren.

Jane Ann Beaumont was a tall girl and quite big and strong. She was typical of that Victorian age, being devout and strait-laced, severe and unrelenting in her views of right and wrong. This attitude was sometimes a problem in the rather unstructured and free life of the Cariboo, but she never faltered in her resolve and never changed. She was a terrific worker and contributed greatly to the fortunes of the Place family in later years.

Jane Ann and J.S. were married from the Douglas home in Victoria in 1887. Sir James Douglas's son gave the bride away as none of her family were present, and Lady Douglas gave her a beautiful brooch as a present. It is still a prized family possession today. They went by boat to Yale and then by horseback from Yale to Dog Creek. Jane Ann rode sidesaddle all that way. I still have the saddle she rode. One can only wonder at the courage and strength of those pioneers!

When J.S. and his bride arrived at Dog Creek, their home consisted of a room over the store, which was located in a two-storey log building. It later became a hotel and eventually my family's ranch home. The logs were huge and had been broad-axed so that they were flat on each side, and the corners were dovetailed. A Mexican horse wrangler named Raphael Valenzuela built it in 1860. An addition was added later, also of logs, and eventually a new kitchen, meathouse, and laundry room, all of frame construction, completed the building.

Dog Creek Hotel and Store in the 1880s, with a good view of the log addition. The bystanders are not identified.

Dog Creek House about 1900. Standing in front, from left to right, are Napoleon Mondada, Old Robbins, John Williams, J.S. Place, Prosper Gaspard, and Beaumont Haig.

*J.S. and Jane Place in the yard by the hotel in about 1908,
the high point of their Dog Creek days.*

The new Mrs. Place found the downstairs of her new home taken
up with the store and the living quarters. The upstairs was one big
room. It contained an iron bed, a cookstove, a table, and some wooden
chairs. Several nails driven into the log walls served as pegs on which
hung a saddle and a few sets of harness. Some axes and shovels were
leaned up in one corner. It is to her credit that she didn't get on her
horse and head back to Yale immediately. Instead she set to work and
over the years built a beautiful home of some 21 rooms out of a very
rough start.

Soon after their marriage the Places started to prosper. Within a
few years J.S. had bought up many of the small holdings around him,
including the River Ranch from Nels Gustafsen, all the stores and
hotels in the little village, the Gaspard Ranch, the View Ranch, Lesser
Dog Creek from the Measons, and the U.S. Meadow from Bill Wright.
He owned just about all of the Dog Creek valley except the Pigeon
Ranch. All this property was in addition to a flour mill, said to be the
first on the mainland of B.C., and a sawmill, a large store business, a
stage line to Clinton and Ashcroft, and a prosperous hotel and bar.

Mrs. Place abhorred the bar business and would enter the bar only to distribute temperance literature and berate the "boys" on the evils of alcohol, much to their silent delight. When she got too carried away, J.S. would escort her out and the merriment would continue on into the night. By 1908 the Place Ranch was considered to be one of the largest and best-equipped ranches in the province.

The Places had six children, two of whom died in infancy. The surviving three sons—Frank, Joe, and Charlie—and one daughter—Annie—lived their lives mostly in the Cariboo. Annie was a beautiful woman, educated at finishing school in Vancouver. Not only did she have the social graces of a debutante, but she could also ride a rough horse and cowboy with the best of the men. She wasn't long out of school when she married a young banker from Ashcroft named Frank Lindsay. They had two children, Douglas and Doris.

Lindsay left the bank and started up an automobile transportation company that was intended to link Ashcroft and Soda Creek. Soda Creek was the terminus of the riverboat system that ran north to Quesnel and Fort George and beyond. The auto transportation scheme did not prove a financial success, probably because it was ahead of its time. Eventually Lindsay got into serious financial trouble and at one point was accused of forging some documents This caused a great hullabaloo in the family, and Annie cried to J.S. to help her husband out. The upshot was that J.S. paid off the debt of some several thousand dollars and took over the assets of the Auto Transit Company. He found himself the proud owner of three great big old cars—a 1908 Winton of 60 horsepower and two 1910 Oldsmobiles, one 60 horsepower and one 90—and a mortgage that would eventually jump up and bite him.

Fortunately J.S.'s oldest son, Frank, was mechanically minded and took over the operation of the cars, but it didn't take J.S. long to figure out that the automobile transportation business on the Cariboo Road was a few years ahead of itself and he quickly shut the operation down. He took the cars back to the ranch, where they were put to private use. Lindsay and Annie parted and were divorced. The whole affair eventually cost J.S. his life's work, but despite this downside the operation established the Places as pioneers in the automobile transportation industry in the Cariboo.

DOG CREEK HOTEL
DOG CREEK, B. C.
J. S. PLACE, - - - PROPRIETOR

My Mother's name appears on the bottom line of this page of the Dog Creek Hotel register, marking her arrival on April 2, 1914.

CHAPTER 2

A Trip to Dog Creek

My Mother would say, especially when she was in an obstreperous mood, that she arrived at Dog Creek on April Fool's Day in 1914, but in fact her name appears in the old Dog Creek Hotel register on April 2, a much less contentious day. She was a good storyteller, and over the years she recounted many times, to me and to other people, the story of her meeting with my Grandmother in Ashcroft, the terminus of the Dog Creek Stage, and her arduous trip on that stage.

It sounds like Mrs. J.S. Place was a bit of a character, a big woman and obviously very set in her ways and determined in her outlook. She had known Ada's mother back in Huddersfield, England, where they had gone to school together. When she heard there was a girl from Yorkshire staying with friends in Nanaimo, she made some inquiries and found out she knew the girl's mother. She wrote and invited Ada to visit a ranch in the Cariboo and Ada accepted.

Dog Creek House in 1910, just a few years before my Mother arrived. There were some cars in the area by that time, but they were few and far between, and not as reliable as the horse-drawn stage.

When Mrs. Place met Ada at the train in Ashcroft, for just a minute there was a tear in her eye and a catch in her throat as she recalled her childhood in England. Quickly the control she had learned over the years of pioneering in the tough Cariboo country returned and the softness faded from her face, but in that brief moment Ada had found a friend and an object for her respect, love, and admiration during the ensuing years at Dog Creek.

Mrs. Place "harrumphed" at Ada's clothes, which were the latest fashion from New York. Ada had lived there for a year, recuperating from a bout of pneumonia and a broken engagement. Mrs. Place particularly "harrumphed" at the high-heeled, pearl-grey, high-topped shoes with the buttons up the side. No doubt she was picturing them slopping through the mudholes on the way into the ranch, but she held her tongue and didn't say anything about it.

They had a nice supper at the Ashcroft Hotel, owned and operated by Mr. William Lyne, and afterwards they went for a short walk to visit Mr. and Mrs. Arthur Haddock. They returned to the hotel early and retired for the night. They had to get up for breakfast at 4:30 a.m.

Ada didn't sleep too well that night. She was excited about the trip to Dog Creek and the prospect of seeing a large cattle ranch. She had read all kinds of stories about the Wild West, with cowboys and Indians and stagecoaches and holdups, and these kept turning over and over in her head all night. She must have slept finally, because the minute she reached oblivion there was a pounding on her door and Mrs. Place was there, calling for her to get up. They had a quick breakfast and were ready to go by 5:30 a.m.

The stage was pulled up in front of the Ashcroft Hotel. There were four horses hitched to a democrat with two seats. The driver and a Chinese man were sitting on the front seat, and another man was holding the bridles of the lead team. The horses were restless, jumping around and pawing the ground. All of the young men from the livery stable and most of the guests from the hotel were lined up on the porch and wooden sidewalk in front of the hotel to see the little English girl who was with Mrs. Place. There was much laughter and banter. The young men were posturing and showing off in the hope that they might earn a look from the young lady when she came out to get into the democrat.

A Trip to Dog Creek

Finally they emerged, Mrs. Place in the lead, Ada following. Ada hadn't been on the stage as a dancer in England for nothing. She knew when she had an audience, and she responded immediately. On went her best smile and she swept the appreciative crowd with her most bewitching look. The "Boys" responded with hoots and hollers, backslaps and jumps. Ada loved it all. She had them in the palm of her hand and would have continued, but Mrs. Place was "not amused." She ordered Ada into the back seat of the democrat. The hotel clerk, white shirt, red armbands, and all, threw the suitcases into the back of the rig. The driver hollered, "Let her go," and the man holding the bridles let loose.

Away they went. With dust flying, dogs barking, chickens squawking, all the "Boys" waving their hats and hollering, the wagon rolled down the street, around the corner, and out across the bridge over the beautiful blue-green waters of the Thompson River, the horses galloping and shying and testing the skill of the driver to the limit.

They started up the Ashcroft hill at a fast pace, but soon the horses slowed down under the strain of the full load. There were supplies for the store at Dog Creek—rice, sugar, beans, some hardware—and of course the mail bags for Jesmond, Canoe Creek, Dog Creek, and Alkali Lake were stashed under the seats and piled high in the back end, covered with heavy canvas and lashed down with rope. Along with the passengers it made quite a weight. The horses started to sweat and the driver had to stop occasionally to let them get their wind. It was at the first stop that Ada looked back along the road and over the magnificent Thompson River valley.

What a sight it was. The sun was tipping the hills with gold, and the hills themselves were like dark soft velvet, with the old dry grasses softening the contours so the hills blended into the sky in the far distance. The blue-green Thompson River glided and tumbled over the whitened rocks past the sleepy little village of Ashcroft. The hills rose from the river, fold on fold covered with dark evergreen forest, to where little patches of white snow bore witness to the recent winter. Beyond were the mountains that remained snowcapped forever.

Ada was captivated by it all. She always got a lump in her throat when such beauty confronted her. It reminded her of the Yorkshire moors with their rolling majesty and soft colours. She fell silent.

Mrs. Place broke the silence by introducing Ada to the driver, Billy Meggot. Ada was to have a good friend in Billy in later years, but now he was very much the hired help as far as Mrs. Place was concerned. He was like a lot of men in the Cariboo in those days—an adventurer seeking the excitement and freedom of the western frontier. It seems that Billy and his father, the mayor of some city in Ontario, did not see eye to eye on what Billy should be, so Billy took off for points west and ended up at Dog Creek driving stage. Ada didn't know it, but this was Billy's second trip as driver of the stage. He was polite to Ada but reserved. Mrs. Place did not countenance much association between her guests, especially her young lady guests, and the hired help, especially handsome young buckaroos like Billy. Billy was well aware of the situation and acted accordingly, but he managed to get in a few swift looks and the odd smile when the old girl wasn't looking.

The Chinese gentleman sat on the front seat with the driver and didn't say a word. Ada was always one to talk to everyone, so she addressed herself to him. He answered her politely in almost perfect English. She inquired what brought him out here from China, and he told her he was on a special mission. Then he would say no more. Ada thought that this was a bit unfriendly, but she had also heard that the Chinese were an inscrutable lot so she didn't press the matter.

She would probably have fainted if he had told her his mission. He was out to gather up the bones of the Chinese men who had died and been buried in this country and to ship them home to China for burial there. On its next trip down to Ashcroft from Dog Creek the stage would be loaded with innumerable little bags of bones, all ticketed and tagged for shipment back to their homeland, accompanied by Ada's inscrutable friend. The Chinese gentleman was very understanding of the little English girl's sensitivity and spared her the horror of spending three days on the road with a ghoul and graverobber. English girls did not understand that sort of thing.

The horses were soon rested and they were off again. Shortly they found themselves hanging, seemingly by a thread, on the cliffs over the Bonaparte River. Ada took one look over her side, which was closest to the drop of at least a thousand feet, and let out a "yipe!" that could have been heard for miles if there had been anyone to hear it. The road was barely wide enough for the wagon. The horses trotted along at a

A Trip to Dog Creek

This is the BC Express Stage near Ashcroft in 1898, about 15 years before my Mother made the trip to Dog Creek. You get a sense of the kind of country she was travelling through—quite a change for a girl who grew up in England.

good clip and the wagon wheels knocked little rocks over the edge. These went bounding down the mountainside to the muddy river below. Ada gasped and held her breath until they were out of the danger zone and up on the flats headed for Cache Creek.

Lunch was at Hat Creek, where Mrs. Place visited with old friends, and then they climbed back into the stage for the rest of the day's journey to Clinton. Once they had climbed Twenty Mile Hill the roadway was no longer dry but alternated between mud out in the sunshine, and ice and snow in the shade. The wagon wheels cut down through the mud and snow, which made the load twice as hard to pull as it was on the dry roadbed. Billy was an excellent horseman and got the best out of the teams in front of him, but the muck slowed the going down and it began to seem longer and longer to Clinton.

Finally they rounded a curve and passed a little salt lake, and Clinton came into view. The horses got a new lease on life and trotted up to the Clinton Hotel. Mud was streaming from the wheels and had splattered up onto the buffalo robes spread over the passengers. They dismounted from the rig and found their legs were shaky from sitting for so long.

The Clinton Hotel was one of the oldest hotels in British Columbia. It began operation in the early 1860s and had been in continuous use by the public since then. It was originally a single-room log building. Then there was an addition and then another, willy nilly, wherever they decided to go. It grew in all directions, with stairs here and hallways there leading off to rooms all over the place. The lobby contained a huge old iron stove that had been made by a local blacksmith out of boilerplate half an inch thick. It was eight feet long and three feet wide and took a five-foot log of wood. This was the heating unit for the lobby and one of the wings of the hotel. There was another stove, not quite so grand, that heated the parlour and some more bedrooms up another set of stairs. The only way any heat got into the bedrooms was by guests leaving the bedroom door open so the air could circulate. This led to some interesting situations, for often there was more than air that would circulate.

The hotel clerk welcomed Mrs. Place and Ada to the hotel. They were stiff and tired, so after registering they were shown upstairs to two of the better rooms in the house, directly over the lobby where they would be warmer. Ada was surprised at the spareness of the room. The only furnishings were the bed in the centre of the wall and a jug and basin on a plain washstand in the corner. The floor was bare boards, with a small mat by the side of the bed. The walls were plain painted boards and she was doubly surprised to find that there were cracks between them that allowed you to see into the next room. Fortunately she had the last room down the corridor, so the only room that she could see into, and be seem from, belonged to Mrs. Place.

Ada washed up and went downstairs with Mrs. Place for supper. The dining room was filled with people, most of whom greeted Mrs. Place politely. The two women were seated at a small corner table and served a meal. Ada was taken aback by the size of the portions and was even more taken aback by the amount she ate. It was good food and the fresh air had given her a tremendous appetite. She was just getting to know the hotel owner's wife in the sitting room after dinner when

Mrs. Place hustled her off to bed with the warning that there was another full day of travel ahead of them.

They were up again well before dawn for the next leg of the journey. It had snowed during the night and there were three or four inches of fresh snow on the ground. After breakfast Ada and Mrs. Place joined Billy and the Chinese gentleman, much to Ada's surprise, in a sleigh. Billy told her that they would be travelling through the mountains and there would be precious little dry ground for a wagon. He had transferred the freight from the wagon sometime during the night, so even though they had converted from wheels to runners, they still had the same load.

Ada liked the sleigh better than the wagon, as it was much smoother. They glided out of Clinton in the predawn gloom, the horses fresh, the air clear and cold, and the new snow hanging from the trees and bushes along the roadside. It was gorgeous. Soon they were past Kelly Lake and then they turned in to the mountains toward Jesmond. The beauty of the country fascinated Ada. It changed with every turn. The day seemed to slip by, but in actual fact it was as long as the day before. The snow and the sleigh slipping along so silently compared to the chatter of the wheels on the stones made it seem so much easier.

Billy's handling of the horses was a delight to watch. He would swing the leaders out around the difficult corners and then bring them back into line with a flick of the wrist. By keeping a steady pace he covered the miles, at the same time conserving the strength of the animals for the heavy pulls up the steep hills. It seemed that they climbed most of the day, and finally they arrived at Jesmond after Billy brought the horses around one last sharp corner.

Ada was intrigued that the old English name "Jesmond" was in use way out here in the wilderness of Canada. In fact, all the old-timers called it the Mountain House, but the owners, Mr. and Mrs. Harry Coldwell, had the name of their old English home accepted by the powers that be as the name for the post office, which was located in their home, so officially it was Jesmond. This was the first post office served by the Dog Creek Stage, and immediately after Billy unloaded the mail sacks at the side door, Mr. Coldwell, the postmaster, started sorting the mail.

Mrs. Coldwell was a hospitable little Englishwoman who took

delight in meeting another young English girl. She and Ada hit it off right away. There were all sorts of people around, waiting for their mail, and Mrs. Coldwell introduced them all to Ada. There was Mr. Grinder, a grizzled old pioneer; Mr. Bill Wright, an American veteran of the Civil War, where he had lost one leg; Mr. Kostering; one or two Indians, the first Ada had seen; and two young fellows, Harry Marriot and Harold Wilshire, both from England. They were all sitting around the big kitchen, sipping coffee and talking and laughing. Ada thought it was one of the friendliest places she had ever been, and though it was different from anything she had seen before, she loved it.

Finally the mail was sorted and each in turn went over to the wicket and got his letters. There was a hush fell over the room as each man returned for a few minutes to his own private life. All these people were from far away, but now each one out here in the wilderness on his own was for a moment taken back through the letters to a family and home far, far away. Ada watched their faces as they read their letters from loved ones. Those like Harold Wilshire, who didn't get any mail, sat back quietly and read the papers, some over a month old but new to them, and smoked their cigarettes in the soft light of the coal-oil lamps. Soon they were all gone with their mail and their memories of home, and only the Coldwells and the travellers were left.

Billy had stabled the horses, and supper was the next item on the program. Mrs. Coldwell was rushing around getting things ready. Ada enjoyed helping set the table and having a running conversation with another young Englishwoman. They all eventually got seated around a big kitchen table. Harry carved the meat at one end of the table and Mrs. Coldwell dished out the vegetables at the other. It was a very homey feeling. The conversation ranged from where and when the stock could be turned out on the range to international affairs and the outlook for war. After the dishes were done they all adjourned to the living room, but it wasn't long before Ada and Mrs. Place were feeling the effects of their two long days in the fresh air and they were off to bed. They sure didn't need any rocking.

They set off with new horses the next morning on the last leg of the journey to Dog Creek, riding in the sleigh again until they got to Indian Meadows, where they changed to a democrat that had been

The Dog Creek Stage in Canoe Creek canyon.

left there on the way up. There were no people at Indian Meadows, so Billy had to make the switch from sleigh to wagon by himself. It took Billy awhile to get this done, so Ada decided to walk on ahead and get picked up when the transfer had been made.

It was a warm spring day. The fresh snow of the day before had not reached Indian Meadows, so the ground was dry. She walked on to the end of the flat meadow and down the steep hill. Suddenly she found herself alone. It was a strange feeling, that sudden solitude. Some people do strange things when it comes over them for the first time. Ada was suddenly overtaken by sadness and she found herself sitting on a big rock and crying, she didn't know why. The sound of the approaching wagon brought her out of her reverie and she quickly dried her eyes and put a smile on her face for Mrs. Place, but Mrs. Place wasn't fooled. She looked at Ada sharply and knew that the girl had experienced the power and strength of this great lonely country.

"Canoe Creek next stop." Billy was pretending to be a trolley conductor and that brought a laugh to Ada's throat. She felt safe and secure again once she was back in the wagon and wondered what had come over her to act as she did.

You can see the cluster of buildings that was Dog Creek at the right of this photo. The school I attended is about in the middle of the shot, and the road to Williams Lake winds off the left side. The open area in the right foreground is Rabbit Park, a small level clearing that was about one third of the way up the south side of the valley. It had a very good running spring, and when I was a kid there was ample evidence of habitation all over the flats, including many keequilly holes, evidence that Indians had lived there, attracted by the fresh water.

The Canoe Creek canyon was very narrow and seemed just wide enough for the wagon. The cliffs rose on both sides, solid rock. Billy whipped the horses through at a good clip to give Ada an extra thrill, and he laughed while doing it. The country here was wild and rugged, the valley getting narrower and steeper as they went, and all at once they were out into a small clearing and in the midst of an Indian village. Dogs were barking and people were peeking out of the doorways of the cabins. Ada was surprised to see grass growing on the roofs of the log cabins. She didn't know that they were all sod roofed, which is the warmest (in winter) and coolest (in summer) roof you can have on a log cabin. The village was as neat as a pin, and the most prominent feature in it was the white-painted church with the picket fence around it, certainly the best structure in the settlement.

Billy wheeled the stage around the corner and up in front of a ranch house and suddenly they were at Canoe Creek. Mr. Hannon greeted Mrs. Place and Ada and invited them in for a bite to eat before they continued on to their final destination, Dog Creek. It was an enjoyable short visit but soon they were off again.

They departed the Canoe Creek valley on a most formidable road, negotiating thirteen switchbacks as they slowly climbed the mountain back of the Hannon home. Billy had to use all his skill to keep the wagon on the road. The lead horses were obliged to go way out on the corners so that the wheelers would be able to keep the wagon on track around the switchback turns. They stopped to rest the horses every little while, and Billy held the wagon from running back down the

Dog Creek in 1917. The big barn at left is the only building that remains. The hotel and store (centre) burned in 1966. The white building at the right housed the store and post office until it burned down in 1961.

mountain with a huge brake lever that he pushed with his foot. It was a tricky business and Ada was nervous, but she didn't say anything, just held on and hoped for the best.

When they got close to the top of the mountain the view was absolutely magnificent. The little Indian village lying below was spread out like a checkerboard, neat and orderly. The log cabins looked like dollhouses set in a dark green forest. Out to the west they could see the Coast Range of mountains, snowcapped and eternal, standing like saw teeth on the skyline.

One more turn and the view was gone and they entered the forest that covered the plateau across the top of Canoe Creek Mountain towards Dog Creek. The road went around this tree and past that one in a maze of twists and turns, over rocks and roots and through mudholes until Ada thought they would all be pulverized. All at once they broke into the open again and found themselves ready to descend into the Dog Creek valley.

As soon as they started down the mountain on the Dog Creek side they were in the shade. The snow hadn't melted off the road. Instead it was packed down into six inches of solid ice. Billy was having a tough time handling the outfit. He did not have much experience in slippery conditions. There was a particularly bad place halfway down the mountain where a spring ran across the road. The ice had built up here due to the continual flooding, and the sheet of ice continued down around the next turn for a hundred yards.

Billy was sweating by this time. He knew he would have to put on a rough-lock to hold the wagon on this steep, dangerous place. (A rough-lock was a chain that was put around one of the spokes in a wheel and then secured to the wagon to prevent the wheel from turning.) He had just put on the rough-lock and was ready to start down this particularly bad stretch when two cowboys broke out of the bush alongside the road and started hollering at Billy to stop. Ada was sure that this was a holdup and dove under the buffalo robe.

"Stay where you are and don't move," the young man with the beard shouted. "You've got the rough-lock on the wrong wheel. If you don't watch out you will dump the whole rig over the bank."

The two men got off their horses and started to change the rough-lock over to the wheel on the other side. Billy was crestfallen at his error, but as soon as the rough-lock was in its proper place he brought the wagon down over the icy spot without any trouble.

When they were out of danger the young man that Ada thought was a bandit turned to Mrs. Place and said, "Hello Ma. I thought I better get up here and see that Billy got over this spot. I know that he hasn't had experience with a rough-lock before and this is a pretty bad spot."

Mrs. Place acknowledged that it surely was a bad place and then turned to Ada and introduced the young man. "This is my son Joseph. He's our ranch foreman."

Ada was pleased to find out that it wasn't Billy the Kid.

In a few minutes they reached the settlement of Dog Creek and pulled up in front of the old hotel, the Place family home. Mr. Place was there to greet them and he made sure that Ada signed the hotel register. After Ada was settled into her room, she went downstairs to meet the others in the private sitting room. Mrs. Place said, "If you are your mother's daughter you must be able to play and sing. Would you do that for me, please?" Ada sat down to the piano and started to play. There was a big mirror above the piano and she saw a handsome young cowboy with a crown of blond hair come into the room as she

My father, Charles Riley Place. He is wearing what I think they called shotgun chaps, from the two legs being like the two barrels of a shotgun. They were made out of the hide of an Angora goat and were warm, impervious to rain, and expensive—and very popular with the old-time cowboys. They came in as many colours as the goats did.

was playing. He stood there and watched until she was finished, then he walked over to her and leaned down and kissed her long and hard on the lips. Mrs. Place nearly exploded.

"Charles!" she screamed. "Have you gone out of your mind? I'll have none of that kind of behaviour out of you!"

Mrs. Place went on at some length, but Charlie just stood there and didn't say a word. It was some time before Ada found out that he had won a twenty-dollar gold piece from Walter Langton for this gesture. What Charlie didn't know then was that he had not only won the bet; he had won the girl too, for that was how my Mother and Father met. It was the start of a life they would share for the next 42 years.

CHAPTER 3

HARD YEARS

Dog Creek was very remote during the war years, 1914 to 1918. News was often a month old before it finally arrived there. When Charlie and Ada drove one of the old cars down from Dog Creek to get married in Ashcroft in 1914, they learned on their arrival that the war had broken out and that they would not be able to make the trip to England that Ada's father had arranged and paid for. They had a simple wedding in Ashcroft and a short honeymoon in Vancouver.

When World War I came along the Place sons were all of an age to go into the army. They all volunteered but were all rejected because they were not tall enough or had flat feet or some other defect. Later they were declared "essential war workers" as agricultural producers. They all had their specific jobs on the ranch. Frank, the oldest, was the mechanic and car driver. Joe Jr. (Young Joe) was the ranch foreman, well liked and respected in this position. Charlie was the cowboy and horse-breaker. During the war he broke over 300 head of horses for the army, all of them standing over 16 hands high (64 inches at the shoulder) or better.

All three sons married within a few years of one another. Charlie was first and married Ada Halstead-Netherwood on August 8, 1914. Joe married Violet Ella Lyne on November 16, 1915. And Frank married Francis Opal Lyne on January 17, 1917. The Lyne girls were sisters, the daughters of Mr. and Mrs. William Lyne who owned the Ashcroft Hotel. Mr. Lyne was the former partner of William Pinchbeck. He and Pinchbeck once owned the property where the town of Williams Lake sits today.

Immediately after the war, the Soldier Settlement Board offered J.S. a quarter of a million dollars for the Dog Creek Ranch. He considered the offer carefully. J.S. had been having financial problems ever since he bailed out Lindsay, his former son-in-law. At that time he

Charles and Ada's wedding day, August 8, 1914. Charlie's mother, Jane, is standing behind them. The newlyweds travelled in one of the first cars that tackled the Cariboo Road.

had made the decision to hang onto the land and sell off stock to meet the debts Lindsay had incurred. This was a bad move as the price of stock, particularly horses, went down and he found himself land rich but cash poor. He was unable to make the payments under the conditions of his "blanket mortgage" and was hanging on by his teeth when the Soldier Settlement Board made its offer. He thought that he could keep the ranch for his sons, so he turned the offer down. It was a big mistake and it cost him everything.

It is hard for us to imagine the severity of the conditions of the mortgage. When the lenders foreclosed they took everything that J.S. owned. He walked out of Dog Creek with only

My brother Geoff at a year and a bit old, sitting with twelve-year-old Lily Harry outside the house called Casey. In 1916 this picture ran on the front page of the English paper The Daily Sketch, *which had a worldwide distribution of several million at that time.*

the clothes on his back. Even the personal pictures of himself and his wife had to be left hanging on the walls of the family home. (They were still there when my Dad bought the property back in 1930.) The bedding stayed, the dishes stayed, every single thing he owned stayed, and he left with absolutely nothing.

Two of the properties that were part of the ranch had been taken up in the name of Joe Jr. and Charlie and therefore were exempt from the mortgage. The two sons immediately signed them over to their Dad, even though they had next to nothing themselves. These were the only things J.S. got out of Dog Creek.

The Dog Creek sawmill in 1914. J.S. lost this business as well as his ranch and the rest of his property.

Fortunately Mrs. Place had been spared from seeing this disaster. She passed away some two years before it all took place, dying from a slow and painful cancer. Her final days were spent in a nursing home in Victoria run by a rather remarkable woman by the name of Ethel Ross. When J.S. had to leave Dog Creek under the terrible conditions described above, he moved down to Victoria. He later looked up Miss Ross and they got married. J.S. died in 1922.

At the end of the war my Mother and Dad decided to make the trip to England that my Grandfather Netherwood had given them for a wedding present. They left for England in the spring of 1919 and had a good summer there. Dad came back to Canada in the fall to finish up the house at the D4—a pre-emption of 160 acres that my Dad took up when it was evident that Grandfather Place was going broke. (The locals called it the Snowball Ranch. That name came from Dad, who was platinum blond as a kid and hence called Snowball.)

In England my Mother was having an awful time. She decided to stay at home after she discovered she was pregnant, and five-year-old Geoff was busy getting every childhood disease that he could get. When I was born in March 1920, Geoff was down with pneumonia. He got a big abscess on his chest, and one night it burst. My Mother

Our house on the D4, inside and out. The interior shot shows the piano that my Mother loved to play.

was infected and almost died, and her doctor told her to get back to Canada and some clean air or her family would be wiped out. Dad came back to England to help on the trip, and we set sail in October 1920.

That was when the tough years on the D4 started, day by day and year by year with little change. I was a baby of six months when we moved in. Dad worked from morning until night every day trying to make a ranch out of nothing, and Mother kept her house spotless and did miles of crochet and embroidery.

Mother and Child 1. Here I am with my Mother in England. I still have the baptismal dress that I'm wearing in this photo. Note my Mother's shoes, held on by laces. She was four feet nine-and-a-half inches tall and took a size 12 child's shoe.

My Dad had built and finished a nice log house on the property during the winter while my Mother waited in England for my arrival. There were two bedrooms, living room, kitchen and pantry, and a good storage space upstairs. There was no plumbing and no electricity in those days, but despite those deficiencies it was a comfortable house. It was completely furnished. There were iron beds in the bedrooms along with dressers. The living room had a table and chairs, a divan, and the little black piano that was my Mother's salvation and delight.

Williams Lake in 1920/21, before the big fire of July 1921. This view up Railway Avenue (now Mackenzie Avenue) shows Fraser and Mackenzie's store (with the light-coloured awning) and the Lakeview Hotel at right.

The kitchen had a table and chairs under the window, a water barrel by the door, and a wood-burning kitchen stove with a hot-water reservoir on one side. The walls were covered with wallpaper and the windows and doors were all painted white.

Although we had a comfortable home, we had practically no money. We survived by living off the land. My Dad grew a large garden and kept the produce in a root cellar. Potatoes, carrots, beets, onions, and turnips were good keepers and we had lots of them. We always had a few pigs, and my Dad was a good butcher and knew how to make bacon and hams. Eating was fairly easy but clothing was another matter. My Dad used to say he wished he could get some seed that would grow a new pair of shoes. We solved this problem by bartering with the Indians for moccasins and gloves and occasionally a coat. My Grandmother in England used to send us gifts for our birthdays and Christmas. Little did she know that we seldom if ever got them in the original form. They were always traded off for some desperately needed shoes or gloves and sometimes berries or fish or meat.

My Mother always spoke of the two worst years as the ones when they had a total income of only $110 one year and $120 the next. It took a lot of careful planning not only to budget the meagre funds, but also to spend them. Bear in mind that they only shopped once a year. If some item was forgotten, all they could do was wait a year and order it the next chance they got.

One year a catastrophe happened. Mom and Dad made the yearly purchase of supplies after Dad sold his stock, which was one steer. There was precious little money to spend. We had our garden produce stored but we had to buy such things as sugar, rice, prunes, tea, coffee, flour, and yeast cakes. So much of this and so much of that—the list was revised and revised God knows how many times.

That year my Uncle Frank was making the trip to Ashcroft (100 miles away) for his supplies, and my parents arranged for him to bring ours also. He arrived back at our place on a frosty night in October. Somehow when he built the load he got our box of prunes up against the tins of coal oil that we needed for our lamps. Of course the coal oil leaked onto the prunes, so we had coal-oil-flavoured prunes for a year thereafter. I think my Mother held this against Frank for the rest of their lives, but my Dad shrugged it off.

Much more serious were the two items that seemed to have been miscalculated on the list: tea and jam. By January it was obvious that these items were in short supply. My Mother loved her afternoon tea. She never missed a day that she didn't dress up and sit down at four o'clock in the afternoon for her cup of tea. As soon as my Dad realized that the tea and jam were getting used up he never ate a speck thereafter. We kids were also cut back. I remember getting a small piece of toast with a thin spread of jam on it for my birthday treat in March. Despite these rigorous conservationist policies, however, the jam was all used up by April. The tea lasted a bit longer by rationing it to one cup per day for my Mother, but by the end of May it was used up too.

There was something about this final deprivation that got right into my Mother's soul. She had stood the years of poverty and loneliness and now it seemed to her that this God-forsaken country beat you down until you could stand no more. She had been a naturally cheerful person with a considerable amount of resilience and more than a bit adventurous, but now she started to go to pieces. Her vitality started to go down and there was nothing that anyone could do to restore it.

We tried making tea out of kinnikinnick berries and leaves but it was no good. We tried making coffee out of roasted wheat. Actually it wasn't too bad, but my Mother hated it all and longed for a cup of real English tea.

Hard Years

My Dad had no way of making any money. There was no work close by and if he left to go to work the garden would go to pieces and we would have nothing to eat that winter. Also, who would look after the few animals we had if he wasn't there? There was no other way but to stick it out. He went down to the store at Dog Creek and found out that he could get a pound of tea and a tin of jam for 95 cents. The only problem was that he did not have a single cent. He got his courage up and asked the storekeeper, A.J. Drinkell, if he could get the tea and jam on credit.

Drinkell knew just how poor my Dad was—he was as poor himself—but he pushed the items across the counter and said, "Pay for them when you can, Charlie. I hope the little lady enjoys them."

It was the first time that anybody had trusted my Dad for anything. He never forgot the favour.

He rode back up to the D4 and hid the tea and jam in the barn for a week, then gave them to my Mother on her birthday. I remember her sitting all by herself in the living room that afternoon, drinking her tea and having her bread and jam with tears running down her cheeks.

☆　☆　☆

My Dad was out pulling stumps. There was very little land cleared and what was cleared was rocky. He set about clearing more land so that when he got some cattle he would have some hay to feed them in the winter. His equipment was a team of pretty good horses and a strong back. It was hard work but he stayed with it morning, noon, and night. Ranching was the only thing he knew how to make a living at and, by God, he wasn't going to be beaten by it! He had a hand stump-puller, which was a cable affair that worked something like a winch. There was a big long handle on it that worked like a ratchet; each stroke of the handle would pull a stump about an inch. Back and forth my Dad would go, five steps forward then five steps back for each stroke, the long heavy handle putting blisters on his hands and pains in his back. Inch by inch each stump came out, was cut off at the roots, dragged away to a pile, and burnt. It was monotonous, it was slow, it was demeaning, and it was drudgery but my Dad stayed with it day after day after day and never gave up.

Dog Creek, A Place in the Cariboo

Tom Stenson was our neighbour, a Norwegian, tall and straight and strong. He was quiet and peaceful, a good friend to my Dad, and he owned the adjoining 160-acre homestead up the creek from ours. It was a little better land than ours, with a meadow of wild hay in the bottom next to the creek. He had a good cabin on it, which he had built himself with the skill of a Norse woodsman, giving it dovetailed corners, fitted windows, and a good sod roof. A small barn and a root cellar were all the outbuildings. He did not have any machinery. Tom cut his hay by hand with a scythe, using great sweeping strokes in a steady rhythm—stroke, pause, stroke, pause, and on down the field to the end, leaving the hay neatly windrowed behind him. Then he'd touch up the scythe blade with a few deft strokes of the stone and go back up the field, never stopping from six in the morning until noon. After an hour for lunch he'd be back at it again until dark.

Tom lived alone. He had no wife or children, no family, and few friends. All his relatives were in Norway and like so many immigrants of that era he was cut off from his family by the great distances and the lack of communication. Shortly after we moved onto the D4, Tom started to visit. He always brought some little thing—fresh picked raspberries or maybe some brook trout or a piece of deer meat. He enjoyed my Mother's bright ways and her singing and piano playing, he enjoyed Geoff and me, but mostly he liked my Dad. I think Tom admired my Dad and the way he was trying to make a home for his family. After all, my Dad was brought up the son of a wealthy man and it must have been hard for him to be broke and have to work like a slave on a stump-puller. Tom was always there when my Dad needed a hand. Many a day he would walk down from his place and take up a shovel or an axe, work alongside my Dad all day until quitting time, then walk off home. Sometimes he would stay and have a meal with us but often he would not. Needless to say, my Dad returned the favour many times, and they cemented a friendship and mutual respect for each other. Tom was a friend in need for my Dad.

We had no radio, no telephone, and newspapers arrived weekly in the summertime and monthly in the winter, if you could afford them. We couldn't. Tom used to get a paper from a religious group known as Judge Rutherford Christian Science. Soon he became engrossed in this literature. He started to study the Bible and harangued my Dad on the subject while they were out pulling stumps. Dad didn't pay much attention to all that Tom said, but he did notice that Tom was getting more and more concerned about Heaven and Hell and more and more irrational about the whole business of religion. He didn't say anything to my Mother, but he began to be worried about his friend's mental state. Since it was winter there wasn't much outdoor work to be done, so Tom had nothing to do but study the Bible and read Judge Rutherford and try to sort the whole religious thing out in his mind alone in his cabin.

As it happened, my Mother had studied the Bible as a school subject in England as a girl. She took great pride in the fact that she had won a competition on biblical history with the highest marks in all of England. She loved to argue on the different texts with whoever happened along, especially the priests and parsons that ministered to us poor benighted heathens. She would tie them up in knots, much to their chagrin and my Mother's delight. She had a most remarkable memory and never forgot one word of the Bible, though she was not a particularly religious person. Her delight in the subject was nearly all academic. I wouldn't say she was irreverent, but she did get a bit flippant about it on occasion.

Poor old Tom was one of her victims. Here he was serious and worried about a subject that was entirely new to him, and my Mother would take off with one of her biblical jokes that Tom could not understand or abide. "Tom, did you know there was a baseball game mentioned in the Bible?"

Tom would immediately start to worry that he did not know about it and my Mother would keep him in suspense as long as she could. "It talks about it the first thing when you open the book. It says IN THE BIG INNING!"

Well, it wasn't a very good joke anyway, but by the time it got through to Tom, past his limited comprehension of English, all he understood was that my Mother was making jokes at the expense of the Lord and he didn't like it. He told my Mother that she would be called before the bar to account for her frivolity one day, and he was quite angry about it.

The first week of March, Dad told my Mother he was going to ride up to the top of the mountain to see if there was enough range open to turn out the few head of cattle he had. She made him a lunch and he saddled up and set off on the trail up to the pasture. Shortly after he left there was a knock at the door and she went to see who it could be. She opened the door and there was Tom. She thought he looked a bit strange but she asked him in. Only when he was inside did she notice that he was packing a gun, a knife, and a double-bitted axe. He stepped in the door but he did not put these weapons aside.

"I want you to say your prayers," he said. "You don't have long to live."

My Mother thought fast. Even though she was shaking inside she replied, "I will in a minute, Tom. I have to fix the heater in the sitting room. It's got a pitchy stick in it and I don't want it to get too hot."

She rushed into the front room and, heart beating a mile a minute, rattled the stove lid and pretended to look after the fire. She turned back towards the kitchen and saw that Tom had followed her into the living room.

"I met Peter, Paul, and Moses on the road down here," he said, "and they told me to come and get you. The end of the world is near and they want you to atone for all your sins before the end. They want me to save you."

"Well just a minute, Tom," she said, "don't you want a cup of coffee? It's awfully cold out. You must be chilled to the bone."

The ruse seemed to work. Tom followed her into the kitchen. She fussed around the stove and started to make some coffee. Tom stood around with that crazed look on his face and the gun in his hands. He didn't seem to know what to do, so my Mother kept him busy by talking as fast as she could about anything that came into her head. As long as she kept talking she felt he would not harm her. The more she talked the less fierce looking he became. She talked about the weather, her family in England, the cattle, anything. Inside she was praying that something or somebody would save her.

Just when she was ready to give up, the door opened and my Dad walked in. He quietly talked to Tom and got him outside. My Mother broke down then and started to cry. Dad didn't get rough with Tom but talked him into going home. Then he came in to see how my Mother was doing. He told her he was nearly at the top of the mountain when he looked back and saw Tom coming down the road towards the house. He thought that he better come back and see what was on Tom's mind. He hadn't liked the way Tom had been acting lately.

Dad stayed close to home for a few days to allow my Mother to get over the ordeal she had gone through. A couple of days after this experience he decided to take a stroll up to Tom's place to see how he was getting along. He knew Tom was in bad shape and he was worried about him. Even though Tom had caused such an upset and scared my Mother half to death, my Dad could not find it in his heart to feel angry at him.

When he arrived at Tom's cabin he found no one. He looked in the barn and the root cellar. Nothing. He returned to the house and went inside to see if Tom was in there and if he was okay. Everything seemed to be in order—the bed was made, the table was neat, the dishes were washed, and it looked like Tom would be back any minute— but something was not right. Dad prowled around and checked over all the things that he could remember about the layout. All of a sudden he noticed what was missing: the Bible. Tom always kept it on the apple box next to his bed. Then Dad remembered that Tom had the Bible in his hand when he visited and threatened my Mother a few days before. He looked for the gun and knife Tom had carried that day. They were also gone. My Dad felt that something was amiss, so he spent the rest of the day looking for his friend, with no results.

The next day Dad went down to Dog Creek and got a search party together to look for Tom. They scoured the area around the cabin and all over Tom's fields. Nothing was found that first day. Some of the men thought that Tom had gone off to Ashcroft for supplies or maybe to look for a job. All sorts of reasons were put forward, but Dad was still worried and said, "Let's search one more day."

In the afternoon of the second day, Harold Wilshire, one of the men from the Gang Ranch, found Tom. He was way up on the hill overlooking his ranch, huddled behind a stump. He had his gun and his knife and his axe with him and also his Bible open on the ground beside him. He had shot himself. The men packed him down to our house wrapped in one of his old blankets and laid him out on some boards propped up on two sawhorses on our front verandah. Tom's body stayed there for the night. The next day my Dad built him a coffin out of some boards that were left over after building the house.

When it came time to put the body into the coffin a problem arose. Tom had been found with his legs bent and rigor mortis had kept them bent, so when they put the body into the coffin his knees stuck up and prevented the lid from going on. Dad solved the problem by cutting the tendons behind the knee with a butcher knife, something few people could do but Dad did it without a moment's hesitation.

The funeral was to be on Sunday. The day before, Dad picked out the place where they would bury Tom. It was on a little hill overlooking his ranch. On Sunday morning Dad and Harold Wilshire put the coffin on the back of my Dad's sleigh. After lunch Dad and Mother got all dressed up in their best clothes, and along with the few men who had taken part in the search they formed a procession headed for Tom's place, a short mile up the road. On his last journey Tom was accompanied by my Mother and Dad on the front seat of the sleigh pulled by the faithful old team of Duke and Dynamite. The coffin was on the back with the friends who had searched for him seated along each side.

It was a beautiful cold spring day. The sun was shining and the cluster of people stood at the graveside to pay their last respects to a friend and companion. As there were no "gentleman of the cloth" available, Mr. Drinkell, the storekeeper and postmaster, who had received the burial certificate, led the mourners in a brief ceremony. My Mother was the only woman there so she shed her tears alone. They quietly buried Tom and filled the grave.

All the participants came back to our house for a warming cup of tea. There were just ten or twelve people but it seemed like a big crowd to me. I had never seen that many people in one place before. After tea they left one by one until we found ourselves alone.

My Dad was missing. Mother called out for him around the house but got no answer. She put on her coat and went down to the barn to see if he was there. He was. Charlie Place was an incredibly strong man. He could do almost anything without becoming emotionally involved, but the strain of the last few days finally took its toll. My Mother said it was the only time she had ever seen him cry. He had lost his best friend.

It was March 13, 1923, my third birthday.

CHAPTER 4

SUZETTE

I think of her quite often.

Suzette is such a glamorous-sounding name. It conjures up visions of high fashion and sophistication and youth and beauty and maybe even Paris. I'm sorry to say that for me the name brings memories of almost the exact opposite.

I must tell you about her.

I was three when my Mother had a complete physical and mental collapse. She had been through all the sickness with my brother Geoff in England and then the collapse of the Place fortunes when J.S. went broke, the privation when we were so poor we had barely enough to eat, and then the terrible ordeal she experienced when Tom Stenson was going to murder her. She just couldn't stand any more. My Grandfather's third wife, Ethel Ross Place, still had her nursing home in Victoria, and my Mother ended up down there for a few months getting her batteries recharged. My Dad made arrangements to have Marc Pigeon and his wife Placida stay at our home and look after us kids, mostly me, while my Mother was away.

Marc was a cousin of the Pigeon family that owned the ranch farther up the valley from ours. He was a quiet and decent man who worshipped the ground that his wife walked on. He was completely without schooling and could neither read nor write, but he had worked as a helper for the teamsters on the wagon road and had in fact driven the horse stage for my Grandfather on occasion. He could remember every parcel and letter given to him for delivery along the way by the look of the parcel. He never got mixed up. People would give him long lists of things to get for them in Clinton and he wouldn't forget a thing. He didn't need to read and write with a memory like that! He was unfailingly polite to everybody and a gentleman in all the aspects of that designation at all times.

Placida, Marc's wife, was the daughter of Raphael Valenzuela, the Mexican horse wrangler who built the original log part of the old Dog Creek Hotel. Placida was a remarkable old gal and as sharp as a tack. She was suffering even then from cancer, and when she was in a bad mood she would berate poor Marc unmercifully. It would just roll off old Marc and he would say, "The missus isn't feeling well today," and pass it off.

My Dad had made some kind of a deal with Old Bill, a local Indian, to do some work for him, and Old Bill and his family were camped down by the ditch below the house. The salmon were running, so Old Bill and the rest of his family went down to the river some seven or eight miles away to fish and dry some salmon for the winter. They left Bill's old mother, Suzette, home at the camp below our house. This would not be so unusual except that Old Bill and the rest of the family were gone for about two weeks, and Suzette was in her eighties and absolutely and completely blind. Her hair hung down uncombed and matted, and her clothes were rags. She wore buckskin moccasins

Marc and Placida Pigeon, who looked after me when my Mother went to Victoria for a rest cure.

on her feet and an Old Mother Hubbard dress made of some dark nondescript material. Her eyes were sore and running and she was crippled up with arthritis and had difficulty getting around on her twisted feet.

One day after taking a sweathouse bath she got lost getting back to her camp. She wandered around nude until she came to the fence a mile down the road from her camp, and then she followed the fence and the ditch back to her camp.

I don't know how she got by living in a tent all by herself with only a campfire, but she did. How did she cook? How did she keep the fire going? How did she survive? She only had old lard pails and syrup tins to cook in, but survive she did, day after day by herself.

In the evening she would sit out by her campfire and smoke her cigarette and seem perfectly content with her lot in life.

I missed my Mother so much when she was away. I was afraid that she was not going to come home. I would look out the window and see the nice warm campfire down at Suzette's camp and I would go down to it. Suzette couldn't speak any English so she couldn't talk to me, but she would talk so quietly and so softly in Shuswap and hold me next to her on the log by the fire that I would soon relax and fall asleep.

Placida would come and get me and take me home. She would give me fits for going down to Suzette's camp and tell me not to go again. It seems that each time I went down there I came home with a new batch of lice for Placida to clean up. But the next night I would go down again and Suzette would comfort me and let me share her warm fire and tell me stories in Shuswap that I couldn't understand.

She had nothing, but she was able to share what little she had and give a small boy comfort and love when it was sorely needed.

Yes, I think of her quite often.

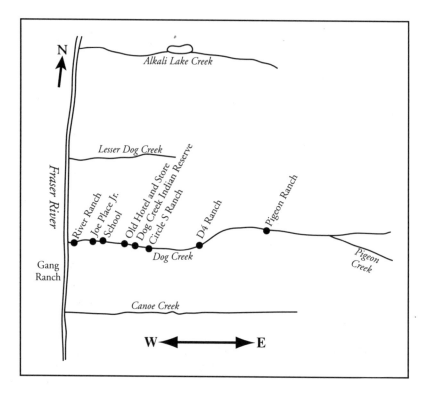

The properties along Dog Creek. My family moved from the D4 to Casey, near the old hotel, in 1926 (see map on page 178). My Dad later traded the D4 for the River Ranch.

CHAPTER 5

SCHOOL DAYS

My Mother returned from Victoria after about three months. She often said her trouble was that she had a racehorse temperament in a workhorse world, a fanciful way of describing it but probably as close to right as you can get. Soon after her return to the D4 she started worrying about school for Geoff and me. There was no schoolhouse in Dog Creek at the time, but the other Place families had children of an age to start school and were having the same worries, so a plan was worked out to convince the government to establish a school. It took a couple of years, and in the meantime Dad sold his cattle and became Mr. Drinkell's partner in the Dog Creek store. He kept the D4, but we moved from the ranch into a small cabin called "Casey" that was about 100 yards east of the store, which was just across the road from the old Dog Creek Hotel.

When we started school in January 1926 I had to walk down the road from Casey right past the old Dog Creek Hotel, which was where the Armes family lived. The Armes family played a big part in our lives at Dog Creek. Mr. James Armes was a great big man in every way. He always came into Dog Creek in a hired car, one of the famous I.T. Stages from Ashcroft, usually with Clarence Stevenson driving.

Armes had acquired J.S. Place's old Dog Creek property in 1923, but his first acquisition in the Cariboo had been the Lesser Dog Creek Ranch. Magnus Meason had founded this ranch at what the old-timers called Little Dog Creek. Mr. Meason was a well-educated man, a Latin and Greek scholar, it was said, who had taught at Oxford University in England. God only knows how he ended up at Little Dog Creek, but he did and he married an Indian woman and raised a good family there. He held the job of Government Agent and also the job of Indian Agent. He built a large frame house on the property and installed running water in the house by way of a ram pump in the creek. All this before World War I.

My Grandfather bought him out, and when J.S. went broke in 1920 the ranch was picked up by a little Jewish man by the name of Billy Holden.

James Armes and Billy Holden were birds of a feather as far as business was concerned. They were both speculators and promoters and opportunists who were into this deal today and that deal tomorrow. Some days they would have lots of money and some days they would have none, but they always kept up a big front even if they had holes in their shoes.

Billy Holden got possession of the Lesser Dog Creek Ranch on one of his lucky days, at a tax sale. He wasn't long finding out that he knew nothing about ranching and he set about getting rid of the ranch as soon as possible, at a profit of course. He tried to sell it to some oil-rich Texans, but he told them so many different stories during their three-day inspection that they left and went back to Texas.

James Armes, meanwhile, had found himself the proud owner of the Monarch Mine at Field, B.C. This mine was located near the top of Mount Stephen, a mountain not unlike the Matterhorn, located in the middle of the Rocky Mountains. Field, at the foot of the mountain, was a Canadian Pacific Railway divisional station, so access was quite easy. Armes wasn't too long finding out that it was a pretty tough mine to operate, sitting as it was one jump short of Heaven on top of that horrendous mountain. It wasn't much longer before he decided to get rid of the thing as soon as possible, at a profit of course.

The two men met and were immediately impressed with one another. Armes talked about his marvellous mine up in Field, and Holden extolled the virtues of country life on his spacious acres in the Cariboo. Like so many good salesmen, they were both suckers for a good sales pitch themselves, and it wasn't too long before Holden had Armes sold on the ranch and Armes had Holden sold on the Rocky Mountain mine. A trade was arranged and the day the documents were signed the two men met at the lawyer's office for the formalities.

After the signing Armes turned to Holden and said, "Congratulations, Billy, you have just bought yourself a mine with no ore!"

Billy burst out laughing and replied, "Alright, Jimmy, you just got yourself a ranch with no water!" Armes joined in the laughter and the two men left the lawyer's office arm in arm. The lawyer never could figure that one out.

It was absolutely true. Neither the mine nor the ranch was worth a hoot, but they both got a new item to peddle and they couldn't care less about value.

Armes decided there was a big future in the ranching industry. He believed that there was a fortune to be made if a person could tie up those vast acres. When the population increased, the property would escalate in value. He was absolutely right of course, but he was 30 or 40 years ahead of his time. At any rate, he became aware of the Cariboo when he bought the Little Dog Creek property, and he decided to get more holdings in the area. He looked around and found the Dog Creek Ranch up for sale by the people who had foreclosed on my Grandfather. He bought the property from them at once.

He sent his three sons—Harold, Harvey, and Frank—up to Dog Creek to run the place for him, and the next year his daughter Kitty joined the boys. As I have said, Mr. Armes was a promoter and speculator and he believed that the less people knew about his affairs the better. He instructed his sons to keep to themselves and not associate with the local Dog Creek people. I think it was his way of protecting his sometimes shaky financial position from gossip that could be harmful. He particularly instructed the boys to stay away from the Places. This may have been good business for Mr. Armes, but it was fatal for good feeling from the people in the valley.

While we were still at the D4 my Dad had a row with Harold Armes over water rights on the ditches. That confrontation ended with my Dad telling Harold that he was here on Dog Creek before the Armes arrived and he would be here after they were gone. It was a prophetic statement as it turned out, but one issued in bravado at the time. After that mix-up the Armes didn't speak to us and used to go flying by our old buggy in their big Graham Paige car, leaving us nothing but the dust. My Mother had many a good cry about that.

I used to wonder what it would be like to ride around in a big car like that. To me the Armes family were like gods, all dressed up and driving around like millionaires, going to Vancouver every once in a

*Our new school! This is the Dog Creek school in 1927,
shortly after it was built.*

while. I was scared to death of them. If I saw one of them coming down the road I would run off into the pasture and hide behind some bushes so as not to be seen.

As I said before, I had to walk by their home on my way to school each day, and I was scared to death of walking by it all by myself. My brother had been given the job of lighting the fires in the school, so he went on ahead. I got my protection by walking to school with the new teacher, Miss Price. We must have presented a funny picture. She was so tall and I was so small. I was half scared of her too, but she was the lesser of two evils.

The first few months in school were about the most miserable time I ever had in my life. The whole beautiful world that I had at the D4 had come apart and the effect on me was disastrous. I was three months short of six years old when I started, and I'd never spent time with anyone but my own immediate family before. My family had always called me "Chubby," but now I was "Hilary." I hated the name and wondered why I had such a terrible name when my brother had such a nice one. The other kids all called me a bloody Englishman and mocked my clothes and my silly name and the fact that I was born in England. My Mother got the bright idea that we would look good in breeches and leggings, so she ordered up the outfits from Eaton's. They never did fit very well and would hang around the waist and gather up around the knees. The leggings rubbed sore spots around our ankles. And these weren't good warm clothes, so in the middle of winter I was always cold. Every day I would cry as I walked to school, hanging three or four paces behind Miss Price, hating the whole damn business and scared at the same time. Then I would come home in tears with my breeches wet because the other kids' teasing made me pee my pants.

There was only one saving grace in the whole disagreeable mess: I could do the work with ease. I didn't like cutting up paper and playing with sticks or modelling clay, but as soon as I saw the letters and numbers, I knew them.

When the one-room Dog Creek school opened, there were ten children in attendance: Eric and Betty Earle, my cousins Kathleen and Harold Place, Geoff and I, and four of the Colin children from Gustafsen Lake, the headwaters of Dog Creek. Of the whole bunch only Eric and Betty Earle had ever been in an organized school before. We ranged in age from Arthur Colin, 16; Willie Colin, 15; Eric and Betty Earle, 12 and 11; Geoff, 11; Kathleen, 9; Harold, 8; down to me, the youngest, at 5 years, 9 months.

The teacher had an awesome job to get us all going. We had to start in Grade 1. You can imagine Arthur Colin and me standing up to read "The little red hen had some chicks. They said Peep, Peep." Arthur was six feet two inches tall, skinny and shy, hands blackened and calloused by the hard work of trapping and skinning and stretching his catch of fur; I was scared and shaking so much I could hardly hold the book, sporting the usual wet spot on my pants. I don't know how Miss Price kept from laughing, but she did.

One day she decided to tell us something about our country. She went into the whole story about the British Empire and how Canada was a Dominion and so on. When she was finished she asked Arthur what nationality he was. He stood up and naturally said he didn't know, so the teacher said he was a Native Canadian.

The next day none of the Colin children were at school. Mr. Drinkell, chairman of the local three-man school board, went to see Mr. Colin to ask what was the matter. Mr. Colin was very upset and indignant. He had written to Victoria demanding that the teacher be fired. Drinkell asked what in the world the teacher had done. Colin replied that she had called all his family Indians and he wasn't going to stand for that insult. Mr. Drinkell knew that both Mr. and Mrs. Colin had some Indian blood in their veins and he also knew they were sensitive about it. He beat it back to Miss Price to see what she had said.

Of course the poor girl was completely baffled and denied having ever said such a thing. It was only after she had gone over the whole of her previous day's teaching that Drinkell caught the phrase "Native Canadian." Native meant only one thing to the Colins and that was Indian.

Mr. Drinkell rushed back to see Colin and explain the wording that the teacher had used, but Colin would not accept the explanation. Miss Price went and apologized and still Colin was adamant. Everything was done that could be done to keep the Colin family in school, but their father said "No." They packed up and went back to Gustafsen Lake the next day.

We were down to six children in school. We had to have six children in attendance to keep the school open, so none of us could miss a single day of school.

Alfred Joseph Drinkell, Dog Creek postmaster, school board chairman, storekeeper, justice of the peace, and uncle to all of us kids.

It was February when the Colin children left, and the weather turned bitterly cold. The thermometer hung around 30 to 35 below zero for three weeks. It was only three quarters of a mile from Casey to the school, but I still froze some of my fingers and my face, and because they were so susceptible they refroze about every day. The weather got so bad that it was impossible to keep the school open. The parents and teacher decided that the school would close when the temperature fell below minus 30 and that we would make the time up when the weather was better—on Saturdays and even Sundays if necessary—so that the records would show perfect attendance. The only thing wrong with this scheme was it cost us our Easter holiday and a few warm spring days while we made up lost time.

After the Colin family left, the teacher had a better shot of getting us in order. She was able to devote more time to each individual. My Mother had taught my brother Geoff for four years, so Miss Price moved him ahead to Grade 3 almost immediately. This put him in a grade with Betty Earle. Geoff wasn't about to be beaten by a girl, so he tied right in and did very well. At the end of the first six months he was able to pass into Grade 4.

Miss Price came back the next fall and moved Geoff ahead and also my cousin Kathleen. They were both doing well, and now Geoff was in the proper grade for his age. My cousin Harold and I were moved ahead one half grade into Grade 1A. By Christmas of that year it was time to move us ahead to Grade 2. The teacher said she would advance me but that Harold wasn't ready yet.

Aunt Violet and Uncle Joe said that they were not going to put up with this. They said that the teacher was coaching me because she was boarding at our place and that if Harold didn't get advanced with me they would pull their children out of school and the school would close. There was no way the teacher would let Harold move ahead, so they kept me back. They told me that I really was started early and was six months under age for Grade 2 anyway, so it wouldn't matter. I knew that I was being shafted and I argued and cried and raised as much hell as possible, but I didn't win. I stayed back with Harold.

This same scenario played itself out in succeeding years. By the time we got to Grade 5 it was painfully evident there was something wrong that affected Harold's ability to do schoolwork. He may have been dyslexic or something, because he seemed normal in every other way. He was like a load on my back, but despite that we were good friends. Harold, who was two years and a few months older than me, was more mature in every way but he simply could not perform as a student. It bothered him and it bothered me. I tried to coach him and help him as much as possible, but it was no use.

I was the opposite of Harold and found schoolwork easy and enjoyed the learning. The only trouble was I was always waiting for Harold to catch up. He never did. I longed to move ahead as my brother had done, but it was not to be. Almost every teacher we had, and we had a different one nearly every year, wanted to move me ahead, but they were always talked out of it to keep peace in the community. We used to get books from a travelling library and I read all of them from cover to cover, so I broadened my horizons somewhat. I also listened to the lessons the teachers gave the older grades and I got to know their work as well as my own. But I stayed in the grade with Harold no matter what.

My brother Geoff (in front) and cousin Harold. They are standing on the back of Knight, the horse I bought with my own money ($5). They are showing off down at Betty Keeble's birthday picnic in the sand at the mouth of Churn Creek on the Fraser River.

CHAPTER 6

BAZIL

The summer of 1930 was hot and dry, and the only rain we got was in the form of a cloudburst now and then. Immediately afterwards the sun would come out, the ground would steam, and then it would be hot all over again.

There is a sound to really hot weather, a sort of rustling singing sound from the insects and the wisps of breezes blowing through the dry grasses. I used to love to go fishing down along the creek on this kind of day. The cool air and quiet murmuring of the water was such a pleasant change from the merciless heat of the sun.

My fishing equipment consisted of a willow pole about six feet long, a piece of black harness thread, and a hook. For bait I used grasshoppers, which were about in the thousands. The intended victims were brook trout, five to seven inches long, that lurked about in the dark back-eddies of the creek. They were delicious pan fried, and I always received praise from my Mother whenever I was able to bring home a big enough batch for a meal, which wasn't that often. My brother was a far better fisherman than I was and therefore he received most of the praise, but occasionally I would surprise myself and bring home a good bunch.

I was on one of these fishing expeditions one day when it had been particularly hot and dry for weeks. Fish always seemed to bite better on such a day. I was making my way along a heavily shaded stretch of the creek towards the Indian reserve. Overhanging birch and willows tangled into a jungle along here, and I was having a tough time trying to get from one pool to another, climbing over old deadfalls, detouring around clumps of willows, getting hung up on sticks, and edging my way around trees that hung out over the running water. I was crossing the creek on an old log when disaster struck. The log collapsed and I dropped into the creek's ice-cold water up to my armpits. I couldn't swim a stroke and the icy water made me howl with fear and dismay.

To my chagrin, I heard someone laughing. I looked up and there on the other side of the creek was a young Indian boy laughing his fool head off. I never did have a very long fuse on my temper, and on this occasion it was probably shorter than usual. I let go with all the cuss words I knew at that tender age (my vocabulary was much more mature than I was), directing them at the grinning ape on the shore. This only brought on more gales of laughter. At the same time as the idiot was laughing his sides sore at my plight, he was jockeying himself around a stump so that he could haul me up out of the frigid water. When I landed on shore I cussed him out some more, as if it was his fault that I had fallen into the creek. He only laughed the louder. Finally my temper subsided and I began to see the humour of the situation myself and joined in the laughter.

I had seen this boy before and knew that his name was Bazil (pronounced Bay-sil). His mother was Eliza Mashue, and he lived on the Dog Creek Indian reserve a mile and a half up the road from home. I had never spoken to him before, although I had seen him around. Once I was out of the creek I got out of the shade and into the sunshine, where I took off my shirt and pants and hung them on a willow bush to dry. Bazil and I talked while the clothes dried, which didn't take long in that dry heat. Then it was back to the business at hand, fishing. Bazil had retrieved my hook and line, and soon we were engrossed in fishing those good pools along the bottom of my Dad's meadow. Bazil was older than me by maybe three or four years, so he could reach a lot farther and knew how to let his hook down deep into the back-eddies where the big ones stayed. He always got more fish than I did.

We liked one another right away and soon fell into that wonderful state known as boyhood friendship. It seemed that I had known Bazil all my life and it was a comfortable feeling. When we parted that first day he gave me three or four of his fish so that I would have something to justify my wet feet and muddy pants when I got home. We arranged to meet again the next day and went our separate ways.

Geoff and I, sitting on the porch of the old Dog Creek Hotel in the early 1930s. Dad gave me the border collie puppy one Christmas. He loved to chase things, but one winter he took a poison coyote bait about five miles up the valley and dragged himself home to die on the porch just about where we are sitting. I was heartbroken but that is the way that country kids got to know about life and death.

I told my Mother all about how I fell in the creek and where I had been, but somehow I never told her about Bazil. Mother didn't particularly like the idea of me having too much to do with Indians. I think her motivation was concern about disease and cleanliness rather than some racial hang-up, and she never really had to face the problem because the Indian children were away attending mission school ten months of the year and therefore were not around to associate with. The result was that up till now I had never had any Indian friends.

Bazil and I soon became inseparable. We met to go fishing, we went exploring up at the Indian caves, or sometimes we would just walk up and down the dusty road and throw rocks or scare groundhogs and talk. Bazil had never been to school and this struck me as odd, even at that young age, so I asked him why. He didn't answer me, but I could tell he was embarrassed and ashamed so I passed it off and changed the subject. When I got home I asked my Mother why Bazil had not been to school like the other Indian kids. She said it was because he had TB and might give it to the rest of the children. I knew he had running sores around his neck that he always tried to hide with a handkerchief so they didn't show. My Mother wanted to know why I was asking these things about Bazil and if I was playing with him. I told her I was just curious and denied that I was seeing Bazil at all. I guess I denied it because if I hadn't she would have stopped me seeing Bazil, and he was the only friend that I had.

Bazil and I often went riding up on the top of Dog Creek Mountain. We would meet where the trail from the reserve and the ranch met, about halfway up. Sometimes we would join in a wild-horse chase with the young cowboys. On one of these occasions we corralled some good-looking animals, and Bazil was given first pick of the slicks (young adult horses with no brand). He chose a beautiful little mare. One of the young cowboys offered to halterbreak her for Bazil so that he could lead her home, but Basil refused and said he would break her himself, his way. He stayed up on the mountain with her for three days and never left her side. At the end of that session she would follow Bazil around like a dog. He brought her home to the reserve and it seemed that he was possessed by that horse. I used to go up to the reserve and watch him work with her. I have never seen such rapport between a man and an animal as there was between Bazil and that horse. It was beautiful to see.

The first time Bazil got on her back she never even quivered. Soon he could do anything with her. He taught her to stand in one place and not move. He taught her to sit. He taught her more tricks than you could teach a dog. Bazil laughed and said the horse understood Shuswap and I darned near believed him. She was a beautiful little animal and Bazil brushed her and washed her till she shone in the sunlight. All the young cowboys said she was the best horse around, and the final word for me was when my Dad said it was one of the best-trained horses he had ever seen.

Marcel Bourgeois was working up at the Pigeon Ranch that summer. He was a fine-looking, clean-cut young man. He was proud and maybe a bit vain. He certainly had the best outfit. Best hat, best vest, best shirt, best boots, best saddle, best bridle, the very best of everything that a young cowboy could have, but he didn't have the best horse. Bazil did, and Marcel wanted that horse more than anything in the world.

One day when we were walking down the road, Bazil told me that his mother said he would have to sell his horse because they had no money. Eliza had no man, and the winter before they'd had nothing to eat but frozen potatoes. Bazil would have to sell his horse before fall so that the family would have food for the winter. I told Bazil that he would get big money for that little mare. Horses were selling at that time for five dollars, and good ones for ten dollars. I told Bazil he could get a hundred dollars for that one. He just laughed and then he started to cough. He coughed and coughed until he was shaking and the blood was running out of the corners of his mouth. He turned away and leaned against the fence. I felt the terror of fear. I knew, somehow, that my gentle sweet friend was dying and I couldn't help him. I couldn't even tell my Mother about it. I was devastated.

A few days later I was sitting on the front porch of the old Dog Creek hotel when down the road came Marcel. He looked like a million bucks. His hat was on just right, his kerchief was flying, his shirt and vest were matching, his chaps, spurs, bridle, and saddle were all the best, and to top it off he was riding Bazil's horse, as proud as punch. I couldn't wait to see Bazil and find out how much he got for the horse. I set off right away for the reserve, but I hadn't made it past the first turn in the road when I heard someone whistle at me from the bushes by the roadside. It was Bazil.

"What the heck are you doing there?" I burst out, and then I looked at Bazil and it struck me. He had followed Marcel down the road. One look at his face told me that Bazil was heartbroken at having to sell his little horse. After the shock of seeing Bazil like this had worn off, I asked him why he had sold her.

"To eat," he said.

I walked back up to the reserve with Bazil. He was very weak and sick. When I left him he was sitting out in front of the log cabin he called home. It was the only time we parted without a smile.

I never saw Bazil alive again. He died two weeks later from the disease that had disfigured him and kept him out of school. Or maybe it was from a broken heart.

The Indians had a custom of laying out their dead, covered with a sheet or blanket, on the floor of the house. Often there would be an offering of flowers in a tin can at the foot and a cross with a carving of Jesus on it at the head. The friends and relations would come and pay their respects. This ritual was done for Bazil. I asked my Dad if he thought I should go. I was surprised when he said he would take me.

We got in the old ranch truck and went up to the reserve, to Bazil's home. It was the first time I had ever been inside an Indian home. The house was a small log cabin with a dirt roof. The windows were small and some of the broken panes had been replaced with pieces of cardboard. It was dark inside.

In the gloom I could see the rough board floor, the heater stove, some harness hanging on a back wall. Old Eliza was kneeling by the body of her son, who was lying on a blanket on the floor. She was moaning and crying. Some relatives were standing by the kitchen stove over in the corner. There was the smell of meat boiling, and the heat was suffocating. The flies were humming around Bazil's face and running around on those godawful sores on his neck. I stood there transfixed with emotion. My Dad grabbed me by the arm and pulled me out of the house, and I rushed around the corner and threw up. Then we got in the truck and drove home. I couldn't eat supper and went to bed. My Mother thought I had picked up a bug of some sort and my Dad just nodded his head and never said a word.

I found out later that Marcel paid Bazil five dollars for the horse. And the church wouldn't let Bazil be buried in the consecrated ground because he had not gone to school.

Bazil was my best friend for one short summer and no one knew a thing about it but my Dad. I will never forget him.

CHAPTER 7

HOCKEY

When school started again that fall we had another new teacher, Doreen Pollitt. In small settlements like Dog Creek, each resident seems to contribute something to the culture of the community. Mother brought music and literature; Dad brought work and dedication. A.J. Drinkell contributed penmanship and writing, while Ed Hillman was known for his studies of classical literature and socialism. Miss Pollitt introduced her students to something entirely different...hockey! Raised in the Peace River country, she had become a pretty good hockey player. Now that she was in Dog Creek, Miss Pollitt felt it was her duty to show her students the finer points of the sport.

Soon we were out staggering around on the frozen meadows and creeks, going at it hammer and tongs. We weren't very well equipped— old automobile skates nailed onto our boots, magazines for shin guards, frozen horse buns for pucks, and stripped willow branches for hockey sticks—but we were still having a great time. Geoff, a natural athlete, took to the new sport right away. I, on the other hand, wobbled around the rough ice on an old pair of girl's skates for the first little while, though I gradually improved.

As we got better at the game, we graduated to real rubber pucks and factory-made sticks, proper uniforms, and padding, too. Of course we weren't factory representatives as most of us still had hockey gloves made of buckskin by the local Indian women.

Miss Pollitt had to drop out of the game after the first year because she married Frank Armes and they were expecting their first child. We pressed on, however, and hockey became our favourite winter pastime. For me, it also became a great way to take my mind off the problems I faced at school.

By the time I reached Grade 6, both my cousin Kathleen and a girl called Betty Keeble were in Grade 8. The girls eagerly awaited the upcoming government exam that they were scheduled to take in June. A teacher from Williams Lake was called in to supervise the test. She was well aware of the fact that I could not be advanced without Harold, despite my best efforts. When the test papers were handed out to the girls, the supervisor offered me her copy and asked if I'd be willing to take the exam also. Of course I jumped at the chance. The supervisor said she'd look over the papers herself, and if my work appeared promising she'd send my exam to Victoria with the others and ask for a mark. This seemed like a great challenge. Perhaps I could prove that I should be advancing much faster than they allowed me to.

I felt fairly confident even though I hadn't officially taken any of the work that the exam covered. During school I had listened in on the Grade 8 lessons and read Betty Keeble's books when she wasn't looking. Part of me believed it'd be pretty tough to get a decent mark, though. After the tests were handed in, the supervisor said nothing more to me the rest of the week. Things didn't look too good.

When the supervisor informed me she was sending my test to Victoria, I was thrilled. Maybe now I'd start to get somewhere with my education. We waited three agonizing weeks for the results. When the grades were announced, everyone was excited to hear that both Kathleen and Betty had passed with flying colours. The news for me wasn't nearly as happy. My paper was never marked. The supervisor who'd given me a chance received a stiff reprimand for her actions. She was upset by the entire incident and told Mother she believed I deserved a higher grade than either Kathleen or Betty. When my mother told me what the teacher had said, I was devastated. Obviously it didn't matter if I knew the material or not. I wasn't going anywhere without my cousin.

By the time Harold and I began Grade 7 together that September, all of us played a pretty good game of shinny. The local Indians joined in on these good times, too. They were usually excellent skaters, having been exposed to the sport at the Cariboo Indian School at 150 Mile House. Not only were they fantastic players, but most were also fine sportsmen and the cleanest players anywhere.

The Indians loved the game. It gave them an opportunity to prove they were the best at a highly demanding sport. But winning the game was not the only thing that counted. For them, the sheer joy of

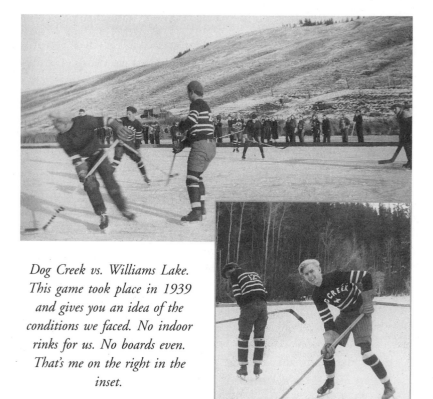

Dog Creek vs. Williams Lake. This game took place in 1939 and gives you an idea of the conditions we faced. No indoor rinks for us. No boards even. That's me on the right in the inset.

the contest of skills was important: a quick turn around the opposing player; skating, turning, stickhandling; all the skills that made hockey the fastest, toughest, and most elegant game ever devised by man were their delight. They played the game not only with grace and power and skill, but with their souls as well.

Conditions under which they played are hard to imagine. Back in 1930, while we were still learning the game, the Alkali Lake team was playing all around the Cariboo. We often heard stories about their games, and a typical match at Williams Lake usually went something like this. The weather would be clear and cold, about ten below zero and looking like it would stay that way for the weekend. A game was set for two o'clock Sunday afternoon at the open-air rink in Williams Lake. On Friday the Alkali boys were getting ready to travel. The old green-and-white uniforms—bought for the team years earlier by Mr.

W.C. Woodward, owner of Woodward's Department Store, who was married to the daughter of the man who owned Alkali Lake Ranch—had been checked over and patched and mended with loving care by the wives and sweethearts of the players. Players packed up their gloves, shin pads, and short pants, the sum total of their equipment, which were usually handmade from buckskin and willow sticks, along with deer hair for extra padding. Their skates were sharpened by hand with file and stones. Some had been sharpened so many times that there was precious little metal left. The skate boots were patched with buckskin and the laces were often rawhide.

After a good night's sleep, the boys were up and ready to go at six Saturday morning. This was no luxury trip; it was 35 miles with sleighs and teams of horses travelling three to four miles an hour. That meant ten to twelve hours' exposure to minus-ten weather, not counting stops for lunch or resting time for the horses on hills. The hockey team of six or seven players formed a caravan of three sleighs and several saddle horses. A few wives and children and even a fan or two piled onto the sleighs for the journey. By the time they arrived in Williams Lake late Saturday afternoon, the sun had already set.

There was no hotel to go to. Indians were not allowed in the hotels. They weren't allowed in the restaurants either. Instead they watered the horses at the Williams Lake creek and got some water for themselves, then proceeded up the hill to the rink on Third Avenue. They shovelled the snow aside and pitched their tents, their accommodation for the weekend. Supper was some deer meat and boiled frozen potatoes they had brought from home. A campfire was the only source of heat and a coal-oil lamp the only source of light. Sleeping under those conditions is next to impossible, but the players got some rest by lying close to the fire.

Breakfast was more of the same food left over from supper. They couldn't buy anything from the store because they simply didn't have any money. When the local players arrived, the Alkali Lake team helped them clean and flood the rink, preparing it for the big game. This exercise was the forerunner of the pre-game warm-up! The team had one more meal of deer meat and potatoes before the game got underway.

As was often the case, the Alkali team didn't have any spare players, so the men played the entire game without any relief. Mathew Dick

The Alkali Lake Hockey Team. Left to right: Joe Clemine, Pat Chelsea, Mathew Dick, Joe Dan, David Johnson, Sylista, Louie Amiele, Peter Christopher, Alfred Sandy.

was in goal, David Johnson and Joe Clemine on defense, Pat Chelsea and Alfred Sandy on each side of Alec Antoine (known as Sylista) on the forward line. Gaby Jack or Francis Squinahan also played with them if anyone got injured. Each of these men brought his own unique abilities to the game and together they made a team few could beat.

Mathew Dick had incredibly quick reflexes. The Indians liked to say that if Mathew saw the puck he'd manage to stop it with something, whether it was his toe or elbow or even his rear end! No matter what, he'd find a way to get the job done.

Then there was Joe Clemine, the master skater. He made the most beautiful swooping turns either way with equal ease. Backwards, forwards—it made no difference. Joe seemed to float around the ice with the puck glued to his stick. The man was a poet with a puck.

Patrick Chelsea was another story. No one ever seemed to notice Pat. He always managed to hide himself when a picture was being taken, and he was the same on the ice. When he played, you would never see him. After the goal was scored, everybody wondered who put the puck in the net until they found out it was Pat again. He scored lots of times, both on and off the ice—he was also the father of 22 children!

Alfred Sandy was another very quiet, soft-spoken man with a shy smile, but his shot could go like a bullet.

The tireless, tough old campaigner on the team was David Johnson. He was also a stickhandler par excellence. When he came down the ice the only sound you heard was the clack, clack, clack of the puck snapping back and forth as he stickhandled around his opponents like they were standing still. I loved to hear the story of old David's marathon race, which proved what an amazing athlete he was. At one of the pre-war stampedes in Williams Lake, the management decided to add a mini-marathon foot race to spice up the program. The race started at 150 Mile House, ten miles from Williams Lake, and proceeded along the lakeshore road into Williams Lake. Participants then made one lap around the track to finish in front of the grandstand. At the end of the day, Wally Naef came in first, followed by Percy Pigeon, and David Johnson was third, having run the race in moccasins on a gravel road. The local paper gave it a nice write-up and even mentioned David's great effort. They missed the most interesting part of the whole story, though. It seems that David couldn't find a ride to 150 Mile House that morning to register for the race, so he had to run the ten miles out there before the race started and then run back to Williams Lake for third place. Not bad for a man over 40.

Sylista was Alkali Lake's secret weapon; as long as they had him, they won. He was a truly magnificent player. For example, during this Sunday afternoon game, the score seesawed back and forth. Every time the teams were tied up, Sylista scored another goal to push them ahead. With only seconds left and the score even, Sylista managed to score again and Alkali came away with another victory. Several people congratulated the Alkali team on their fine play, and then the crowd gradually drifted off as everyone returned to the comfort of their warm homes. The Alkali boys, on the other hand, had another ten-hour journey ahead of them that night. Still wearing their uniforms, they

Alkali Lake Indian Reserve. Everyone on the reserve lived in log houses back in the days I played hockey here on the rink that was created just east of the church.

took down their tents and headed back to Alkali Lake. No one invited them in for a meal or cup of coffee or even to get warmed up.

Alkali eventually won the Cariboo championship. This meant they were invited down to Vancouver to play an all-star team of players from the Pacific Coast League, a group from the professional ranks. Peter Christopher and Louie Amiele, both from Canim Lake, joined the team for what were to be Alkali Lake's greatest games.

This trip to Vancouver could be likened to a Chilliwack junior ball team playing in Yankee Stadium. None of the Alkali Lake men had ever been to the big city. They had never played on artificial ice in a stadium and they had also never played, or seen, for that matter, a professional hockey player.

Vancouver hockey fans were intrigued by the idea of having an all-Indian team competing, and the games were sold out. The players came dressed in their normal working attire: buckskin gloves and coats, blue jeans, cowboy hats, and boots. The Vancouver papers were full of pictures and write-ups about them.

When the games began, every radio in the Cariboo was tuned to the station broadcasting the series. Reception was terrible and the station kept fading in and out. Just when you heard that Alkali was starting down the ice, the radio faded out and the results of the rush were lost in the static. The last big fade-out happened at the very end of the game. When we heard the final score, Alkali had been beaten by one goal. Vancouver sportswriters had predicted a walkover, with scores of 15 to 1 for the Vancouver team, so we Cariboo people were more than satisfied with the showing. Their second game was a repeat of the first, and again Alkali was beaten by only one goal. All things considered, it was a terrific performance.

Sylista had shone once again during the games. Lester Patrick, the New York Rangers general manager, knew a good thing when he saw it. He offered Sylista a job playing for the Rangers, but Sylista refused, saying that he already had a job cowboying at Alkali Lake Ranch for fifteen dollars a month. Even though he was a superb player, Sylista was more naive than most of the other boys on his team. Sylista's admirers could only imagine how far he might have gone with a career in hockey. There were few hockey players as gifted as he was. A power skater with tremendous speed, he needed just one stride to be in full flight. Sylista turned with equal dexterity in either direction, stickhandling at full speed all the time. He skated backwards with the puck better than most of the other players could carry it going forward. He had a natural talent for shooting as well; the players regularly lined up bottles or tin cans on the backboards and Sylista picked off each one of them from the blue line. His accuracy was uncanny.

Perhaps Sylista chose to stay because that was all he knew and understood about the world. He had never been to school a day in his life. An orphan who actually belonged to the Chilcotin tribe, Sylista was raised by Napoit and his wife at Alkali Lake. He was different from the Shuswaps, built heavier and stronger. The biggest difference, however, was in his personality. Sylista had the grit and determination to win and simply would not be beaten. None of the other Alkali boys would hurt another player to win, but Sylista would.

At the height of Alkali Lake's hockey success, a major mine named the Cariboo Gold Quartz was discovered close to the old Barkerville diggings. The town of Wells, named after the discoverer of the mine, quickly grew up around it. Wells supported a hockey team made up mostly of big, tough, hungry boys from the prairies and northern Ontario. Their biggest, toughest, and hungriest was a guy named Red Waller. Dirty was his method and mean was his nature.

Hockey

The same year they joined the league, Wells ended up playing in the Cariboo Championship finals against Alkali Lake. It was a hard-fought game, played in Williams Lake. Sylista was having one of his greatest games, scoring most of the Alkali goals. His opponents soon figured out that without Sylista in the picture they could beat Alkali and get the championship. Waller came out on the next shift and deliberately brought his stick down across Sylista's foot, breaking three bones in the arch. Alkali Lake's star player was taken off the ice and examined by a doctor present at the game. The physician immediately ordered Sylista up to the hospital, but the player made it clear he wasn't going anywhere.

"Put my skate back on, put me on the ice, and give me the puck." Sylista's voice was like steel; there was no stopping him.

He returned to the ice and one of his teammates passed him the puck. Waller was skating away and Sylista shouted at him. As Waller turned to hear what Sylista was saying, Sylista let fly with a shot. The puck caught Waller on the side of his head and he went down like he'd been poleaxed. He never knew what hit him; in fact, he didn't know anything for about three days. It took a week in the hospital before Waller was able to function normally again. He was just plain lucky to have survived at all.

That was the last year Alkali Lake won the championship. After that the team started to disintegrate. They continued to play hockey, they quit the Cariboo league. By this time, though, they'd left such an impression on their community that everyone continued to watch whatever games they played and proudly cheered them on.

Sylista continued in his job as a ranch hand at Alkali Lake Ranch. He was sent out to build a fence on a day when one of those thunderstorms we used to get during hot, dry summers came up. Lightning was flashing all over the place, and just a second after Sylista let go of the crowbar he was working with, the lightning hit it. Other members of the work crew found Sylista out cold on the ground. He was unconscious for several days but finally came to. With his remarkable physique he was back to work in a few days, but he was not the same. He couldn't walk quite right and his speech was slurred. His health kept going downhill and within a year he died—I think it was in 1933. He was truly a most unusual and gifted man.

The Dog Creek hockey team at Alkali Lake about 1938. Back row, left to right: Ford Glasco, George Thompson, Norman Worthington, Ray Bill, Archie Sampson, Gilbert Harry, Hilary Place. Front row, left to right: Ernie Glasco, Geoff Place, Ray Pigeon (goalie), Eric Hillman.

The story takes a strange jump here. In 1968, 35 years later, I moved to Vancouver from the Cariboo. One day I was shopping at a Safeway store and as I pushed my cart around the end of an aisle, BANG, I ran right smack into a cart that a woman was pushing. "Excuse me," I said, "I guess this Cariboo boy isn't very good with one of these things."

The woman laughed and said, "From the Cariboo?"

"Yes," I said. "I can't stickhandle around like I used to."

"My," she said, "you sound like a hockey player. My brother was a great hockey player, you know. He always talked about a young Indian boy from the Cariboo that he saw play once in Vancouver years ago. My brother said many times that young man was the finest natural hockey player he ever saw in his life, and my brother should know."

It seems her brother was Lester Patrick.

Thirty-five years had passed, but Sylista was not forgotten!

As our team at Dog Creek improved, we began playing the Alkali team quite a bit. Their love of the game still showed, and it inspired us to play our best. Their rink was out in the open air in the Indian village at Alkali Lake, and a big fire always burned alongside the sheet of ice where we sat to put on our skates. All of the people from the reserve, about a hundred of them, gathered around talking and laughing and enjoying themselves, along with a few whites. Chrissie Pigeon, the wife of our goaltender Ray Pigeon, was there for every game. Unfortunately she was a great Alkali Lake fan and cheered whenever they scored on her husband, which happened to be quite often. Chrissie gloried in our discomfort every time we were beaten 20 to 0, and she rubbed it in with great glee.

A game was scheduled near the D4 after Christmas 1933 while I was still in Grade 7. Even though I was younger than most of the other players, I played a pretty good game and got a lot of ice time. When the game ended we wearily rode our horses the five miles back home as the temperature sank to twenty below. I was exhausted by the time we arrived and began to feel a bit queer during supper. Shrugging it off as fatigue after a hard day on the ice, I fell into bed and drifted off to sleep in no time.

CHAPTER 8

A TERRIBLE BURDEN

The next morning I got out of bed, intending to get ready for school as usual. Suddenly my heart started to pound and hives broke out all over my skin. I sat down on the edge of the bed until the feeling passed. Again I stood and reached for my clothes. My pulse quickened immediately and the hives returned even worse than before. I felt my eyes swelling, then my tongue, and I began to choke.

Gasping, I called out to Mother as I collapsed onto the bed. She rushed into my room and when she saw the state I was in she grabbed a shoehorn and was able to hold my tongue down so that I could breathe.

Fifteen minutes later the attack subsided and I seemed okay. Mother believed the episode must have been brought on by something I ate, so she ordered me to stay in bed and sleep it off. Soon the rest of the hives disappeared and I believed I was fine. I tried a third time to get up only to have the same symptoms. It was scary.

The following morning nothing had changed. I could not stand up without my heart pounding, hives breaking out, and my tongue swelling. My mother felt it best that I stay put in my room until this problem passed. The days quickly turned to weeks, and soon months were passing with no sign of this nightmare ending. I felt perfectly healthy yet I could not move without breaking into hives.

Lying in bed day after day was horribly boring. Our radio did not work in the daytime so my only entertainment was reading. And I read everything in sight—every magazine, book, and paper in the house. Fortunately Mr. Keeble, the bookkeeper and storekeeper at the Gang Ranch, belonged to a mystery book club and he kindly sent his books over for me.

When I wasn't reading I gazed out the window. By this time we were living in the old Dog Creek Hotel. In 1929 the Dog Creek store had gone broke and the Armes family lost control of the Dog Creek Ranch. In 1930 my Dad had bought back a portion of my Grandfather Place's ranch with no money down and a first-year payment of $100, and we'd moved into the old hotel in 1931. Now I lay in bed and watched the trees leaf out in spring and the summer sun on the hills. The fall colours came and went and the winter snow settled on the valley. Still I could not even get to the edge of my bed without causing an outbreak. My skin was itchy beyond belief, and every time I tried to get up I suffered for my efforts.

At Christmas, Dad and Geoff packed me downstairs and laid me out on the couch in the big living room of the hotel. This was the first time I'd been out of my room in twelve months. I admired the holiday decorations around me, grateful for something new to look at. My muscles had withered so much from inactivity that I couldn't stand on my own, leaving me little choice but to eat Christmas dinner propped on the sofa. Even though I'd had visitors throughout the past year and they knew my condition, it seemed everyone was acting strangely around me now that I was downstairs.

After we moved into the hotel we started hosting a huge turkey dinner each Christmas, inviting people from the community to join us. Most of those who came were men who worked as placer miners on the Fraser River. They would all contribute something to the dinner such as a bottle of wine or some Mandarin oranges. My Mother, who was a great hostess, would ask them each to do something to entertain the others. We were treated to displays of magic, music, dances, poems in God knows what languages, and one performance I remember vividly, performed by a former German soldier, "How to Kill With a Bayonet." We were still very poor, but we grew the turkey and vegetables, and with the donations we got from the attendees, it cost virtually nothing.

Ed Hillman, who helped my Dad on the ranch, would usually have a few too many Christmas drinks, then rise from the table to propose a grand toast to my mother in his thick Swedish accent. Although he knew she'd be half mad at him, Ed loved to expound at great length using his finest flowery language. After his speech he'd bow deeply to Mother, then toast the room.

Not one to disappoint, Ed was in fine form again this Christmas, offering a tribute to Dad for his generosity. He moved on to acknowledge the other guests gathered at the table, then quoted everyone from Socrates and Plato to Immanuel Kant. With the customary bow to my mother, Ed complimented her beauty of form and face as well as her delightful culinary arts. It appeared after his lengthy praise of Mother that Ed was finished. Instead he turned to me as his expression grew more serious.

"We have all of us borne our burdens this year, but none of us has had the terrible burden of sickness that you have carried." His voice soft, the tears that had welled up in the corners of his eyes now fell freely down his face. "You have borne it well. I only hope that this year God will give you good health." Until that moment I hadn't comprehended how wasted and weak I'd become. Ed's touching speech revealed that he was actually afraid for my life.

Not until the following spring did I receive a visit from a doctor. After his examination, Dr. Grafton could not provide any explanation for what was happening to me. A month later a young doctor arrived while Dr. Grafton was away on holidays. The doctor asked me to stand, but this exertion brought on a terrible attack of hives. I was close to passing out as I watched the doctor plunge a hypodermic needle into my leg, injecting a yellow fluid. Within seconds I felt normal; the hives disappeared, the itching stopped, and my heart slowed to its regular rhythm.

He warned me that this was a temporary fix. He had injected adrenaline and his diagnosis was that my adrenal glands had stopped working. He didn't know if they'd ever function normally again. I could, however, ward off future attacks by injecting more adrenaline. The doctor showed Mother how to insert the needle and he gave us several vials to use when necessary. Mother informed him that she didn't like the idea of my learning to shoot stuff into my body like a junkie every time I felt I needed it. This statement caused him to cast a rather odd look my mother's way, but he didn't respond and soon left for Williams Lake.

It turned out Mother's comments about junkies must have hit a nerve with the doctor. Several days later we found out he'd been caught stealing drugs from the Williams Lake hospital. I was sorry to hear it;

he had been the only person who offered me any explanation about my poor health and gave me slight hope that someday I'd recover. He was a clever young man with a serious problem.

Any doctors travelling through Dog Creek would stop in to have a look at me, but they had little success in treating me. Dr. Grafton finally said I'd never be cured and was clearly pessimistic in assessing my chances for a normal life. In fact, he predicted I wouldn't live past the age of 21, although he suggested I keep this information from my Mother so I wouldn't cause her any more anxiety. And then he left.

From that day on I had little use for him. I had no respect for a doctor who could treat a very ill young patient in such a callous manner. Fortunately for me, I was beginning to do a little better and could move about by holding onto chairs. Whenever I felt my heart rate increase, I sat down and rested. It might take an hour to get out of bed and go downstairs, but at least I was mobile. A chair was my biggest helper, steadying my weak legs and giving me a place to sit quickly when I needed to. (I never did use the adrenaline. My Mother did not believe in needles and it was just never used. Somehow things got better on their own.)

Shortly after Dr. Grafton's grim prognosis that I'd probably kick the bucket some day soon, Geoff had to go pick up parts from the Gang Ranch. It was such a beautiful hot summer day that I decided I'd make the trip with him. My brother helped me into the car and we were off by ten o'clock that morning. Breathing in the fresh air on such a gorgeous day, especially after being housebound for well over a year, filled me with a sense of elation and freedom. We met Mrs. Keeble at the Gang Ranch and had a lovely lunch with her. She was always warm and funny and I enjoyed our friendly banter while we ate.

By three o'clock that afternoon, Geoff and I were ready to return to Dog Creek. Over the hills in the distance we could see that the dark clouds had opened up and the rain was falling hard. After crossing the Fraser River we began the climb up the other side of the valley. Geoff slowed down where a section of mud and gravel had been washed across the road by the rain, but he managed to steer the car through. A little farther down the road there was another washout, only it was much larger than the first and we were not able to get past it. My

*My Dad's 17-hand saddlehorse Whitey looks across the Fraser River to the
Gang Ranch. This ranch, at one point the largest in British Columbia,
was started by the Harper brothers at the end of the 1800s. The ranch
got its name because Jerome and Thaddeus Harper were the first in the
area to use a gang plough—one with two or more ploughshares (a "gang
of ploughs") so it can make several furrows at once.*

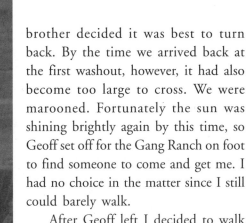

brother decided it was best to turn back. By the time we arrived back at the first washout, however, it had also become too large to cross. We were marooned. Fortunately the sun was shining brightly again by this time, so Geoff set off for the Gang Ranch on foot to find someone to come and get me. I had no choice in the matter since I still could barely walk.

After Geoff left I decided to walk to the bridge over the Fraser River so I could watch the swift, muddy water rush by. It was only 50 yards from the car, yet it took me a long time to get there as I had to stop every few feet to rest. Finally I sat, legs hanging over the edge of the bridge, and stared at the river beneath my feet. I felt terrible; I was shaking and itching and my heart pounded in my chest. All the beauty of the day, along with the laughter and jokes, was forgotten. I couldn't stand this life anymore. I knew that only one short step off the side of the bridge would end my problems.

There comes a time in everybody's life when a vital decision has to be made. I made mine on that bridge. From that moment on I vowed I would live each day with as much strength as I had. Standing slowly, I walked away from where I sat at the edge of the bridge and made my way to the car. By the time I reached it, Geoff and J.H. McIntyre, the Gang Ranch foreman, had arrived and we returned to the ranch, staying the night there. The next morning a crew from the ranch cleared the road for us and we drove back home. What began as a little road trip of ten miles became one of the most important journeys of my life. I knew that I wanted to live no matter what obstacles I faced.

✫ ✫ ✫

I was determined to return to school, and I made it back when classes began in September 1935. Ironically, Harold quit school on his sixteenth birthday, which was two weeks after I first got sick, so now I could study and advance at my own pace. When I became ill, my teacher kindly gave me a pass mark for Grade 7 based on the work I'd done up until Christmas. A year and a half later I was finally starting Grade 8.

The schoolwork was still familiar and I quickly picked up where I left off. Walking to and from the school was another matter though. My natural inclination was to move fast, but I was forced by my lingering illness to take each step slowly. If I forgot myself and picked up my pace, the hives were an abrupt reminder of my limitations. Some days I rested two or three times along the half-mile walk, but I was gradually getting better. In November I took on the job of school janitor—lighting the fire in the morning and doing other chores around the school. It didn't pay anything, but it did prove that I wouldn't be completely useless all my life.

Mr. A.R. Lord, the school inspector, paid us a visit in May the following year. He was impressed with all of the students and gave the teacher a good report. After he had watched the different classes in the room, Mr. Lord dismissed everyone but me. "I have an experimental exam for you to take, if you'd like," he told me. "Should you pass this test I'll advance you to Grade 9 immediately. However, if you don't pass you'll still be able to take the government exam at the end of June." He stood quietly, waiting for my reply.

It certainly wasn't a long wait. "Yes sir, I'd like to take this test. When do I start?"

"Right now."

Slightly bewildered by this sudden opportunity, I went to my desk and he handed me the exam paper. I began the test at one o'clock and I was allowed four hours to complete it. By four o'clock I was finished and had reread my answers twice. There was nothing more to do so I handed the paper in.

"If you'd like to wait, I'll let you know the results." I nodded and returned to my desk. He carefully read through each page while I watched for any clues as to how I had done. Finally he added the totals and looked up, appearing dumbfounded by the outcome.

"I can hardly believe it. Not only have you passed, but I will bet you have the best marks in British Columbia." He paused, looking back down at the papers. "You've got 99.6 percent."

Of course I was thrilled with my good showing, but most of all I was happy to be through Grade 8. Three long years had passed since I'd taken the government exams with Betty and Kathleen. I had made it over that hurdle at last.

Mr. Lord submitted my name and marks for the Lieutenant Governor's Medal, awarded each year to the pupil with the highest marks in the province. I was disqualified, however, because I had been

Sheila Doherty, shown here with her horse Fiddle, was the teacher at Dog Creek school when I returned to Grade 8 after my illness. She introduced me to Keats, Browning, and Shelley. Later, under her married name of Sheila Watson, she wrote a couple of novels based on her time in Dog Creek—The Double Hook *and* Deep Hollow Creek.

graded on an experimental examination. I didn't care about it though; to me, the year had been a huge success. I was walking with greater ease now and I was through with Grade 8!

Now I moved on to high school and found that the rules that once applied to my brother had changed, and certainly not for the better. High school was a three-year course when Geoff attended and he was still considered a pupil of the school. The trustees hired teachers with higher qualifications to instruct and paid more for their services.

This system worked well for the students, including my brother, who graduated with no problem.

Under the new rules I was no longer a student of the Dog Creek school and I wasn't even allowed in the classroom. A qualified teacher would not be brought in for me and I was forced to complete high school by correspondence from Victoria. The trustees wanted me to continue as janitor since all of the remaining students were girls and they had to travel farther in the mornings. This suited me fine, but the fact that I couldn't stay in the classroom where I'd spent so many years caused a little controversy between the school trustees and me. We finally reached a compromise. In exchange for my janitorial work I was allowed to sit in the cloakroom at the back of the building and study for my diploma among the coats and overshoes. To make matters worse, high school now took four years to complete instead of three. Talk about bad luck.

Working on my correspondence courses and being partitioned from the other students soon had me feeling isolated. The young men and women teaching at the school helped me if I found something difficult to understand, but occasionally even they couldn't help me if I was studying a subject they had never taken. I was left to wrestle with these problems myself, and it overwhelmed me at times. My courses included French and Latin, which were mandatory, along with algebra, geometry, physics, English, history, automotive engineering, electricity, and art. With weekly mail service in the area it took a month to get a corrected paper back from Victoria. If I was making a mistake I wouldn't find out for a month. Similarly, if I needed instruction it took a month to receive any guidance.

Grade 9 passed without too many problems. Or at least without too many problems at school!

CHAPTER 9

JOY

That same year, 1936, I had other things on my mind besides schoolwork. At the age of sixteen I was on the verge of learning much more about life.

Mother had had a series of Indian girls who worked at the house, but that year she heard of a white girl in Likely who was looking for work. My mother wrote to her and offered the eighteen-year-old a job. After accepting the position, Joy arrived with Geoff on the stage. She was of Norwegian descent, though not at all the blond Nordic type I expected. Joy was dark-haired, slim, and beautiful.

She was given a room up our stairs. (There were two sets of stairs in the house. One led from the bar room to the workers' side, where the rooms were quite plain. The other set connected the main sitting room to our more lavishly decorated family quarters.)

Joy soon fit into the routine in our house. She was a great worker, doing extra

Here I am with Joy, who was such a good friend and companion to me when I was getting back to living after my long illness.

little things like dressing up the table, which pleased Mother immensely. Dad always cooked breakfast, joined by Mr. Drinkell, Ed Hillman, and anyone working for us at the time. They didn't want any women around during breakfast, so Joy's day didn't start until half past seven. I was never an early riser and after being sick so long I was used to fixing my own breakfast before school. Mother never woke before nine each morning and by then everyone was out of the house.

This arrangement found Joy and me eating breakfast together every day. Shy with each other at first, our awkwardness soon passed as we began to enjoy conversations about our mutual interests, leading to discussions involving our hopes and dreams for the future. She told me about her childhood, living on a houseboat on Kingcome Inlet where her father was a handlogger. Joy revealed how she lost her little brother when he fell overboard and drowned, and then she told me about her mother's depression, which led the family to move to Likely. Her father had to give up logging on the salt chuck, and the family was penniless when they arrived in the Cariboo. At one point they made a chimney for the stove out of old four-pound jam tins they found in the dump, cutting out the bottoms and wiring them together.

Each time Joy spoke of her parents, the love she felt for them would shine brightly in her eyes. She was particularly proud of her father's fiddle playing, and she was very musical herself. At that time I was learning to play the fiddle, along with the piano and guitar. The mutual love of music brought us closer together. Soon we were spending all our spare time at the piano, trying to figure out how the chord patterns were put together. We were elated when we found out how to play "The Waltz You Saved For Me." It was a glorious feeling to have someone to share the learning with, one I had never experienced before.

One spring day it was raining heavily. We always saved rainwater for washing our hair because the water from the creek was as hard as nails and left our hair like straw. Joy and I ran for the old galvanized tub used to collect the rainfall and placed it under the eavestrough. At that moment there was a magnificent flash and the most terrible bang I'd ever heard. Lightning had struck the hill behind the house. Joy fell back into me, speechless with fright. I would later find out that her mother was nearly killed by a lightning bolt at their cabin in Likely. I held on to Joy while she looked at me, still scared and shaking; then I

Betty Keeble boarded at our house while she was attending school, and later she had her own car so she could get back and forth from the Gang Ranch, where her parents lived. Everyone thought Geoff and Betty (right) would get married—but it didn't happen. (The car was a 1932 [I think] Auburn straight eight, built in the same factory as the Duesenburg and the Cord—this will mean something to car buffs. If you had one today it would be worth a fortune.)

leaned down and kissed her. I think we both knew at that moment that we were in love.

Taken aback by this sudden turn of events, neither of us was sure what to do. Mother was at Mrs. Keeble's, so at least we had time to compose ourselves before she returned. We decided to keep our newly discovered feelings a secret, because Mother would not approve. The problem with this plan was that keeping something like love under wraps at our tender age was virtually impossible. Everyone around us knew how we felt about each other in no time.

That's when the trouble started. Mrs. Keeble was furious and declared it was disgraceful to have a son consorting with the hired help. She was particularly upset because her daughter Betty was contemplating marriage to Geoff and she didn't want Betty associating with a family that condoned our "shameful" relationship. This upset me and I couldn't see why Mrs. Keeble, along with everyone else, had such difficulty with Joy and me being together.

All the pleasure we had felt in our little romance ended abruptly. We could no longer even be seen together without more vituperation. When Geoff and Betty invited me to go for rides in Betty's car, Joy was excluded. It seemed that no one was on our side. The friendship and innocent love Joy and I shared was reduced to tears and heartbreak.

The situation started to take its toll on Joy. She was unhappy and run down, getting one cold after another. One night she went to bed early, suffering from a bad chest cold that gave her trouble breathing. Around midnight I lay in bed in my room down the hall and could hear her gasping for breath. George Thompson was sleeping on Geoff's old bed in my room, and as I got out of bed I told George that I was going to check on Joy and see if she needed anything.

Joy was sitting up in her bed looking miserable. She asked for a hot drink, and I went downstairs and fixed a hot lemonade, grabbing a couple of aspirin on the way back to her room. She sipped at the warm liquid, then slowly rested her head back on her pillow. I sat beside her a little while before returning to my own room. George was still awake and asked if Joy was feeling any better. Crawling into bed I said yes, then blew out the lamp and went to sleep. The next morning I woke and left for school as usual.

After I left, all hell broke loose at the house. Mother learned I'd been in Joy's room during the night and made her own assumptions as to what went on. She berated Joy for entertaining me in her bedroom in the middle of the night and would not listen to any explanations. Joy was not given any opportunity to defend herself and Mother fired her on the spot.

When I returned from school, Joy was gone. Mother told me she was in the hospital at Williams Lake. I phoned the hospital to inquire about Joy, only to be informed that no patient by that name had been admitted. It was then that Mother revealed what had transpired. After she fired Joy, Mother insisted the girl be on the next stage, which was close to departing at that time.

When I began to protest, Mother justified her harsh actions with accusations. "I know you were having a sexual affair with that girl.

Don't deny it! You don't go to a respectable lady's bedroom at midnight without some intent."

"It was hardly a clandestine meeting, Mother. I told George where I was going. We weren't hiding anything. I even went downstairs to the kitchen to make her a lemonade. When I got to her room, I left the door open. Besides, I was only in there a few minutes."

I could see my words were having little effect on my mother. It really didn't matter what I said anyway. Joy was gone.

Nobody seemed to care, let alone believe, that we had simply been genuinely happy in each other's company. Joy and I had no one else and we had shared so much. There was nothing I could do now except face the fact that it was over. I sat on a rock up behind the house and sobbed, hoping that the tears would diminish my pain. Numbness settled over me as I tried to compose myself before returning home.

It was a long time before I was able to get to Williams Lake. I had learned that Joy was working as a waitress at the hotel. When I saw her, my heart almost stopped. Feeling slightly uncomfortable, we talked with some reservation until she told me she was getting married in a few weeks. I felt as though the wind had been knocked out of me and left as quickly as I could. Despite everything I intended to say, I had remained silent. I wanted to wish her happiness, to thank her for her friendship, and to apologize for the way we parted. And to say that every time I heard "The Waltz You Saved for Me," I thought of her.

CHAPTER 10

ROMANCE
AND OTHER ADVENTURES

When I started Grade 10 in the fall of 1937 I resumed my job of getting firewood, sweeping the floor, and cleaning the room at the end of classes each day. While I was busy with my tasks, the teacher wrote the next day's lessons on the blackboard. She was a pretty girl, only nineteen years old, and I found my gaze drifting in her direction as we both worked. Two people of our age probably shouldn't have been left alone together.

One day after we'd finished our chores I was helping her on with her coat. The next thing I knew we were kissing and holding each other and I felt a thrill run through me. School had suddenly become my favourite place to be.

It quickly developed into an afternoon ritual, one that I looked forward to with great anticipation. Soon, as is the wont of young lovers, the lips were not enough; the neck must be kissed and so on and we eagerly explored this exciting new world. She was the only girl around for miles and I really liked her, yet something told me to back off before it was too late. I resolved to discuss the whole matter of our relationship with her the next afternoon.

It wasn't easy, but I mustered up courage enough and during our tryst I broached the subject. I'd gone over it a thousand times in my mind and thought I had it down pat. The way I had it figured, by the time I finished my recitation she'd still want to throw herself in my arms but would resist in favour of the more circumspect path I believed we should follow.

Obviously in all the reading I'd done I missed the part about a woman scorned. I soon learned there was no graceful or painless way to back out of an affair. Her response left me dumbfounded; that girl's vocabulary was far more extensive than I'd ever expected. I was also painfully aware that our necking matches were over for good.

She flounced out of the school without another word. I knew I'd get no more tutoring from that teacher. She wasn't alone long, however, finding solace in Harold's arms for the rest of the year. This was well and good for them but, damn it, I could have used some help in French!

The next year was another game again. This time the teacher was a young man, only 22 years old, by the name of Graham Fuller. We called him Teach. He was tall and gangly, with a hank of unruly hair hanging over his face. Although he was a fairly good teacher, his heart just wasn't in the job. He craved action, and there was precious little of that to be found around Dog Creek. By that time I was healthy enough, and along with Harold we set out to stir up a little excitement every now and then.

Uncle Joe had an old GMC truck that could haul a ton when it was working okay. We got the bright idea that if we hauled a load of potatoes to Williams Lake and sold them door to door, we'd have enough to pay for the trip, with money left over to take in one of the Saturday night dances in town. Both my Dad and Uncle Joe grew good spuds, which they sold to two stores in Williams Lake, Moore's

"Teach" (Graham Fuller) horsing around at Dog Creek.
He was a good friend and lots of fun.

and Mackenzie's, for 75 cents per sack. We scraped together $15, with Teach contributing most of it, and bought a ton of potatoes. Harold borrowed the truck from his dad and that Saturday morning we set off for Williams Lake to make our fortune.

We arrived in town about noon without a penny between the three of us and began peddling our spuds on the residential streets right away. Graham covered one side of the road while I walked the other. Harold followed behind us in the truck. Whenever we made a sale we'd load one of the hundred-pound sacks on our back and carry it into the house. We were charging two dollars a sack and business was good.

By five o'clock we had sold the entire load and even had orders for the following week. Now it was time to enjoy the fruits of our labour. We took a room at the Lakeview Hotel and washed up before heading to the lunch counter. Hungry as wolves, we each ordered a good meal and teased the waitresses. At least Teach did. Harold and I were still too shy. Teach had taken a run to the liquor store for some cheap rye whisky that the three of us sampled before sitting down to dinner. After we cleaned off our plates, we decided to put in time walking around the streets, plotting what we'd do at the dance, which started at ten o'clock.

We could hear the music going full blast before we even walked through the doors. The place was full of young people and I could feel the excitement and energy in the room. It didn't take long for Teach to find his way to the dance floor. Harold and I hung back, both of us lacking the courage to ask a girl to dance and worrying about our dancing abilities. Harold had never danced before and all I knew were the old, out-of-fashion steps that Mother had taught me. We stood around in the stag line, talking smart to one another and watching the couples go by. I was feeling left out and alone and I could see Harold was too. We decided we needed another shot of courage and went out to down a few healthy snorts from the bottle of rye in the truck. Harold may have had some drinks before, but this was my first time.

It didn't take long before things started to spin around and I had trouble walking right. Harold was laughing his fool head off, watching me reeling around and talking stupid. Of course he was half drunk too, but I wasn't thinking straight and started cussing him out. This

*In 1938, Geoff went to Vancouver in Betty Keeble's car to get Mrs.
Keeble and Betty and deliver them to the Gang Ranch. I went along for
the ride. We were one night in Vancouver and back to Dog Creek the
next day. On the trip down, the road was so bad that a man who was
stopped in the middle of the road south of Ashcroft paid me five dollars to
drive him to Hope. He was from the prairies and was scared stiff.*

only made my cousin laugh louder. I was so furious I decided to walk
back to the hotel and let Harold tough it out at the dance by himself.

The hotel was only a few feet behind the dance hall, but in my
condition I started off in the wrong direction and quickly became lost.
I was thrashing my way along some back lane when a car appeared,
heading toward me. The bright lights dazzled me and I stepped off
the end of a culvert, falling face first into a muddy ditch half full of
water.

I heard the car stop and one of its doors opened. I just lay there.
The cold water in the ditch was bringing me back to my senses a
little. Voices drifted down from above me in the dark. I hoped they'd
go away and leave me alone.

"That's Hilary Place, Charlie Place's boy from Dog Creek. We'd better get him into the car and take him home." Whoever was speaking let out a low whistle. "If his mother could see him now...would she ever be upset."

I recognized the voice of Mr. Taylor, the Indian Agent. He'd been to Dog Creek many times and we had always enjoyed his company. Now he hauled me out of the ditch and put me in his car. When we arrived at his home, he and Mrs. Taylor led me to the basement where they had an extra cot for me to sleep on. I flopped onto the mattress, still fully clothed, and passed out cold. Only once during the rest of the night did I have to move and that was to throw up.

The next morning I woke with a splitting headache and couldn't figure for the life of me where I'd ended up. I had a horrible taste in my mouth that made me feel more nauseous. Standing up as gingerly as possible, I looked down at my muddy clothes. God, was I ever in rough shape. First things first, I somehow managed to clean the horrible mess I'd made on the floor without making another one. There was no way I wanted the Taylors to see their basement in such a state. Then it was time to do something about my own appearance. Luckily there was a bathroom in the basement, so I quickly stepped into the warm shower to wash up. It was only then that I realized I had nothing clean to put on after. I finished washing and put a towel around me, then went back to my dirty clothes. The muddy mess of laundry I'd left on the floor was gone; instead there was a clean shirt and pants folded neatly on the cot. I dressed and combed my hair down with my fingers. A female voice called out softly, "Are you decent?"

"Uh, yes I am."

I heard footsteps descending the stairs and a pleasant-looking woman appeared. "I'm Mrs. Taylor," she said. "My husband tells me you are one of Charlie Place's boys from Dog Creek."

"Yes, I am." I studied the floor intently, suffering from the embarrassment of my situation. "I'm really very sorry to put you to this trouble. I don't want to be any more of a nuisance to you. If you'll return my clothes, Mrs. Taylor, I'll be on my way."

"No. You won't leave without breakfast. I have it all ready for you." She smiled and motioned for me to follow her, "Come on upstairs, Hilary."

I had never felt so ashamed of myself in my life. This lady would not take no for an answer and she led the way upstairs. It was even worse than I thought it would be. There at the table were Mr. Taylor and the couple's five children, two boys in their early twenties and three beautiful girls in their teens. I tried to be as inconspicuous as possible, but I felt extremely uncomfortable. My appetite was gone, the result of a bad hangover mingled with humiliation.

Fortunately the Taylors were a talkative family and soon the focus was on last night's dance. All of the children had been there and each one excitedly shared stories about what they heard and saw. For the time I forgot my discomfort and listened to their tales. Then Mrs. Taylor tried to include me in the conversation, asking if I was the boy who had sold her potatoes yesterday.

"Yes, that was me." My face turned crimson as I answered. I felt cheap now, having to peddle spuds on the street for money.

"Were you at the dance last night, Hilary?" I realized she was trying to make me feel comfortable, but her questions had the opposite effect. I tried not to squirm in my seat as I responded that yes, I had been at the dance.

The girls all focussed on me now. "We didn't see you there." I'm sure the statement was innocent enough, but at that moment it only caused me more misery, knowing they were waiting for an explanation.

"Well, I stood over against the wall. I don't really know the new dances so I decided to watch instead." I neglected to add that I was too shy to ask a girl to join me whether I knew the steps or not.

Breakfast finally ended, much to my relief. Mrs. Taylor had kindly washed my clothes for me and hung them out on the line under the warm sun. Now all I had to do was wait until they finished drying and I could leave. Sitting in their living room, I watched the Taylor children bustling around while they prepared for a Sunday outing. After the children left, Mr. and Mrs. Taylor joined me.

Mr. Taylor spoke first. "You had a bit of an experience last night, didn't you?" I nodded in agreement.

"You are not the first person who has made a fool of himself, you know. But it really doesn't matter as long as you profit by it. We are not going to tell your folks about this and I don't think you should either." He paused a moment. "There, I've said my piece. Hilary, our family likes you and we'd like you to come and stay with us whenever you come to town. My daughters informed me they'd also be happy to teach you to dance." He smiled. "You would be welcome here any time."

I could hardly believe my ears. I thanked the couple from the bottom of my heart for their generosity and their invitation. I made up my mind at that moment that I would avail myself at the first opportunity. Mrs. Taylor brought my clothes in to me and I changed quickly. Expressing my gratitude to them again, I left their house and went in search of Teach and Harold.

Back in Dog Creek, our potato business came to a screeching halt right away. Mr. Western and Mr. Mackenzie, the bosses of the two stores in town that purchased spuds from Dad and Uncle Joe, said they refused to buy any more if we continued to peddle potatoes on the street. Without our profitable business, trips to Williams Lake were now out of the question. So I didn't see the Taylors again any time soon.

✲ ✲ ✲

Teach never did help me with my schoolwork. On the other hand, he did teach me how to get drunk, which we did often. We even made moonshine right in the school. The rest of the kids believed that it was a scientific experiment of mine. Teach and I rigged up a fractional column and ran off some alcohol that burned with a clear blue flame that didn't even sputter. Harold, Teach, and I laid back a pint of that one weekend and I don't think we sobered up until Wednesday.

The three of us had some wild times together. Wild, but not good. I found myself thinking about the dance in Williams Lake and all the good times I was missing out on. With each passing week I felt more lonely and discouraged.

Teach left in June and several of the boys gathered for one big final drunk with him. This time Mother caught wind of the party and we all caught hell. I wasn't particularly bothered by her lecture; I was getting so that I didn't care much about anything. Even my schoolwork had fallen behind but I managed to get through Grade 11.

The following September I was back at it again. I was going to be twenty years old before finishing Grade 12. The correspondence courses and the cloakroom were getting to me. For three long years I'd been trying to learn this way and I was sick of it. I longed for company and friends, but there were none. Before the year had started I told Mother and Dad I wanted to attend university and eventually law school. They said there was absolutely no way they could afford any further education for me. Mother believed it was time for me to start contributing some work around the ranch, since I hadn't really done anything in the last four years following my illness. Our talk ended on a discouraging note and I came out of it feeling I had been a burden to the family long enough.

Harold Henry Place was my cousin, best friend, and hero. During World War II he was in the army at North Africa, Sicily, Italy, Holland, and Belgium. When he came home he took off his uniform and said, "I hope that's the last I see of that."

I managed to stay with the schoolwork until spring. Finally I knew I'd lost all interest in learning and simply stopped going to school. There was a big row with my parents over my decision, but I quit anyway.

The morning after our argument I started work on the ranch. My job was to ensure the mud, stones, and brush didn't inhibit the flow of water along a five-mile ditch. A shovel was my only implement. My higher education was definitely over and as I considered my new career, it seemed that anything I'd learned in my schoolbooks had been a waste of time.

CHAPTER 11

ED HILLMAN

I'm sure the average city person sees ranch work as riding off into the sunset with a beautiful girl while music plays on—just like in a western movie. The reality was far from romantic. Dad had around 4500 acres by the time I came on the scene as a worker, so there was plenty to do. I went from the spring ditch-cleaning job to the manure wagon. That job entailed hauling the manure from the back of the barn to the fields and spreading it out to fertilize the alfalfa crop. Through the rest of the year I helped with other duties like irrigating, planting potatoes, gardening, and all the haying jobs from raking to pitching and stacking. The cattle had to be branded, de-horned, cut, and cowboyed back onto the range. And of course we also milked the cows and fed the chickens. There was always something to be done. I didn't mind the work half as much as the hours we had to keep in order to get things done.

Dad, Ed Hillman, Geoff, and I did most of the work on the ranch. Geoff also drove the Dog Creek Stage, which took him to Williams Lake on Tuesdays and back to Dog Creek the next day. My Dad had got the contract to haul the mail to Dog Creek from Williams Lake in 1928. He used a motor truck during the summer and horses in the winter, when it turned into a four-day trip—two days to Williams Lake and two back, with a stopover at Emilio Frizzi's place each way. Dad drove the stage until Geoff was old enough to handle it, and then Dad went back to tending the cattle out on the range. Ed and I did chores.

Ed was a remarkable man. He was born and raised in Sweden by a father who painted houses and a mother who worked as a wet nurse for the Swedish royal family. Following in his father's footsteps, Ed began a career in the painting trade. This did not last. His parents

One of the annual jobs was branding. Someone would keep the fire hot and the other workers would separate a calf from the herd and wrestle him to the ground for the branding iron. We did most all our corral work on foot, or else the animals were run through a squeeze chute. My Dad said it was easier on the animals and harder on the men.

were strict and conservative in their behaviour and outlook. At the age of nineteen, Ed had a love affair with a young lady his family felt was below his class. When they refused to allow Ed and the girl to marry, he hopped on a boat bound for New York and sailed away from his home for good. Ed's older brother was already in New York City, so Ed stayed with him until he learned enough English to get by. Then he lit out on his own for the great Wild West.

Ed could do more work by accident than most men do by design. He worked on the construction of the Great Northern Railway in the United States, and after sowing his share of wild oats across the northern states, he wound up in Tacoma. Things got a bit hectic in his association with some young ladies there, so Ed decided to move on to Canada as quickly as possible. He found work on the railroad and became active in union affairs, which meant taking several bonks on the noggin for his diligence. One morning in 1912 he woke to find himself unemployed and hung over in Ashcroft. As luck would have it, the foreman from the Gang Ranch was in town looking for some haymakers. Ed signed on and was soon happily pitching hay at the Gang.

This haying crew was working in New Westminster during the 1880s, but the photo gives you an idea of the number of men and horses who were needed to get a harvest in. And it shows a couple of well-loaded hay wagons.

The Gang was an enormous ranch, and when the haying season started in June it took a crew of 40 men to get the job done. All the power they had was horse power, and it wasn't unusual to see 20 teams harnessed and ready for the field at five o'clock in the morning. Great big Belgians and Clydesdales and Percherons were used to pull the mowers for cutting hay and the rakes for gathering it up. They threw their weight and strength into their collars, straining to bring the fully loaded wagons to the stackyard and powering the derricks that lifted the hay up the boom pole.

A fully loaded wagon consisted of four forkloads that the derrick driver would pull up to the top of the stack. The fork was U shaped and each prong was three feet long. When the prongs were driven down into the hay as deep as they would go, a lever at the top activated a hinge that set three inches of the fork's tip at right angles to the tine. This held the hay on the fork until the stacker hollered "Dump!" Then the driver pulled a rope attached to the trip on the fork and released the load onto the stack.

A boom pole was used for stacking at the Gang. It was similar to the mast of a ship and worked much the same way as it unloaded wagons. The tall boom pole was placed beside the site where the stack was to be built, guyed by four ropes set well out from the base. Then the crew attached a yardarm and adjusted the guy lines so the yardarm would swing in the right direction when the load was lifted. It took considerable skill on the crew's part to set this up so the rig worked properly.

There was a hierarchy among the workers out in the field. The stacker was the top man while the derrick driver was at the bottom of the heap. Young men worked their asses off to get into a more respected

job, which required a great deal of skill and perseverance. Mower men never left a blade of grass standing; their backswath was guaranteed to get every last bit of hay right up to the edge of the ditch. Rakers were careful not to drag the hay too far in the rake teeth so that the leaves weren't knocked off. They also made sure there was no hay left on the field when they were through.

Wagons were loaded evenly and squarely. The teamster, who was also the wagon loader, was helped by pitchers who could lay a cock of hay up onto the load so that the full load never fell over on its way to the stackyard. Many a green pitcher got his ass kicked for dumping a haycock on its side up on the load. A well-built load could be lifted in four even forkfuls onto the stack without requiring the stacker to expend a lot of effort spreading them out. A poorly built load might come apart either on the way to the stackyard or when it was being lifted up the pole to the top of the stack. The experienced men knew what a nightmare a badly built stack was. The centre of the stack would end up solid ice in the winter, with the hay knotted together, and it would take a great deal of sawing and chopping and grunting to get a load of feed out in twenty below weather.

There must have been a thousand tricks that an experienced man could bring to the job. Little things like loading the wagon going downhill instead of uphill so the horses wouldn't have a heavy pull to start the wagon between haycocks. Or finishing the load close to the stackyard so the horses had a shorter distance to pull it. Ed was right there in the thick of things, no doubt lending his own bits of expertise to the process.

At that same time my Grandfather Place ran the only bar in the area at Dog Creek. The crew from the Gang Ranch, including Ed of course, made weekend trips into town for refreshments and good times. As was his nature, Ed celebrated perhaps a little too well on more than one occasion and ended up fathering the child of a pleasant Indian girl named Mary Ann. She had had other children by various men before, but the liaisons that produced these offspring were short-lived. Each man drifted off to other ranches and left Mary Ann to fend for herself. Ed did not abandon her like the others. He took his responsibilities seriously and looked after the mother of his child. When their son, Eric, was born during the height of World War I, Ed put his wandering days behind him. Mary Ann raised Eric in a little log cabin across the creek from the Indian reserve, and Ed visited on weekends. He also set up a charge account for Mary Ann at the store, which he paid every month. They did not marry. It was clear that they weren't really compatible, but the arrangement worked fairly well. Mother occasionally rebuked Ed, insisting he should marry and live a decent life. Ed, in turn, would just shake his head and go out to work to avoid any more of Mother's lecturing.

When the Dog Creek school was built in 1925, Ed pitched in and helped along with many others. Our house was the kitchen for the operation, and most of the men slept on our floors throughout the project. After the building was completed, Ed became a part of our extended household, staying with us for several months at a time and sometimes for more than a year.

At around five feet nine inches tall, Ed wasn't a big man but he was strong, there is no doubt about that. If there was an easy way of doing physical work and a hard way, he never failed to choose the latter. His thin, wispy, blonde hair was parted in the middle, revealing bright blue eyes and a ruddy complexion. It was obvious that Ed's nose had been remodelled more than once in sundry bars during his days in the U.S. He wore ill-fitting, store-bought teeth that tended to rattle and click, particularly when he eagerly discussed classical literature, something he studied with great interest. Two of Ed's favourite books were *The Decline and Fall of the Roman Empire* and

Ed Hillman

Ben Hur, neither of which was a real potboiler, but he certainly delighted in them. This was not at all what you might expect from a man who wore a wool lumberjack shirt, heavy wool pants held up by police bracers, and red lace-up rubber boots that usually tracked muddy water across Mother's clean kitchen floor. But then, Ed was full of surprises.

He gained an excellent command of the English language by reading great literary works by the light of a coal-oil lamp in a bunkhouse. Ed enjoyed reading everything from Nietzsche and Schopenhauer to Socrates and Sinclair Lewis. His education extended beyond literature to include the American Civil War, and he prided himself on his knowledge of the various generals and battles. The only problem was that he still spoke with a heavy accent. This, along with the fact he had derived certain pronunciations phonetically, meant it sometimes took people a moment to figure out what he said and how he said it. On one occasion he stumped Mother while discussing the

Bible when he kept referring to someone named "Rack-el." She finally realized Ed was talking about Rachel.

One of Ed's favourite pastimes was listening to the wrestling matches broadcast on the radio from Seattle. Joe Stecher and Ed "Strangler" Lewis were Ed's heroes. When a bout was on he listened intently, even giggling when the announcers remarked on John Freeberg's size sixteen shoes and his flat feet. When Geoff and I were little, Ed taught us all the holds he knew during impromptu wrestling matches on the sitting room floor. With one of us tucked between his legs in a scissor-hold, he'd hold the other one off with one hand. My brother and I loved the roughhousing with Ed, laughing every time until our sides hurt.

In many ways Ed was more of a father to me than Dad was, particularly as far as communicating was concerned. Dad just wasn't a talker, while Ed and I enjoyed many lengthy discussions on everything from philosophy and religion to the ills of our society. Most of these conversations took place as we dug potatoes or spread manure, which made the day go by a little faster.

Ed wasn't always an intellectual. Truth be known, he was about the most impractical man alive. Given a set of conditions, he tended to come up with the most difficult and least profitable way of resolving them. It was his nature—as well as one of his most endearing qualities— to reject all the easier ways of doing things as not being worthy. Another quirk of his character was that every so often he'd get stinking drunk and make a complete ass of himself. He was good for two or three of these episodes a year. After a lot of drinking he'd get himself angry over something, then stagger around yelling swear words at the top of his voice. Act two came the next day when he'd turn up again, all contrite, and receive a suitable dressing down from Mother on the evils of drink. For some reason Ed seemed to enjoy getting into her bad books.

On one occasion, one of Ed's drinking spells happened to coincide with a school Christmas concert, the premier event of the year. I was eleven or twelve at the time. Both my parents were involved in the concert. Dad dressed as Santa Claus while Mother was the musical director of our group of eight. Our program for the evening included a song, some poetry, and a play. Betty Keeble chose to sing "When

Love is Blind, Tra La La," and my cousin Kathleen had memorized a poem about ten pages long. Eric Earle, Betty Earle, and Geoff were set to deliver their knockout dramatic performance, which even included six French words. Once the entertainment was over, A.J. Drinkell, chairman of the three-man school board, intended to thank the teacher in a carefully worded speech.

Old Ed prepared for the rigours of sitting through the performances by knocking back several hot rums. Somewhere between Kathleen's high monotone delivery of her 30-odd verses and Geoff's best French pronunciation, Ed sneaked outside for a few more belts of the great fortifier. As he came back in, Mother caught him with a withering look before he made it to his seat in the back row. Aunty Violet dug her finger into Uncle Joe's ribs and said in a stage whisper that could be heard for a mile, "Ed's drunk again, Joe!"

This remark rolled around in Ed's befuddled mind for the rest of the concert. From time to time he muttered to himself, though I couldn't make out what he was saying. When our great production came to an end, Aunty Violet had more to say. "Hasn't that Ed Hillman got sense enough to keep quiet during the performance?"

That was the last straw for Ed. He sat up in his seat. "Good God, woman," he replied. "As if it weren't penance enough to have to sit through two hours of excruciating boredom, now I also have to submit myself to taking lessons in deportment from an old tit!"

Aunty Vi screamed at Uncle Joe. "Don't you let him say those things to me. Hit him! Hit him!" Her voice was rising in volume and pitch with each repetition as her face flushed in fury. "HIT HIM!"

Uncle Joe wasn't about to pit his 130 pounds against Ed's 190, so he decided on a different solution. "Let's just go home."

This suited Aunty Vi, but it didn't sit well with their younger kids, Millie and Jean. Santa Claus hadn't made his visit yet and be damned if they were going to be cheated out of their annual bit of hard candy and orange. They took as long as they could to find their overshoes and coats, then proceeded to lose them again.

Meanwhile, Drinkell appointed himself the great peacemaker, trying to get Ed to apologize. Ed, however, was not about to retract a thing and he kept mumbling about that damned old tit, plenty loud enough for everyone to hear. Harold and I tried to avoid the whole scene by hiding in the outdoor privy, but it was twenty below and we froze out.

Santa made a rush trip and the stockings were handed around in haste. Aunty Vi was still after Uncle Joe for being such a coward and not protecting her dignity like a real man would do. Drinkell, who had also had a rum or two, tried to settle Ed. Uncle Joe was desperately avoiding Aunty Vi's tongue-lashing, focussing instead on getting Millie and Jean into their outdoor clothes. Old Saint Nick kept milling around, doing his best to look jolly despite the circumstances, and Ed was still going strong, throwing in the odd off-colour comment to make sure he wouldn't be ignored.

Finally the children got their stockings from Santa, and Uncle Joe piled his family into their sleigh and left for home. We decided it was time for our exit as well and loaded Mother's piano onto the sleigh. Ed left the school on foot before us, but when we caught up to him Dad helped him aboard. Mother, completely disgusted by Ed's behaviour, said nothing at all. To everyone's relief he quickly passed out in the hay. Then it was silent except for the crunch of the horses' hooves in the frozen snow. I sat at the back of the sleigh, watching the iron runners strike fire off the odd rock. It was a glorious clear, cold, winter night and the stars twinkled brightly above us. Smiling in the darkness, I thought about the evening's events and realized just how much fun it had been.

As was his character, Ed went down to Uncle Joe's the next morning and apologized for his bad behaviour. He endured a bit more abuse from Aunty Vi, but Uncle Joe passed it off and life went on.

Ed took small contracting jobs, haying or fencing for the ranchers during the summers. While he made sure the men working for him earned good money and were well fed, Ed seldom had much money left over from the jobs for himself. Perhaps this suited him because then he would stay on with us for longer periods of time, turning his hand to any job on the ranch that needed to be done. When Ed worked with us he slept in a plain old room up the bar room stairs. It was definitely not a luxury suite—a single bed and small dresser were the only furnishings, and his clothes hung on some nails pounded into a board on one of the walls. Ed preferred the simplicity of his lodgings and never asked for anything more.

Among the more interesting and famous people that visited Dog Creek was a Mr. Marius Barbeau, the historian and authority on Native culture. He was a fast-acting, somewhat pompous little Frenchman who spoke with authority and honesty. He was one of the first to recognize the genius of Emily Carr, the famous painter, and of the great Haida artists like Edenshaw. Like most visitors to the ranch he wanted to dress up in cowboy regalia and get a picture to take home and show the folks.

I think what drew Ed to our home was the sense of togetherness. He loved the conversations that took place around the supper table. Mother and Mr. Drinkell, both of whom were well educated, often engaged in discussions of one topic or another with Ed, as did Mrs. Keeble, who joined our family on occasion. Other guests included clergy and government officials who ministered to us poor heathens out in the woods. We also entertained visitors from around the world. It seemed that if you visited the Cariboo you had to come to Dog Creek and partake in one of Mother's famous afternoon teas.

I remember when we had some professors from the University of British Columbia staying with us. Their field of expertise was classical literature. They were astonished when Ed, dressed in his wool and flannel workclothes, joined in one discussion with some intelligent, well-substantiated arguments on the subject of Socrates' philosophy or some such thing. When they left the following day, one of the men remarked that he had met few people as well versed in ancient history as Ed. Perhaps if he'd stayed longer he might have discovered Ed's wealth of knowledge on the American Civil War, too!

Although he became quite animated when engaging in his history studies and literary pursuits, Ed was otherwise not easily excited. Toby Clyne, a sister of the famous lawyer and judge J.V. Clyne, learned this fact the hard way. When she married Harvey Armes, Toby moved from Vancouver to live with her husband at the D4 Ranch, which he was renting from my Dad. Doreen Armes, who was teaching at the school again, and her husband Frank stayed with them. Each day Toby drove Doreen the five miles to and from school in her little car.

One day Ed was cleaning the ditch that ran behind our house and across the road. As was common practice, when he came to the culvert under the road he lifted off the planks and proceeded to dig his way across. Soon after, Toby and Doreen came speeding down the road on their way to the school, running a little late that morning. Toby nearly drove into the gap in the road, stopping just short of it. When Ed made no move to replace the planking right away, Toby's temper got the best of her and she jumped out of the car. She gave him hell for nearly causing an accident, then blasted him for not getting the planks back in place so she could pass.

Ed was used to the Cariboo way where nobody got so excited over such things. Most of the people he knew in the area would have been happy to stop and chat a while before getting back to business. Not Toby. She continued her tirade until she ran out of wind and expletives. At that point Ed stopped shovelling and turned to the large girl glaring at him.

"Ma'am!" This was Ed's favourite word when addressing a woman he was displeased with. "Not all of us have been blessed with the advantages of a university education such as you have. So please don't blame us for our ignorance, but show compassion for those of us who do not know the error of our ways."

Toby was fit to be tied, yet there was nothing she could do but wait until Ed finally replaced the culvert top. Eventually she was on her way, still mad as a hatter, and Ed chuckled as he watched the car speed off into the distance in a cloud of dust.

At some time during those years Dad became the proud owner of an old 4-90 Chev. The back seat had been removed and replaced with a wooden box, creating an early version of the pickup truck. Dad used it to haul 700-pound loads of freight from Ashcroft. With a little four-banger engine it was a pretty good rig for a 1924 model.

One spring when the Chev wasn't being used around the ranch, Ed decided the vehicle presented an opportunity for him to finally join the twentieth century. Usually he was averse to all things mechanical, but now he struck a deal with Dad to purchase the rig for $100. One condition of the sale was that Dad would teach Ed how to drive.

All morning the 4-90 lurched around the pasture between the store and Casey, with Ed at the wheel and Dad hanging on for dear life. When Ed wanted to stop he'd yell "Whoa!" at the top of his lungs, completely forgetting that he had to put his foot on the brake. On his first visit for gasoline he nearly obliterated the only gas pump within 50 miles of Dog Creek. By noon, Dad decided Ed was ready for a solo run. Along with everyone else watching, I held my breath as he lurched off in the direction of the Gaspard Ranch. Cringing at the sound of grinding gears, we saw the dust and exhaust smoke billowing skyward as Ed followed the road into the trees and out of our sight.

There were two nasty corners before the Indian reserve, both of which Ed successfully navigated. Feeling much more confident, he decided to speed up a little. Another tricky part of the road was quickly approaching, however, as he got closer to the Gaspard Ranch gate. There was a sharp left turn to be negotiated at the bottom of a little hill. The alternative was a straight drop of several feet directly into the creek below. Ed noticed that the car had picked up considerable speed down the hill before he remembered to push his foot down hard on the brake.

Unfortunately, being a new driver, he forgot to remove his other foot from the gas pedal.

A yell of "Whoa!" that Dad swore he heard clearly three miles down the valley was to no avail. The damned car appeared to have a mind of its own. Suddenly faced with the hard left turn, Ed pulled hard on the steering wheel's left side with the same motion he'd have used to turn a team of horses. He completely forgot that the wheel turned.

Instead of making the turn, the car flew off the end of the road and head-on into a lone cottonwood tree about twelve inches in diameter. The old 4-90 took it square in the middle of the radiator. On impact, Ed was thrown out through the canvas top, landing in the water below, where he damn near drowned. Fortunately he was able to pull himself, coughing and sputtering, onto dry ground.

An assessment of the damage revealed no permanent injuries to Ed, just a good shaking up and a welcome bath to cool off after the wreck. As for the old car, the radiator certainly needed some repairs, but everything else seemed to work as well as it ever had. Ed was happy to sell the vehicle back to Dad for $50. Like I've said, if Ed could do something the hard way, he would. After that he was quite content to return to the horse and buggy, confident that when he hollered "Whoa!" at least the animals knew it meant stop.

Moments like these made the harder times a little more bearable. This was particularly true throughout the Depression years. Our family made do as best we could, and Ed did the same for his family. When Eric was six years old, Mary Ann sent him to the mission school, much to Ed's chagrin. He would have preferred Eric attend the Dog Creek school, but Mary Ann did not want her son brought up as a white man. Eric grew distant from his father as a result of being away for such long periods of time, and it wasn't until he finished school that their relationship began to heal.

The first year Eric was out of school, Dad and Ed got a contract to put up all the hay on the Gaspard Ranch, in addition to our own. It was going to be a lot of strenuous work since we still relied on horsedrawn machinery. We set up camp at the Gaspard Ranch, three miles up the valley from our home. We had a crew of eight to get the job done, as well as Dad when he wasn't driving the mail stage two days a week (this was before Geoff took over the job). Ed was the crew boss, Eric and Geoff were the mower and rake men, Frank Armes and Lance McPhee did the pitching, while I was the derrick boy. There was also Henry Dave, who was half crazy most of the time, and Mary Ann, who did all of the cooking.

Eric Hillman. Eric was working for my Dad at the D4 in about 1941. One day I saw him coming down the road to Dog Creek as fast as his horse would go. He was reeling around on the horse and almost falling off. I grabbed the horse's bridle and Eric slipped off the horse and landed at my feet, covered in blood. I loaded him into the car and took him to the nurse, Mrs. Anderson, who found that he had fallen on a razor-sharp axe and severed the main artery in his leg. She put on a pressure bandage and told me to get him to the hospital in Williams Lake as fast as I could as the injury was going to kill him. The normal time for the trip in those days was two and a half hours. I had my Dad's car, a new Chevy, and I made the trip in an hour and fifteen minutes. It saved Eric's life.

Each morning we rose at five, then drove up to the ranch. After harnessing and watering the horses we'd sit down for a full breakfast, then head out to the field by seven. Depending on how close we were to the cookhouse at lunchtime, we'd either eat there or have our meal on the job. Quitting time in the field was five o'clock, but there was usually still plenty left to be done. Once the horses were tended to we'd take our supper, then see what we had to prepare for the next day. Sometimes the machinery needed repairs or maintenance, like sharpening mower blades and changing rake teeth. By the time we finished, often around eight or nine each night, our beds looked pretty inviting.

We had a good crew of men and enjoyed some good times. Lance, a retired professional boxer, often donned the gloves and gave us a few pointers. For the rest of that summer we tried our best to hit Lance in the face—but we never could. Eric often persisted in trying to get the better of Lance and ended up getting knocked flat on his back for his efforts every time.

When there was some free time we'd swim in the ice-cold creek. Of course no one had trunks, so we'd strip down to nothing and hop in. Poor Henry was too shy for this. He'd sit on the shore while we splashed around. On one particularly hot day, Lance and Eric decided that Henry really should join us. They grabbed him without warning and threw him in the water, clothes and all. To make matters worse for Henry, they wouldn't let him out until he nearly froze. Things like that happened every now and then, just to keep life interesting I suppose.

Wages for our work were low. The top hands received $20 a month. I clearly remember my pay for the two months was 75 cents! Dad and Ed probably didn't end up with too much more than me, but at least we were working.

CHAPTER 12

DAVEY ANDERSON

When we looked down the road from the house, we could hardly believe our eyes. Up the road came a small boy carrying a pack on his shoulder. He was a skinny little fellow with pointed features, big jug ears, and wearing glasses. Each step was an effort for the little guy, for when he got closer we could see that he had been cursed with clubfeet. Not one but both of them. He lumbered along with both arms swinging, lurching from side to side. His feet were wrapped in canvas and tied up with string. When he got closer we could see that he was a white boy and we wondered where he came from.

It turned out he was the son of Mr. and Mrs. Bill Anderson of the Gang Ranch. His dad was the bookkeeper and storekeeper there. His name was David Anderson and he had run away from home. He said it was because his father had beaten up on him and he showed us the scars and bruises to prove it. Up close you could also see the stains on his pinched face, left there by tears that had flowed. He said he was not looking for charity but that if my Dad would give him a job he would show that he could earn a living. He looked you right in the eye when he was talking and you had to believe him. He said he was nine years old.

My Dad could see he was just a child but he spoke to him like he was a man and surprised me by saying, "Alright Davey. You can stay here and feed the chickens and look after them, but there is one thing you will have to do and that is go to school and behave yourself."

Davey stuck out his hand and they solemnly shook on the deal.

Davey came into our house and my Mother gave him the other bed in the twin bedroom that my brother and I had shared. The first night he almost scared the daylights out of me by screaming and carrying on in his sleep. He apparently was reliving the horrors he had experienced at home. These episodes lasted for three months or so until he finally settled down.

In time we learned the story of his life according to his mother, Mrs. Anderson. He was an adopted boy who really belonged to Mrs. Anderson's brother. This brother had fathered the child by some unknown girl and then gone off to fight in the Spanish Civil War. He never returned. Davey had a few mementos of this shadowy character and that was all. We only partially believed the story as there was a rumour that Davey actually belonged to Mrs. Anderson and that the father was the man lost in the civil war. There was always this kind of rumour running around the country. Some you believed and some you didn't. In this case, God knows Mrs. Anderson and Davey were dead ringers for one another. They had the same looks exactly and the same poor eyesight. Davey certainly was not Bill Anderson's kid as there was no resemblance there at all.

Bill Anderson was a merchant of some considerable skill. He had opened the first Safeway store in Vancouver in Kerrisdale and was a successful business man until the booze caught up to him and he worked himself down the ladder of success until he reached the bottom at the Gang, drunk and violent. Davey was the object of most, if not all of his frustration and anger and he beat the kid regularly and often and hard.

We contacted his family at the Gang Ranch immediately after he turned up at Dog Creek. Of course they wanted him to go back home. My Mother and Dad talked it over with Davey and he absolutely refused to go back to the Gang under any circumstances. He said he would sooner die than go back. An RCMP officer came out from Williams Lake to investigate the matter. Fortunately he was a sensible man with a heart and he recommended that the boy stay where he was in Dog Creek as he was being treated well and was attending school. There was no school at the Gang Ranch at the time.

The chickens never had it so good. They were fed regularly and the henhouse was kept clean, with the nests full of fresh straw. Davey attended school, where he was a good scholar and behaved himself. My Dad gave him a few dollars each month, as if he was on the payroll, and he stayed in the room with me for a year. Then one day he asked if he could have one of the rooms up the old staircase where Ed Hillman

Davey Anderson (left) and his two brothers, Kenny (above left) and Gerald (above right). Davey is standing behind a good example of a perfect Christmas tree. Each whorl of the tree had eight branches instead of the usual four.

stayed. I guess he felt more like a working man there. His request was granted and he moved.

A few years went by and Bill Anderson lost his job at the Gang Ranch because of his drinking problem. Mr. and Mrs. Anderson moved over to Dog Creek with their two small boys, Kenny and Gerald, and stayed in our old house, Casey. Davey did not join them but stayed put where he was. Bill got a job in Wells, B.C., as a store manager, but he soon lost it due to his drinking. The family stayed at Dog Creek.

I will digress here and tell you a couple of stories about Mrs. Anderson, Davey's mother, who was a remarkable woman in many ways. She had gained some measure of fame and notoriety back where she used to live north of Edmonton. It seems that the settlement she was in was snowbound when one of the neighbours became very sick. The man's wife called Mrs. Anderson in to look at him and see what was the matter. Mrs. Anderson, who was a nurse, took one look and immediately knew his problem was an infected appendix. She was able to phone a doctor she knew in Edmonton and after describing the symptoms to him, had her diagnosis confirmed. There was no hope of getting the man out to a hospital, so the decision was made that Mrs. Anderson would operate on the man where he was, under direction of the doctor in Edmonton who would be in contact on the telephone. There was a small emergency clinic in the town that had enough drugs to put the man out while the operation went on, so he was prepped as soon as possible. Mrs. Anderson said it was a routine operation, there were no complications and she had seen dozens of them done, so she was quite familiar with the procedure, but she said she almost didn't do it at the last minute. It was only after the man said "Please go ahead" that she was able to start the incision. Once she started she said it was easy from then on. The whole thing was written up in the *Edmonton Journal* and she was quite famous for awhile.

The adventure that I personally know about took place when Mrs. Anderson was at the Gang Ranch. She hadn't been there long before she was looking after the ranch help and any of the local Indians who required attention. The first winter they were there there was an epidemic of flu that was a killer. Word came down to the ranch that the Kalelse family was in deep trouble. Could Mrs. Anderson come and help them out? She immediately threw some clothes in a sack and got in the sleigh with the young Indian who had come with the message, and they headed out to the Kalelse home. It was a full day's travel on the snowdrifted road and it was dark when they got to their destination.

The cabin was a single room with a low-pitched roof. In front there was an overhang that covered a porch about six feet wide. When Mrs. Anderson entered the cabin, the interior was lit by a single coal-oil lamp that barely broke the gloom. She had brought a flashlight and with that took stock of the situation. There were two beds in the room. She went around to look at the people in the cabin and found that there were five children under ten years old, two women, and one man, all terribly sick. As well, there were two people lying dead on the floor.

She and the young man who had fetched her dragged the bodies of the dead people out onto the porch. It was 20 degrees below zero, so she made sure they were properly laid out before they froze stiff. Then she set to work to try to save the living. It was a tremendous task. There was practically nothing to eat in the house—just some rice, some frozen potatoes, and the carcass of a deer, frozen stiff, hanging from a tree outside. First she had to try to clean the place up and clean up her patients. It wasn't easy but she did the best she could. She bossed the young man who had brought her and made him get wood and water and keep the fires going. She boiled the deer meat into a soup and fed it to her patients.

This went on for two weeks with not one contact with the outside world. When finally a cowboy from the Gang Ranch arrived he found that Mrs. Anderson had not lost one of her patients and that they were all getting well and were being properly cared for. She was proud of that and she had every right to that pride. She had shown a remarkable amount of courage and dedication.

When she lived at Dog Creek, Mrs. Anderson was given a medicine cabinet by the Indian Department. Her duties were to look after the Indians. I was her driver and took her around to fulfil these duties. My experiences on these safaris are a whole separate story, but not for now. Eventually Mrs. Anderson got a job as Red Cross nurse at the Alexis Creek Hospital and the family moved there.

Davey stayed with us. In fact he stayed with us until my Dad died and then for two more years after that, 21 years in all. He quit school as soon as it was legally possible and went to work full time for my Dad on the ranch. He milked the cows night and morning every day, and despite the fact he had those terrible feet to deal with, he grew incredibly strong, especially in his arms.

I remember one time when we were digging spuds and sacking them up and hauling them to the root cellar by the old mill. Among the sacks was an old peanut sack that was three times the size of an ordinary gunnysack. We filled it up with potatoes and left it there just for laughs for Davey to pick up and throw on the truck. Sure enough, he came along, grabbed it, and threw the 300-pound sack up on the truck like it was nothing.

He was as weak in the eyes as he was strong in the arms and back. I don't know what his eyesight problem was, but I know he couldn't see a darn thing without glasses. I do know what his glasses problem was. They were broken and twisted, wired and glued and soldered and taped and stuck together with chewing gum and God knows what else, and the glass part was cracked.

One time when Davey was about eighteen years old he was breaking a horse for riding. It was one of those animals that you could never be sure when it was going to buck. It generally chose the most inopportune moment in which to indulge itself in the pleasure of dumping Davey in the dirt. Davey had decided to ride this horse up to the top of Canoe Creek Mountain, where the Indians were holding a jackpot stampede (where all the contestants pay entry fees into a jackpot and the winner takes the pot). He was halfway up the mountain when he stopped and dismounted to give the horse a breather. When he got back on, as soon as his rear end hit the saddle, the horse decided it was time to buck. Davey wasn't settled in the saddle yet, so on about the second jump he went flying off and landed in a clump of fir trees. No great harm had been done except the darned glasses had fallen off. He couldn't find them anywhere. Of course he couldn't see anything without them, so he was having a hell of a time. He searched for awhile and then gave up and went on to the stampede. On his way back he looked again for a couple of hours, then returned again the next day and for two days more, but to no avail. Finally one of the young Indian boys joined him in the search and was successful. The glasses were found

Davey Anderson

not on the ground, where Davey had spent the last four days on his hands and knees looking for them, but hanging from one of the top branches of the fir tree where Davey had landed. More tape and chewing gum and solder and he was back in the land of the sighted again.

When he had got the horse straightened out after the glasses were lost, Davey decided to continue on to the stampede even if he couldn't see what was going on very well. There was a dance that night in one of the cabins, and Davey managed to get into a fight with one of the Tressierra boys from Clinton. Davey was smaller than his adversary and that, coupled with the fact that all Davey could see was a blur, meant he wasn't doing well. In fact he was getting the daylights pounded out of him. Tressierra was doing great as long as he stayed out of Davey's clutches, but it was inevitable that Davey would grab him and the game would be over. Sure enough, Davey finally grabbed him by the shirtfront and the crotch, lifted this 200-pound man like a doll over his head, and brought him down flat on his back on the floor with a bang that could be heard for a mile. Davey was going to give him another one the same as the last one, but a few of the boys grabbed him and persuaded him to stop. Tressierra came to about noon the next day. I heard that Tressierra was slightly cross-eyed after this and spoke with a stutter, but that is just hearsay and only very probably true!

We used to have dances at Dog Creek every once in awhile, and it was natural that Davey was chosen as the bouncer. We never had any serious trouble after the first dance. At that one, two of the young bucks decided to have a fight in the middle of the dance hall. Davey went over and grabbed them and tucked one under each arm and marched them outside where he proceeded to knock their two heads together until he got a solemn promise from them that they wouldn't do that again. End of trouble.

When Davey was nineteen he moved into a tarpaper shack that was between the powerhouse and the store. He had a dog called Useless that stayed with him there, and also on occasion he would have a visit from one of the local Indian girls named Nora Rosette. Davey was a guy with strong convictions. He didn't believe in living with a girl and so he made arrangements to get married, which they did the first time there was a priest around to perform the ceremony. Nora was a quiet, soft-spoken girl who really loved Davey, and she made him a good wife. They had two children, a boy and a girl, and spent most of their lives around Lac la Hache and 100 Mile House. Nora got some kind of flu one day that attacked her lungs, and she slipped away before anyone realized how ill she was. It was a terrible loss for Davey, but with his remarkable spirit and resilience he weathered the blow and carried on.

I never think of Davey without thinking of his epic walk from the Gang Ranch over to Dog Creek when he ran away from home. He was only a child, just nine years old, and it was a ten-mile journey: down the twisty road in Dismal Gulch and across the Fraser River on the old suspension bridge; up the five-mile mountain to the top where there was an abandoned Indian cabin or two; then down the Dog Creek Valley side to our place. What was going through his head as he trudged along on those twisted feet? He had never been on the road before and there was not a living thing along the way, just the wind swishing through the grass and the hiss of the mighty river. What sort of determination did it take to keep going, mile after mile? What sort of guts did it take for him to stand in front of my Dad without a tear and ask, not for charity or help, but for a job? All he had in the world was a skinny little body with twisted feet and eyes that could barely see without his broken glasses, and a flour-sack pack containing one patched pair of pants and a faded jacket.

Davey walked down this long road (right) between Gang Ranch and Dog Creek to escape his father's abuse. I still have trouble imagining the grit he needed to make the trek.

In many ways Davey was more of a son to my Dad than either Geoff or I. He worked alongside my Dad every day and he was a terrific worker. He loved the outdoors and the ranch life and he loved my Dad with all his heart. As far as I know there was never a harsh word between them and they enjoyed one another's company.

After my Dad died, Davey stayed on at the ranch and tried to do his best for my Mother. Unfortunately, Drinkell felt it was his right to be the boss and run the outfit. Drinkell had been my Grandfather Place's secretary and storekeeper and my Dad's partner in the store, and he'd lived with our family since the 1930s, but he was completely incompetent and he blamed his disasters on Davey. My Mother was always influenced by Drinkell rather than my brother or more especially me. Her diaries are full of her arguments with me about what should be done, and she would always side with Drinkell in the end.

Davey finally moved on and built a successful life for himself elsewhere. He took up the sport of arm wrestling and with his enormous strength and courage won many trophies and honours. He was popular with the fans, highly respected throughout the sport and the community, and an inspiration to many who were handicapped as he was.

A remarkable man.

CHAPTER 13

SAM SAULT JOHN

My earliest memory of Sam Sault John is from the fall of 1923. He and his family were camped down by the blacksmith shop at the D4 while he helped Dad get in the second crop. After they finished, Sam decided to stay put for a few days while he did some hunting.

Bright and early one morning, Sam mounted one of his team that doubled as a saddle horse. The scene was certainly not the same as you might see in a western movie, where the rugged cowboy mounts his restless steed and gallops off in a swirl of dust. In reality, the horse plodded calmly and deliberately out of the yard with its head down while Sam sat slightly hunched over in his saddle. His legs hung loosely against the horse's sides and he twitched the willow stick in his hand occasionally in order to keep his horse awake. There was no great show, just a horse and rider who shared a complete harmony of purpose.

Sam headed out for the Stenson meadow east of the D4. He was barely out of sight before we heard the report of his gun. One shot was fired, then silence. Minutes later, Sam rode his horse into our yard at full speed, pulling up in front of the barn where Dad was working.

"Hey, Charlie! You better come and look at this thing I shot!" He spoke loudly and his voice was shaking with excitement. "It's the damndest-looking animal I ever saw!"

It took an awful lot to get Sam excited, especially when it came to animals and wildlife, and soon everyone gathered around to see what on earth had Sam so riled. Mrs. Sam was talking in Shuswap as fast as she could while their son Wilfred jumped up and down along with Geoff. They wanted to get a look at this creature right away. Even Mother came out of the house, with me at her coattails, to listen to Sam's description of the animal.

We decided to walk down to the lower section of the Stenson meadow, less than a mile from our house, where the animal was shot.

Geoff and Wilfred took off running right away. Following the boys, Dad drove the team so that he could drag the dead animal out of the wet part of the field where Sam had left it. Mrs. Sam had not let up on her running monologue in Shuswap, which only Sam could understand, although he appeared completely oblivious to his wife's chatter. Mother and I brought up the rear, gingerly picking our way through the sticks and rocks.

Standing by the ditch where it was dry, we watched as Dad took the team down near the water to retrieve the carcass. The horses didn't like the smell of the dead animal and snorted, showing the whites of their eyes while they splashed about in the water. Dad was getting soaked to the bone because of Duke and Dynamite's performance. He knew the horses well after spending three years working them daily. Dynamite was generally good at taking commands from Dad, but Duke was being difficult, as usual. After flailing away at the stubborn horse, Dad, madder than a wet hen by this time, finally got Duke into position with Dynamite, then hooked the dead animal up. The horses pulled their load up onto dry ground and we stepped forward for a better look.

At first we thought it was a horse until we saw its great big horns. Horses certainly didn't grow horns, although Dad was a bit dubious about old Duke every now and then. If it was an elk, the horns certainly didn't look right. We debated back and forth until my Mother stepped forward and solved the mystery. "That's a moose."

Dad and Sam eyed her curiously, along with the rest of us. She could see no one knew whether to believe her or not. "I've seen lots of pictures of them. And that is definitely a moose. I'm sure of it."

Mother was right. It turned out that it was the first moose to be killed in the area. The Indians around Dog Creek had never seen one in the Cariboo up to that point. After Sam's big kill, however, moose seemed to become much more common in the area.

We soon found out moose meat was good to eat, and Sam became a local celebrity for his efforts. He wasn't too concerned about receiving extra attention. He'd just smile and go about his business.

Sam was born on the reserve at the top of Canoe Creek Mountain. Old Sampson, the hereditary chief, was his uncle. As was required, Sam left the reserve to attend the St. Joseph Mission school at 150

Mile House when he was old enough. Far from his home and his family, Sam was subjected to the same horrible conditions that so many Indian children faced. They were forbidden to speak their own language and there was no communication between boys and girls. This meant that even brothers and sisters were not allowed to speak to each other. Every moment of the day was filled; if the children weren't in

Sam Sault John

classes they were chopping wood for the institution or feeding cattle and cleaning ditches at the nearby ranch. As far as the church was concerned, this turned out well-trained individuals. However, I think little consideration was given to how it affected the children's morale to be told their own culture was sinful and wrong.

Fortunately Sam survived the system and came out of it with a better-than-average education, along with the desire to continue learning throughout his life. When Mother was finished with the papers and magazines she received from my Grandmother in England, she'd pass them on to Sam. As a result, he had a pretty good idea of what was going on in the world and where he fit into the scheme of things.

Sam was a big man, especially when you stood him up alongside the other local Indians. Most of them were short and stocky, with an average height of five foot six to eight, while Sam was nearly six feet tall and more rangy than bulky. One side of his face and his top lip were permanently scarred when a horse he was breaking kicked him in the face when he was young. Damaged nerves caused the scarred areas of Sam's face to droop slightly. Despite the severity of his injuries, the whole effect now gave him a look of distinction more than anything else.

Not long after he got out of school, Sam got married. His petite wife, who was no more than five feet tall and a hundred pounds, bore twenty children over the years. Seventeen of them died in infancy, while one boy named Wilfred and two daughters, Celestine and Violet, survived and lived into adulthood. In spite of the tragedy of losing so many children, Sam and his wife never gave up but continued to work at maintaining a good life for themselves. They lived in a solid log cabin at the reserve where Sam was born. Along with a good team of horses, the couple also had a wagon and sleigh and all the necessary rigging. Sam was known as an excellent worker and easily found jobs at any of the local ranches whenever he needed cash.

Their life seemed little different from ours. I've often thought that during those days not much separated Indians and whites either economically or culturally. Yet the colour boundaries were there and Indians were denied many things because of their race. Even my own Grandmother Place refused to have any Natives or those with Native blood in her home, and her attitude was very common. Like the hockey players from Alkali Lake, no Indian could get accommodation in hotels or even meals at some of the roadhouses. They weren't allowed to vote or own land, and among a long list of other restrictions, Indians were forbidden to buy or consume alcohol.

This particular rule galled Sam. He resented being told what he could and couldn't do, so he set about making his own homebrew. It wasn't long before he was turning out some mighty good stuff, as Dad could attest to since he was known to enjoy a bottle every now and again with his good friend. Sam had to be careful as to when and where he made the alcohol. He set up his still by the big spring behind Rabbit Park, far from any roads. This was to ensure that the police or Indian Agents wouldn't come poking around where they were not wanted. Despite his extra measures, however, Sam's extracurricular activities were eventually discovered and blamed for an accident that devastated him.

When Sam's son Wilfred was school age, he left for St. Joseph Mission school, much to Sam's dismay. He'd have preferred to keep his son at home, but he complied with the church's wishes and enrolled

St. Joseph Mission in 1922. The Indian children who went to school here worked in the fields when they weren't in class.

Wilfred. Around 1920, while Wilfred was there, an incident occurred at the school that shocked everyone in the country. Several Indian boys ran away from St. Joseph. They were soon rounded up and returned, except for one little fellow from Alkali Lake named Duncan Sticks. He started back to Alkali Lake on foot but succumbed to exhaustion before he made it home. The day after the search for Duncan began, Antone Boitanio found him alongside the road. He was dead and his face had been partially eaten by some wild animal. Realizing the absolute desperation the boy must have felt to risk his life returning home, Sam was immediately concerned for Wilfred's well-being. He wrote a plaintive letter to the authorities asking that his son be dismissed from the school. Of course no heed was paid to his request and nothing was done to ease Sam's apprehension. Sam remembered this inaction for the rest of his life.

Finally Wilfred's schooling was completed and he returned to his family. He became his father's constant companion. The two shared similar temperaments. Like Sam, Wilfred was especially kind and considerate to his sisters and mother. Sam always regarded his son with pride and joy. His boy had grown up well.

Another trait that the Sampson family possessed was the ability to ride horses. And not simply ride, but ride them at full speed through timber. Anyone who has chased an ornery cow through the bush on horseback knows how much skill and stamina is required. Old Sampson was great at it. When I was a kid there was a stampede at Dog Creek, and one of the events was a timber race. The idea of a timber race is to get from point A to point B as quickly as possible. There are no trails to follow. Each rider makes his own route as he goes. It's a wild race and an entertaining one to watch as the men and horses combine their skills to get through, over, under, and around whatever gets in their way. I tried it myself once and nearly killed myself, finishing last, about half an hour behind the others. At the Dog Creek stampede, Old Sampson, nearly 70 years old at the time, won the race handily— wearing a wide leather belt to help brace up an old back injury!

Old Sampson taught Sam how to ride through bush, and in turn, Sam taught Wilfred. They'd find about any excuse they could to go pounding off through the timber as fast as possible. At the drop of a hat they'd challenge one another to race.

One Easter a celebration was being held at Canoe Creek. Sam had run off a couple of batches of homebrew to take along for the boys, and his family loaded up and headed off for the festivities. Along the way everyone drank his fair share, especially Wilfred. When they arrived at Canoe Creek they discovered a five-mile timber race was being planned, and Wilfred jumped in right away to sign up.

Wilfred was the heavy favourite to win this race and he lined up with the others, trying to keep his high-strung horse in line before the start. Suddenly the race was on and Wilfred was off, his long black hair streaming out behind him as his horse tore across the ground. A wild yell of pure joy rang from his lips as he disappeared into the timber ahead of the others.

Sam, Mrs. Sam, and their daughters stood by the finish line to welcome Wilfred in. They giggled in excitement, waiting for the first glimpse of him as he raced out of the trees. One of the daughters gasped when she saw the leader break out of the bush. It was Francis Camille. Right on his heels was Dave Sampson, followed by a couple of others. The tension climbed as Sam's family watched each rider cross the finish line. Finally all of the other competitors were in, except

The view from the top of Canoe Creek Mountain was spectacular. This is where Sam Sault John lived and also where the occasional jackpot rodeo was held, like the one Davey Anderson attended.

for Wilfred. Feeling frantic, Sam ran up to a couple of the riders and asked if they'd seen his son. No one had. They all climbed back onto their horses and set off over the route to find Wilfred.

His horse must have stumbled...maybe his cinch broke...These thoughts raced through Sam's head as he paced near the finish line. Dave Sampson returned from the search, riding very slowly. Before Dave spoke, Sam knew what he was going to say. Wilfred was dead.

Dave's voice was like an echo as he explained what must have happened. He figured Wilfred had been swept out of his saddle by a tree branch and his foot got hung up in the stirrup. The terrified horse would have bolted, dragging and smashing the life out of Sam's helpless son. Sam was broken. His thoughts immediately went to the liquor his son consumed prior to the race. It had to have put off his timing, he'd drunk so much of Sam's homebrew. And now he was gone, leaving Sam to live with this for the rest of his life.

Not only did Sam have to fight the guilt he felt, he also had to contend with the police. They laid a charge against Sam for selling moonshine. The fact that the charge didn't stick was small comfort to Sam; he'd already paid dearly for his "crime."

Life went on for Sam. He worked on the ranches when he needed cash. Otherwise he picked berries, fished salmon, shot deer, and trapped when the season was right. Sam lived what I called the Indian way, along with his wife and daughters.

Their oldest daughter, Celestine, met and fell in love with one of the ranch hands and eventually became pregnant. She was a lovely girl and would have made the young man a good wife, but he was not prepared for any such responsibilities. Instead he went off to war and never returned. In time, Celestine married a good Indian man from Lillooet and they had more children together. She took good care of her children and despite severe headaches that plagued her occasionally, she was content with her life. The headaches gradually got worse and worse. Although aspirin had given relief in the past, it no longer had any effect on her pain. Her death a short time later finally ended her suffering. An autopsy revealed she had died from a brain tumour, the source of the headaches she had tried to treat with mere aspirin.

After Celestine died, her husband returned to Lillooet while their children—Clara, Bert, and Sammy—remained with Sam and Mrs. Sam. This was a big load for the old couple to take on. Fortunately their daughter Violet was still in the area and she helped them whenever necessary. Sam did not receive any financial assistance for taking on the care of his grandchildren, nor did he expect any. The Indian Department offered to place the kids in separate foster homes, but it would not lend any support to Sam. Foster homes were not an option. Sam and his wife were collecting the old age pension, and they chose to make do with that as their only source of income.

The next problem facing Sam was getting an education for his grandchildren. He was determined that these kids, unlike Wilfred, were not going to end up at the mission school. By this time I was running the store in Dog Creek and was chairman of the school board, and one day Sam visited me to ask if it'd be all right for Clara and Bert to attend Dog Creek school. To my knowledge, to this time there had never been an Indian child at a white school in the Cariboo. I assured Sam his kids would be welcome. In fact, I added, consider them enrolled as of right now. What I didn't say was that I'd still have to run it by the other members, although I was sure it'd be accepted with no problem. And it was—the kids were in.

What I hadn't anticipated was the church's sudden involvement in the situation. The Roman Catholic Church vigorously guarded its position as educators of the Indian population. Church officials considered the enrolment of Clara and Bert at Dog Creek an affront to their authority. Sam and Mrs. Sam were immediately refused admittance to any church services. The only thing about this ban that concerned Sam was the fact that being shunned from the church bothered his wife a great deal.

Regardless, it was not going to change Sam's mind. His only dilemma now was how to get the children to school. They were living at the top of Canoe Creek Mountain, and there was no way the kids could commute that distance each day. He solved the situation by building a small shack on the Dog Creek reserve, two miles from the school. It certainly wasn't the best of homes; he couldn't afford nails or lumber, so he scavenged the materials from old shacks. Dad also gave Sam some rough-cut from the mill to use. By the time school started, Sam and his family had moved into their new house.

Each morning Sam delivered the kids to school, then picked them up afterwards. On the really cold days throughout the winter, Sam stopped in at the store on his way to the school so he could warm up. It didn't take long before Sam became the unofficial bus driver in the area and all the kids piled on for a ride. He did this for years without any kind of compensation, and I don't know that he was ever even thanked for his efforts.

A couple of years after Sam's grandchildren began attending Dog Creek school, one of the Indian girls at the Gang Ranch attempted suicide. She ended up in the Ashcroft hospital and died a short time later. Her daughter, eighteen months old, was left alone. And who should end up looking after the little girl but Sam.

The added burden on Sam's resources began to show. Mrs. Sam started keeping Clara at home to help out, and Clara's schoolwork suffered. At the store, Sam's account was falling behind. It was clear to me that they couldn't handle the extra person in their household. I decided to speak with the Indian Agent the next time he visited.

As fate would have it, Mr. Christie, the agent, stopped in soon after on one of his trips through the region. An understanding man, he listened while I explained the situation facing Sam and his wife. Mr. Christie agreed when I suggested that he find the child another home in order to relieve Sam of the responsibility, and the two of us set off for the reserve to talk to Sam.

Mr. Christie and I learned a little about the Indian culture as a result of our involvement. After we told Sam that sending the girl to another home would be best for him, he didn't hesitate with his response.

"It was an honour that the chief chose me to keep the girl, and I'm proud to have her here. As long as there is food to eat on the table, I am happy to share it with her." Sam went on to say that it would do Clara good to learn that there were other things to do besides schoolwork, especially something as important as helping to support her family when they needed it. By the time Sam finished speaking, we knew there was absolutely nothing left to say in defence of what we'd once believed was a sound solution. Mr. Christie and I left the reserve somewhat taken aback by this enlightening conversation.

The little girl stayed until Mrs. Sam became ill. As it happened, a young couple, relations of the girl's mother, asked Sam for the child. Using his good judgment, Sam knew what was best and let her go.

Mrs. Sam's condition steadily grew worse. The small, frail body that had borne twenty children could finally fight no longer. She quietly fell asleep and never awakened. The usual wake was arranged and she was laid out on the floor of their cabin. I felt the need to see Sam, to express my sorrow and offer my old friend some comfort.

When I arrived, Mrs. Sam was covered with a bedspread, as if she were sleeping. A candle burned on each side of her and a crucifix was propped at her head. I watched Sam, who was seated at her feet with his back to me. The room was very quiet even though it was full of people. All eyes were on me, and I stood there for several minutes, unsure of what I should say or do. Finally I slowly walked over and knelt down by Sam.

"I'm very sorry, Sam." His twisted old face was drawn and tired. I could see he was suffering terribly.

"It's all right," he said, his voice tight. "It's all right. They let her be buried in the church." Sam swallowed hard, nodding his head slightly. "She wanted that, you know. More than anything."

Only on her deathbed had the church finally forgiven Mrs. Sam for her "sin" of keeping her grandchildren out of the mission school. I was pleased that Sam gained some small comfort knowing his wife would have felt more at peace when she died because of the church's change in its position.

Sam Sault John

Sam lived on. His grandchildren grew up, and when Clara got married he went to live in her home. It was about that time that I left Dog Creek and I only saw Sam once more several years later. He was an old man then, proud to tell me that he'd shot a moose that fall and provided the meat for his family one more time. That winter my good friend Sam died in his sleep.

Of all the men I have met in my life—the wealthy and the poor, the meek and the aggressive, white, black, yellow—I don't believe there was one any better than Sam Sault John.

CHAPTER 14

RITA
MARGARET HAMILTON

150 Mile House was a bustling little town in 1915. Cecelia had been living there for some time in a cabin across the road from the telegraph office. She planned to move down to Lac la Hache, but first she would stay at 150 Mile until her baby was born.

It was a beautiful summer night in August. The music was going full bore in the cabin next to Cecelia's. She could hear the feet hitting the floor and the fiddles singing. She had to smile even when the pain hit her. Moffat was out there dancing and enjoying himself in the other cabin, and Cecelia was half mad at him for doing so, but that was the way it was so there was no use getting too upset about it. She had been through all this five times before, so she was used to the feeling of anger and frustration that accompanied a confinement. It should be over pretty soon. The pains were getting sharper and more frequent. Every time they started, her good friend Mrs. Wineberg would let out a yell and poor old Dr. Feare would try to plug his ears. Mrs. Wineberg was starting to get hoarse from all the yelling.

Lac la Hache, where Rita grew up.

Rita's parents were Cecelia Eagle (left) and Moffat Hamilton (right).

Rita Margaret Hamilton with her mother, Cecelia Eagle.
Compare this to my baby picture in Chapter 3. We started out
with half a world between us, from vastly different cultures, yet
ended up in the same place, together.

Finally the last big push and the last big yell from Mrs Wineberg and the baby was born. Dr. Feare held up the baby and announced that it was a girl. Cecelia was pleased it was a girl and she knew Moff would be too. And she was a beautiful baby, all wrinkled and angry looking. When everything was cleaned up and the baby was nestled in her arms, Cecelia quietly drifted off to sleep as the fiddles continued to play. She had already picked the name for the child.

Rita Margaret Hamilton grew up at Lac la Hache, though her family had no real home. They stayed in log cabins where the boys—Alfy, Clifford, and Buster—could get work either haying or cutting ties for the railway. Their life was very hard but they were a happy family. Rita remembers as a little girl being sent to live with her cousin. She didn't realize that she was sent there to keep her away from her older sister, who was dying of tuberculosis. At the time, the family was living in tents beside the government road, and Mary, her sister, was in her own tent where Rita wasn't allowed. Rita was in her teens before she had a house to live in that they could call home.

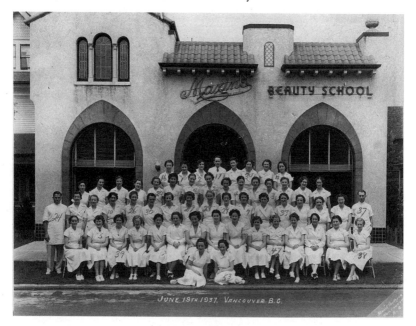

Maxine Beauty School in Vancouver, where Rita took a hairdressing course. She worked as a cook for haying crews and in tie-cutting camps for a year to raise the $100 she needed to go to school.

By that time she was working as a cook for haying and tie-cutting crews to save up enough money to go to Vancouver and take a course in hairdressing. She eventually got the money together, and while she was taking the course she met her future partner, Vivian Billing. When the course was finished they went up to the Cariboo and decided to open a beauty parlour in Williams Lake. With much trepidation they approached Julian Fry at Lac la Hache for a loan to buy equipment. They asked for and got $1000, which seemed like an astronomical sum at the time. They bought equipment from the ReVita company, so they decided to call their business Vi-Rita Beauty Salon. They operated it for five successful years and paid Mr. Fry his money back. It was one of the first beauty parlours in the area and ran from 1937 to 1942.

✲ ✲ ✲

I first saw Rita when she was nineteen years old and was the Queen of the Williams Lake Stampede. I was just able to walk around a bit after being sick for almost a year, and we had gone to Williams Lake to take in the stampede. Geoff drove the mail truck, with Betty Keeble and Mother beside him in the front, but it was a dreary ride for me in the back. Every time Geoff slowed down for a bump, the dust billowed in to where I was huddled under the tarpaulin with the mail bags. I got car-sick, too, and whenever I had to throw up I would get another batch of dust. By the time we got to Williams Lake I was happy to stay in our cabin at the old auto court in town, resting and listening to the birds and the crickets singing, while the others went downtown to see the parade.

When they returned, my Mother told me what a beautiful girl the queen was and how nice she looked riding her horse at the head of the parade. I didn't go down to the stampede grounds that day, but in the evening I wanted to hear the music at the big dance at the Elks Hall, so I got myself ready and away we went. We had to wait in line to get in, and then I found myself a seat along the side of the hall. It was very exciting for me and I was breaking out in hives, so I had to sit still and get control of myself. I was just settled down when there was a big commotion in the crowd as the queen arrived. I stood on the bench to get a better view of what was going on, and my Mother got

The Williams Lake Stampede began in 1920—or in 1919 depending on who you talk to. The event in 1919 was an informal affair, but the next year it was held "to celebrate the making of this new town by the arrival of the Pacific Great Eastern Railway." It was suspended during the war, but by the 1950s it had become a major Canadian rodeo.

In 1934 Rita was one of the Stampede princesses (bottom left). That year the queen contestants and their supporters sold tickets, and the queen was chosen by the number of tickets sold. Rita was winning when an older admirer of one of the other girls spent all his money on tickets and bought the other girl in. The next year the committee asked Rita to run again as they said she wasn't treated fairly in the first contest, so she did and won easily (above). She was a good queen and always supported the Stampede through the years and was accorded a lifetime pass to the Stampede grounds for her efforts.

In 1978 there was a reunion of Williams Lake Stampede queens and princesses. Rita attended, wearing the same outfit she did when she was crowned, riding Jim Roberts' champion roping horse in the parade, still beautiful, still "Queen."

up on the bench with me because she was so short she couldn't see unless she did.

Rita, the queen, entered to cheers and clapping. She was lovely, with big dark eyes flashing as she smiled at everybody and waved. Her gorgeous white dress set off her dark skin and her beautiful smile.

My Mother turned to me and said, "What do you think of her?"

"I think she's beautiful," I said. "I think I will marry her someday."

My Mother had a big laugh at that, but I had the last laugh because that is exactly what I did seven years later.

* * *

Four years later, when I was twenty years old and working for a Christmas tree company, I was registering for a room at the Lakeview Hotel in Williams Lake when an old friend, Barney Anderson, came into the hotel lobby. He greeted me and started to sing a sad song of being left by all of his "so-called friends" who were all out at 150 Mile House for a dance, leaving him stranded with no transportation.

"Ah heck," I said. "It's only ten miles out there. I'll take you if you promise to quit belly-aching."

He laughed and we piled into the old jalopy I was driving. We stopped at the Maple Leaf Beer Parlour, where Barney worked, and loaded up a few cases of beer out of the cooler, then set off for 150 Mile on the washboard road.

We hadn't gone a quarter mile when we hit a particularly rough spot in the road and the car shuddered and the lights went out. Barney was perturbed, but I assured him the problem was only temporary and that the lights would come back on in a few minutes when the car had stopped shaking and the relay had cooled down. In the meantime we should settle ourselves with a cool one.

"Done," said Barney.

Down went the beer and the lights came on. Away we went until the exercise repeated itself a few hundred yards further. This called for more rejoicing and another beer while things cooled down and light returned.

It was a very rough piece of road to 150 Mile House, but eventually we made it with only the contents of a great number of beer bottles missing. I intended to turn right around and go back to Williams

Our wedding day, June 26, 1942. Left to right: Irene Moxon; Henry Zirnhelt; Mrs. Scott; my Mother; the bride, Rita; the groom, Hilary; Vi Zirnhelt (Rita's partner in the beauty parlour); my brother Geoff. None of Rita's family was there and only my Mother and Geoff from my side.

Lake, but Barney persuaded me to stay until it was daylight, just a couple of hours away. He also persuaded me to come into the dance where it was warmer. I didn't need much persuasion. The next thing I knew I was in the hall, dressed in my old workclothes—plaid wool shirt and pants all covered with pitch, with fir needles stuck in the pitch. All I had on my feet was a pair of moccasins, and my hands and face were covered with pitch. I was a mess.

I was also face to face with the Christmas tree company bookkeeper who was supposed to have had my paycheque ready and didn't, which was why I had been staying over in Williams Lake.

"So here you are you little S.O.B. Where the hell is my cheque?"

He said something smart back. I had a bellyfull of liquid courage so I took a swing at him and down he went. Then the peacemakers took over and the main peacemaker looking after me was Rita.

Somebody dragged out the remains of the bookkeeper, and Rita soon had me forgetting about him. Soon after that, however, I wasn't feeling as good as I should, so I sneaked outside and threw up by the back fence. Somehow I got my neck down between two pickets on the fence. I think I could have died there if Rita hadn't come and found me a few minutes later. She got me out of the predicament and I drove her back to Williams Lake and dropped her off at her beauty shop.

A year went by.

My brother Geoff thought it would be fun to have some females at my twenty-first birthday party. He was driving the mail truck down the street in Williams Lake when he saw Betty Keeble and invited her. She agreed to come out to Dog Creek. Then Geoff saw Rita and hollered to her, "Would you like to come to Dog Creek to my brother's twenty-first birthday party?" She agreed too, so much to my surprise, Geoff arrived at Dog Creek with two guests for my birthday party.

I fell in love with Rita that first time I saw her as the Stampede Queen. Her visit to Dog Creek for my birthday certainly sealed it. When I asked her to marry me in 1942 I had nothing. No job, no business, nothing but a saxophone, a fiddle, an accordion, and something less than 50 dollars in my pocket. The only work experience I had was ranch work and the Christmas tree business. She, on the other hand, owned with her partner a beauty parlour, fully equipped and paid for, and a house full of furniture they shared.

We were engaged at Easter and married on June 26, 1942. When Geoff got married there was a great big wedding party and people came from miles around. When Rita and I were married in Kamloops, there were only ten people attending. None of Rita's family came, and my Dad wasn't there either, though Geoff and my Mother were at the church. I stood up there and said my vows in a second-hand suit that I had bought for five dollars from a pawn shop. The light shining through the stained glass windows fell on my face and cast a pale green tinge on me, but Rita was lovely and said her vows with a smile as she looked at me on my knees beside her.

Rita sold her share of the beauty parlour to her partner and came to live with me at Dog Creek.

CHAPTER 15

DRIVING TRUCKS

Rita and I got home to Dog Creek from our honeymoon in the first week of July 1942. There was great excitement in the valley because the Canadian government had decided to build an airbase on Dog Creek Mountain, seven miles from the Dog Creek post office on the road to Williams Lake. The surveyors were already there at work. The top of the mountain was a great big flat prairie that was ideal for a landing strip, but this was no single landing strip. It would be a full-fledged three-runway airport that could land anything that was flying in those days.

By the first of August the construction work got going in earnest. The contractor was a Calgary firm by the name of Fred Mannix and Son. The Son part of the name showed up at Dog Creek with fifteen men to set up camp. There was nowhere for them to stay except the old hotel-ranch house that we lived in. Up to that point the main users of the hotel under my parents' regime were police officials and Indian Agents and such with the odd traveller, usually lost, thrown in, but now my Mother hired a couple of extra Indian girls and set to work accommodating the Mannix crew. Dad and Geoff made a deal with Mannix to haul all the construction crew's supplies from Williams Lake. They were also to supply all the lumber to build the camp. This was a pretty tall order, but they got the contract and we started work.

Geoff made a quick trip to Vancouver to buy a new (second-hand) truck. He got a long wheelbase International Model KS5 with a fishplated frame in good shape. It could handle five-ton loads pretty good because it had a double reduction differential and a five-speed transmission that gave it ten speeds ahead and two backwards. The motor was an International Green Diamond. The main feature of this motor was that it did not have power enough to hurt itself, so it lasted forever. It also took forever to climb a hill with a load on. Geoff was proud of it and he was ready to go.

The other piece of equipment was the old ranch truck. This was a short wheelbase Chevrolet Maple Leaf with a four-speed transmission, no double reduction differential, and a six-cylinder engine. It could also pack a five-ton load if you got enough of the load in front of the hind wheels. If you didn't it had a tendency to rear up on its hind wheels like a dog begging for a bone, which scared the hell out of you. This was to be my vehicle.

I had never driven a truck in my life. I had lots of experience driving a car, and I was kind of proud of my ability on the poor roads that we had to deal with, but Dad or Geoff had always done all the truck driving. However, on August 1 I found myself at the wheel of the old ranch truck, ready to start my trucking career. Geoff had already left for Williams Lake to pick up a load of lumber, and I was to take the airport crew from Dog Creek up the mountain to the airport site. Then I was to continue on to Williams Lake and pick up a load of gasoline and diesel oil and bring it out to the camp.

A man by the name of Lynch (a Mannix son-in-law) was the head honcho for Mannix. He jumped in the front seat of the truck with me, the fifteen-man crew got in the back, and away we went. The road up the mountain was narrow and steep and the truck seemed gigantic to me, but I made it up the first part, corners and all. The next part had a section we called the rockslide. I didn't do so good there. I missed a gear just at the worst part and the truck started to roll back. The brakes weren't too good so I had to swing the back end of the truck into the bank to get it stopped. This manoeuvre caused some consternation in the back and one of the men yelled out, "Have you ever driven a truck before, for God's sake?"

"No!" I yelled back and jammed the thing into the company gear and took off. Lynch was looking a little pale. He was sitting on the low side and he didn't relish the idea of us ending up on top of him in the rock pile at the bottom of the grade if we went over the side. I wasn't feeling too good myself, but we eventually made it and I dropped them off at the airport site, then continued on to Williams Lake. I practised changing gears on the way. (The "company gear" I mentioned above is a term commonly used by truckers to refer to the lowest gear

*Williams Lake from the Dog Creek Road. This became
a familiar sight to me in the 1940s.*

you could use to pull the most freight and make the most money for
the "company.")

These old trucks didn't have synchromesh gears, so if you wanted
to change gears you had to double clutch: depress the clutch, shift
from the gear you were in to neutral, let out the clutch, speed the
motor to match vehicle speed, depress clutch again, shift to your new
gear, let out clutch. You could do it without ever thinking about it
after the first 500 times or so. After I got good at it I could show off
and do it without touching the clutch pedal, but this was dangerous
because if you missed the timing you could chip the transmission
gears and that cost money.

But to get back to my first day, when I got to Williams Lake I had
to take off the side racks and put on several tanks at the Imperial Oil
bulk plant. Bob Blair, the agent, helped me get the tanks safely on
board and filled with gasoline and diesel. I was ready to start back. I
had never pulled a load before, and gasoline and diesel are not the

safest of materials to haul, so I took it pretty easy. I finally got unloaded at the work site and got home by midnight. It was a long, stressful day, but there was another one the next and the next for 330 days straight without one single day off.

August, September, and October went by with Geoff and me on the road every day. As soon as the camp had accommodation ready, the earthmovers came in and the construction went into high gear. We had five or six trips a week for fuel alone. Construction had started on the quarters for the airforce men who would eventually occupy the premises, so we had all that material to haul also: all the lumber, roofing, nails, plumbing supplies (including five miles of five-inch cast-iron water mains), 800 tons of coal, wallboard, etc., etc.

The old ranch truck had a terribly noisy transmission. When the thing got hot climbing a hill it would just scream. I remember one time I was climbing up from Little Dog Creek towards the airport. It must have been 95 to 100 degrees outside and about twice that inside the cab of the truck. The transmission was screaming and I was tired out from the interminable work. My head was aching as if it would burst so I pulled over and got out of the truck and lay down in the dirt. After a while I got up and got in the truck and went on. There didn't seem to be anything else that I could do.

At the end of October I was home on Sunday afternoon when the phone rang. It was Jack Lepinski. Jack had the garage in Williams Lake that we were doing our business with. He was also a friend of Geoff's. He sounded a bit worried on the phone. "I think you better come in and attend to business. Geoff has left."

I immediately got my Dad and we headed for Williams Lake. When we got to town, Jack Lepinski told us that Geoff had run off with one of the waitresses from the Lakeview Hotel. That was pretty upsetting in itself, but it wasn't all. The International truck was on its side in a ditch a quarter of a mile out of town with a load of diesel oil leaking out all over the place. It was one hell of a mess!

My Dad just gave up on the whole thing. He said he was not able to leave the ranch to drive truck and that he needed the ranch truck back at the ranch. He said if I wanted to I could take the International truck and see what I could do. He would put up the truck and I would operate it and we would split whatever we made 50-50.

KS5 International truck with ten speeds ahead and two backwards and without heat in the cab or anti-freeze in the radiator. This was my home nearly every day for three and a half years.

By three o'clock that day I was in business. I got the truck out of the ditch, topped up the diesel tank, and headed for the airport. The truck's bulkhead was pushed over from the upset in the ditch but otherwise there wasn't any damage. This was a lot better truck to drive than the old ranch truck, but it did have one major fault: it did not have a heater. For three months that winter I drove the thing without heat in the cab or water in the radiator (there was no antifreeze available because of the war). I can remember crossing Springhouse prairie when it was 30 degrees below zero, scraping the frost off the windshield and driving with sheepskin-lined flight boots, wool-lined mitts, and heavy parka, with a pair of coveralls pulled over the top to try to stay warm. Finally Jack Lepinski made me a heater out of an old radiator and a windshield fan. It was a lifesaver.

Geoff had been making $200 per month as driver and manager of the trucking business. I was getting $50 for being a driver. At the time it didn't seem unfair, as he was experienced and capable whereas I was not, but he also got his groceries paid for and there is where it hurt. I was paying my own store bill out of my lousy 50 bucks. All that changed. Now I was in charge of the trucking business and I paid myself out of whatever I could make. Eventually I bought a half share in the business by paying my Dad half the value of the truck. I think the amount was $800—big money for me in those days!

I only had one truck, the International, to work with, whereas we had two before. I solved that problem by hiring a driver, Bill Frizzi, and keeping the truck on the road 24 hours a day. Bill was a good enough driver, but he had one problem: he could not drive at night, so I had to do all the night-shift driving myself.

It was wartime of course, and there were no repair parts available. What we did get a hold of was a book that listed interchangeable parts. I had made arrangements to work in Jack Lepinski's garage at night to effect any repairs, and I did most of the work myself. It wasn't long before we had Ford gears in the transmission and Chevrolet springs on the front end, but we kept her going no matter what. I remember lots of nights that winter when I would finish a repair job, go over to the "Gag and Hack" Chinese restaurant for a sandwich, then head out to the airport in 30-below weather at two o'clock in the morning.

I remember one incident that illustrates the conditions we were working under. It was winter and it was cold, and I was headed out to the airport with a load of diesel and gasoline. Going down the grade towards Sam Sorensen's place I heard the engine start to make a funny noise. I identified the noise as an indication the connecting rod bearings were gone. These were a shell bearing and could be replaced. I asked Sam for the use of his phone and called Jack Lepinski. He ordered up some new bearings and had them sent up on the express from Vancouver. I hitched a ride back to Williams Lake and left the truck at Sam Sorensen's. The next day Jack and I went out to put in the new bearings. We rigged up some canvas around the front end of the truck and set a blowtorch going underneath for warmth. It's a fairly big job to install six new connecting rod bearings when your truck's in the middle of a snowbank, so we were working on it all day. About three o'clock Sam came out and asked if we could use a cup of coffee. He wasn't long getting a reply.

"By the way Sam, how cold is it?" Jack asked.

"I just looked on the way out," he said. "It's 45 below zero right now!"

By some means I was able to keep up with the work and I hung onto the contract with Mannix. While I was running around like a chicken nicked on the head, trying to handle the whole mess, Rita was left at Dog Creek in the house called Casey, the same house my family had lived in when we first moved down from the D4 years before. It had been enlarged from a two-room cabin to a seven-room house, but every time someone added a room they tagged it on the end of the building, so it ended up seven rooms long and one room wide!

Marc Pigeon, a retired old-timer, occupied the original two-room log part at one end, and we had the rest. It wasn't much of a place at best, and it had been occupied previously by a family that left it run-down and dirty. Rita had to

Marc Pigeon

clean it up herself as I was on the road every day. My Mother had a girl working for her and she very kindly helped Rita move in. Rita's mother came and helped too, so Rita soon set up a comfortable home by the standards of the day. I must say here what a help old Marc Pigeon was to us at this time. This was the same man who had looked after me with his wife Placida when my Mother went to Victoria for a rest in 1923. Placida had died about the time Rita and I were married. Marc packed the water for Rita when I wasn't there. She felt safe when I wasn't home, and he was a perfect gentleman at all times. He was helpful, considerate, and kind and even though he could not read or write, he was a wonderful good neighbour.

I remember the first winter it was so cold in the bedroom that we used to sleep on the chesterfield because we could drag it up close to the heater stove in the living room. We would bring in a big pile of wood for the heater before going to bed, and we'd keep stoking the stove all night to keep from freezing. We could lie in bed and see the stars through the holes in the roof.

We had to pack water from the creek with a pole and two buckets like the Chinese did. There was no bathroom, just an outside toilet.

When we wanted a bath we had to pack extra water, heat it up on the kitchen stove, and have our bath in the middle of the kitchen floor in a galvanized tub.

We had no car. Rita was stuck at home and of course with our vast knowledge of birth control she was pregnant and sick from it too. It was a tough life for Rita, and it could have been a lot better if my Mother had treated her right. Rita would visit her one day and everything would be fine; the next day Mother would turn away and not even speak to her. Rita had never seen such behaviour in her family and could not understand it in mine. I, on the other hand, was used to it as I had been exposed to it all my life. What made it doubly hard was that when Geoff had been around, his wife Gladys was not treated this way. In fact, she was always treated like royalty. She and Geoff were at my Mother's for dinner every night, they got their laundry done, they didn't pay their grocery bill, they had the use of Dad's car, and they had a cosy little house where they stayed and where the roof did not leak. My Mother was of the old English school that believed the firstborn son was to inherit the fortune and the secondborn could either join the church or go off somewhere and quietly drink himself to death. I guess this extended to his wife as well.

I don't know why we stayed at Dog Creek, but we did—for seventeen years.

As far as we knew, Rita was expecting in March. We had never been near a doctor so it was guesswork at the best. In January we decided that Rita should go to Kamloops to have the baby, as the hospital in Williams Lake was closed due to the war. Arrangements were made and off we went to Williams Lake in the old International truck on the morning of February 3, 1943. It had snowed about a foot the night before and we had a hell of a time getting up Dog Creek Mountain. I had to chain up and load a pile of snow behind the rear wheels for added traction. We dug and shovelled and spun wheels for hours getting up to the airport, and then we had to contend with drifts and blowing snow across the top of Dog Creek Mountain. The tracks were blowing in behind us as we inched our way across the wide open spots. We left at seven in the morning and we got to Springhouse at six that night, about 35 miles in all. Rita's uncle and aunt, Antone and May Boitanio, lived there and they had us in for

Antone Boitanio (left), cowboy and fiddler,
married May Hamilton (right), a relation of Rita's father.

dinner. Both Rita and I were exhausted, but we had 20 miles yet to go
to get to Williams Lake, so we left right after dinner and arrived in
Williams Lake at midnight. We got a room at the Maple Leaf Hotel,
run by Mrs. Moxon at the time, and fell into bed, played out. I was
up the next morning and made a trip to the airport with diesel fuel.
Rita stayed at the hotel and spent most of the day in bed trying to rest
up from the horrendous trip. I got back about eight that night and
had supper, and we got to bed as soon after as we could.

About midnight Rita was awakened by labour pains. We had found
out that day that they had reopened the local hospital two days earlier
so, thank God, we had somewhere to go. I loaded Rita into the old
truck and up the hill we went to the hospital. It was about 20 below
zero and there was no water in the truck and no heater, so it was a cold
but short ride. As soon as she was admitted they kicked me out and I
went back to the hotel. I stayed awake and worried about her until
finally sheer exhaustion put me to sleep.

The next morning the first person I met on the street was Bert
Levens, the janitor at the hospital. He said, "Good Morning Daddy,"
and that was how I found out that I was a father. I went up to the
hospital right away and found out that Rita and our son were okay,
but of course they would not let me in to see her. They had visiting

hours, you know—two till four and seven till nine. I loaded up and made a trip to the airport and back by eight that night and was allowed in to see Rita for one hour. She didn't look too bad considering the trip in, but the baby was another matter. They actually didn't expect that he would make it, so the doctor and nurses had shoved him off to one side while they went on about their business. When they finally got around to dealing with him, he was still there putting up a fight.

This routine of getting up at four o'clock in the morning and making my trip to the airport and back for visiting hours went on day after day. Rita wasn't getting any stronger and the baby was hanging on by a thread. Ten days, eleven days, twelve days, thirteen, fourteen, fifteen. On the seventeenth day I got back to the hospital at seven for the visiting hour. I was about to enter Rita's room when the matron came running down the hall and stopped me.

"You can't go in there, the priest is in there!"

"Like hell I can't," I yelled as I pushed her out of the way and barged into the room. I grabbed the priest by the shirt collar and told him to get to hell out of the room. He bolted out the door with me in hot pursuit. I called him everything I could think of and told him I would knock his bloody block off if he ever entered Rita's room again.

On my way in I had spotted a baby bottle on the kitchen stove, half full of curdled sour milk, with Baby Place written on it, so now I grabbed the matron and gave her hell about that. I also told off the cook and I think there might have been some others. They all got a cussing-out. Then I went in to visit Rita.

She was discharged the next day. I don't think she was any better, but they probably wanted to get rid of me before I murdered somebody.

Rita moved down to the Lakeview Hotel, where Jack Chow gave us a nice room and saw that Rita was well cared for by his staff. She was there for almost three weeks before she was ready to go home. She had a tough time of it, but the reward was we got a great little guy in our first son, Adrian Charles Place.

There was no health insurance in those days, so we had the problem of paying for the doctor, hospital, and hotel bills. All told they amounted to more than I made in a year, so it took a little finagling to do. I dug up enough cash to pay the doctor, then made a deal with the hospital to pay them off in two months and asked Jack Chow to wait for his money until I got the hospital paid. When the hospital bill was out of the way I paid Jack so much per month over and above our regular hotel bill until the debt was cleared.

While Rita was at the hotel the roads were getting worse and worse. There was no maintenance being done because of the war. We just beat a road through the snow every day. We shovelled when we had to and we chained up when we had to and we kept a narrow lane open that way. If we were unlucky enough to meet somebody, which fortunately was rare, we shovelled a passing place around him. That March there were some bad snowstorms and the road became entirely blocked.

Mannix started to get low on supplies and I couldn't get through. They were not too co-operative about it and said that if I wasn't able to get through they would get somebody who could. They contacted George Luscomb to haul their stuff out to the airport.

George was a great big hulk of a man, a former policeman. He was a tough-looking customer and he was as tough as he looked. His idea of enjoying himself was to pick a fight with George Murphy, one of his employees, and go a few rounds in the back shop of his garage. Luscomb owned a couple of trucks and the Ford garage in Williams Lake, so he was happy as all get out to get the contract away from me. He sent Murphy and a guy named Murdock out in his two trucks the next day with a load of supplies for Mannix.

Two days later they were only halfway to the airport, off the side of the road about 200 yards somewhere between Springhouse and Alkali Lake. All the groceries were frozen, one truck was down with a broken spring, and the other was frozen up solid with a busted block. At about this time the Alkali Lake Ranch needed supplies too, and they sent their bulldozer through to open the road. I quickly loaded up and started out to the airport. I had to shovel all the bad spots for about three miles when I got past Alkali, but after eighteen hours on the road I got to the airport with my load intact.

I also got my contract back.

In the spring I had an opportunity to buy another truck. It was a short wheelbase, three-ton Ford that had belonged to Ivan Walters. Ivan lived out Likely way and had the mail contract for that area. The truck had been used to haul mail, freight, and passengers and was in reasonably good shape. Ivan had installed a small airtight heater in the cargo space for the comfort of his extra passengers. This ended up providing great amusement to the people around, as the truck would head down the road with smoke pouring out the chimney like some misguided freight train. Everybody called it the "Blue Goose." Needless to say I got rid of these comfort features and installed a freight box when I got a hold of the thing. It was then that I noticed another feature that Ivan had installed: a bullet hole in the roof of the cab. It seems that Ivan carried a loaded gun so he could get the drop on any

Hilary the Truck Driver. Note the ever-needed chains. I hauled every pound of freight to Dog Creek airport and operated trucks 24 hours per day, seven days per week, for the first year.

game that might wander onto the road during the hunting season (or any other season for that matter). One day he had a woman and her eight-year-old son riding with him into Williams Lake. The young hopeful got playing around with the gun and pulled the trigger. Ivan claimed that he could never hear as well as he could before, but no other harm was done. I fixed the leak with two washers, a stove bolt, and some rubber cement.

That spring Geoff returned home with his new wife Betts, the waitress, and started back to work driving for me. He seemed perfectly happy to let me make the decisions, except that I had him driving the Blue Goose and he hated the darn thing. We were hauling lumber out to the airport and I had been using an old trick to make unloading easier. I would put pieces of pipe under the lumber, then chain the load down well. When I got to my destination I undid the chains, backed up, and jammed on the brakes. The pipes acted as rollers and the load would roll off in one piece, nice and neat. I used to leave one chain wrapped around the load so it would stay together. It was a good way to handle lumber and it saved hours of labour.

For some reason Geoff had never done this manoeuvre and wasn't quite up to the situation that arose. He was loaded and away from Williams Lake ahead of me with the Blue Goose, and I got to the airport just in time to see him sitting there with the old Goose half unloaded. The front wheels were about six feet off the ground and the lumber was still holding down the back end. When this happened, the best method of solving it was to put the truck in reverse and torque the front end down. Geoff didn't know this so he slapped the truck into a forward gear and jumped it out from under the load. Down she came BANG! onto the ground. Geoff jumped out of the cab, half knocked out from the fall and hitting his head on the steering wheel. He stepped over and took a kick at the front fender of the old Goose and generally put on quite a show. It looked funnier than all get out to me.

In June 1943 Rita and I took a few days off. It was the first holiday I had since starting to drive truck. I had even been on the road on Christmas and New Year's Day and all Sundays and holidays since the August before. They were not short, easy days but long and hard working days.

We drove down to Vancouver and got settled in our hotel. When I went to the bathroom to wash up, I passed out cold on the bathroom floor. As luck would have it there was a knock on our room door at that precise second and damned if it wasn't Harold Stuart from Redstone, a good friend from the Cariboo. He helped Rita call a doctor and an ambulance, and the next thing I knew I was in St. Paul's Hospital—in poor shape. I only weighed 125 pounds and my diagnosis was double pneumonia.

Rita went to stay with my Aunt Frankie, Uncle Frank's wife, but soon we were running out of money. The hospital bill was climbing day by day and the only solution was to get out of there as soon as possible and get home. After six days in the hospital I discharged myself, and the next day we set off back to Dog Creek.

We got as far as Lytton the first day and were nearing Clinton the second day when disaster struck. The roads were unimaginably rough due to the total lack of maintenance. The car was bouncing over this stuff when all of a sudden the battery flew out of its case under the floorboards and smashed on the road. When I stopped the car to find out what had happened, the motor stopped. There was no way to get it started with no battery, but I knew that if I could push it over the crest of the little hill ahead it would start and I could run in to Clinton on the generator alone. I pushed and struggled till I was about to pass out again, but I didn't have the strength to get it over the rise of the hill. There wasn't a single car along that road for at least an hour, but finally there came the Clinton Stage, which was operated by Joe Barr who was some sort of relation of Aunt Frankie. I hailed him and asked him to give me a push over the crest of the hill.

He refused.

I asked him if he would take a message in to Boyd's Garage for me and he said he would...for one dollar! So I wrote a note to Baldy Boyd and gave Joe a dollar.

Then we waited...and waited...and waited...at least three hours in the blazing sun. Finally Baldy came flying out and gave us a push and we drove into Clinton. It appears that Mr. Barr delivered first things first, then had his lunch hour, and delivered our message to Baldy last. So much for relatives.

I needed some new equipment, there was no doubt about that. The old trucks I was working with had just about had it. The war effort was going full blast and there was no way that I could get any new trucks, so I applied to the Wartime Prices and Trade Board for authorization to buy a truck. The Board was a government agency that had control of all transactions so that it could maximize the war effort. I got a ten-page form to fill in and the Board sent around a guy to evaluate the equipment we had. I had to get all my customers to sign a petition attesting to our essential service in the line of general freight and mail. I also included our contract with the builders of the airport to show our contribution to the war effort. All to no avail.

Among the companies dependent on our service was the Diamond "S" Ranch, owned by Colonel Victor Spencer. We hauled in all their cattle feeds and general freight. Colonel Spencer happened to be in Dog Creek at the time, and I talked to him about our equipment problem. He said I should take all the papers down to Vancouver and see his store manager, a Mr. Bartlett, who was the head of the Wartime Prices and Trade Board for B.C. Colonel Spencer was sure he would get it through for me.

Mr. Drinkell and I made an appointment with Mr. Bartlett and we hitched a ride to Vancouver with Sam McRae to see him. Drinkell was along primarily because Victor Spencer loved to get him down to the Vancouver Club to spin yarns about the Cariboo. A couple of stiff drinks and the fun would begin.

As for the meeting with Mr. Bartlett, when we arrived at his office Mr.

A.J. Drinkell had been in the Cariboo since 1912, so he had a wealth of stories about the region's history and characters. He'd get his pipe stoked up and sit around yarning for hours.

Drinkell was invited in for coffee and cakes and laughs and I was left sitting in the waiting room. After a half hour or so Drinkell was escorted out and I was invited in. Bartlett started out something like, "I wonder who the hell you think you are to be trying to get a fancy new truck to ride around in while all those boys are overseas getting killed. You ought to be ashamed of yourself for asking for help to hinder the war effort."

I was so taken aback that I let him continue for a few minutes until my head went into gear. Finally I stood up and asked him if he had anything else to say and he said no, that was final. Then I told him that if he thought I came all the way down there to be spoken to like a dog, he had another think coming. As far as I was concerned he could take his Wartime Prices and Trade Board and shove it up his ass, and if he thought I would accept any help from a pompous poop like him, forget it! Then I walked out.

All in all it wasn't a very successful trip. When I got back to Williams Lake I went the political route via the Liberal party, which had the sitting member for Cariboo at the time. A suitable donation to the party brought the necessary approvals and in due course we had all the papers to get a new truck. I learned that in business you do what you have to do if you are going to survive.

When the new truck arrived, Jack Lepinski went down to Vancouver to get it and drive it up to Williams Lake. He arrived back in the middle of the night. The next day he was at work when I got there and sure enough, the new truck was sitting in the yard. I looked it over and could hardly believe that we finally had it. We went into his office and he started adding up the cost. "Well," he said, "it's going to set you back $2500. Now how are you going to pay for it?"

"Holy smokes, Jack, that's a big chunk of money," I said, and then I reached into the back pocket of my jeans and got out my wallet. I pulled out two $1000 bills and a $500 bill and put them in his hand. He almost crapped himself he was so flabbergasted. I had been to the bank and got the bills before going down, and the banker, who had the same kind of sense of humour as me, dug up the bills for me.

I put Geoff on the new truck. It was bigger and more powerful than what we'd had and it made us more efficient. Geoff did most of the full-load hauling and I looked after the way freight. In 1944 the airport construction was starting to wind down. The airforce took over and hauled its own supplies. As it happened, that was a very hard winter and we had a lot of grain and feed to haul for the ranches at Alkali Lake and Little Dog Creek. The situation on the ranches was almost desperate, so we were running night and day to keep up with the demand. The grain was all in hundred-pound sacks that we loaded out of the boxcars in Williams Lake by hand and unloaded at their destination the same way. I vividly remember getting to Alkali at about two o'clock in the morning and unloading by myself in the dark. I

We came up with ingenious ways to move things in the old days. Here Tommy Hodgson loads a bridge timber on two trucks so he can manoeuvre it around the hairpin turns of the Cariboo roads.

never got any help there. The next night I would be at Little Dog Creek. I would no sooner get backed up to the barn, again at two o'clock, than out would come old Quin Able and his son Henry to help me unload. After we had finished unloading, Old Quin would say, "You better come in for a cup of coffee." I would be greeted by coffee and also by deer steaks and fried potatoes that Mrs. Able had whipped up while we were unloading.

I often think of the different treatment that I got at the two ranches. At Alkali the owner, Mr. Reidemann, a wealthy man, had a personal dislike for me and issued orders to his employees not to give me any help at all.

Lesser Dog Creek Ranch was owned by Colonel Victor Spencer, who also owned the Diamond "S" Ranch. The Ables, Spencer's employees and very poor people, were not instructed to help me unload or give me a meal. They did it out of the kindness of their hearts. They knew what it was like to work alone at night and they knew how it felt to get a helping hand. They earned my undying gratitude and my highest respect.

By 1944 I had bought another new truck, so now I had two good vehicles and all the paraphernalia that goes with the job: good canvases, tire chains, logging chains and tighteners, ropes, tools, the works. At that time we were under the supervision of the Motor Carrier Branch of the provincial government. The inspector was a man named DeBlaquiere. In 1944, when I had all the good equipment that I have been talking about, he came to me with a proposition. He said that he was going to cancel the Hodgson licence for the Chilcotin and recommend to the government that it be granted to me. He said that the Hodgsons had been giving poor service and they did not have any decent trucks and that he was fed up with them. I knew the situation well and I knew that the Chilcotin licence was a valuable one, so I had some decisions to make. I told DeBlaquiere I wanted to think it over and would let him know what I would do in the morning.

The Hodgsons were an old-time family in the Cariboo, well liked by all. The two older sons were in the army overseas, so Tommy Hodgson, the father, was trying to run the business with Cookie, his youngest son, who was fourteen at the time. The old dad would get laid up from time to time, and poor young Cookie was left with the work. He did remarkably well, but he could only do so much and it was falling short of what was required to give good service.

I met Mr. DeBlaquiere the next day and turned the offer down. I told him that I was not going to be party to taking the licence away from the Hodgsons while their two sons were overseas fighting for their country. I also said that if the Hodgsons ever required help to make deliveries I would be happy to make whatever equipment I had available to them, but that I would do everything I could to see that they retained the licence. I don't think the Hodgsons ever knew that this episode took place, but I know they kept their licence until the boys got home from the war.

One cannot write about trucking in the Cariboo without commenting on the condition of the "roads." In 1939 when the war broke out, all roadwork was suspended. The Dog Creek road did not see a single grader, snowplough, or gravel truck for the next six years. It is hard to imagine how terrible the roads got. In the summer the dust was so thick it penetrated everything. It billowed up in what looked like monstrous cloudbanks. If you were following another driver, you ate dust till your teeth would grind on the grit. If you wore sunglasses, as I did, they would have to be cleaned every few miles. In addition to all the dust there were the chuckholes and rocks left over from the spring break-up. In the fall after freeze-up was the best travelling. The potholes iced over and that smoothed out the road a bit. Winter was an ongoing competition with the snowdrifts.

*The Springhouse prairie road that caused
so much grief in the winter and spring.*

I had some pretty tough trips that first winter of 1942-43. It was a particularly cold winter with more-than-average snowfall. The bad spots were the top of Dog Creek Mountain, Alkali Lake Valley as it climbed out of the creek bottom, and Springhouse prairie. My only tool was a snow shovel and I literally shovelled for miles. I found that if I partially broke the trail I could bunt the truck through. Another trick was to leave the road and look for high ground where the wind had blown the snow away, or to get into light timber where there were no drifts. We used all those tricks to get to where we wanted to go. I particularly remember shovelling the road ahead at the halfway gulch on Dog Creek Mountain at night. I would shovel ahead as far as the lights of the truck would shine, then go back and get in the truck and drive up to where I stopped shovelling, then get out and shovel some more to as far as I could see, then back to the truck and drive ahead again. It was drifted all the way to the airport gate and that was about three miles. When I finally got home at midnight the thermometer showed 30 below zero Fahrenheit.

Springtime was the delight of all truckers in the country. This was the season when you proved yourself as a survivor. This was the season for putting on chains with the muddy water running down the back of your neck and the icy water seeping into your coveralls. On one occasion there were three of us waiting to leave Williams Lake at four o'clock in the morning "on the frost" (when the mudholes were still frozen so there was less chance of getting stuck in the mud)—my brother Geoff, Gordon Brown (Brownie), and myself. Brownie was driving for the airforce and had a four-wheel-drive, three-ton truck equipped with a winch. We thought we had it licked.

We got away and it was clear sailing as far as the church on Springhouse prairie, then trouble. Brownie was in the lead as he had the lightest load and the four-wheel-drive and the winch to pull us through when we got stuck. That was the way it was supposed to be, but it was not the way it played out. Brownie started into the mudhole that was about a half mile long and, as we soon found out, about four or five feet deep. In no time he was sitting in the middle of the morass with all four wheels spinning and going nowhere. He let out his winch line. It was 30 feet long so it went nowhere too, and there was nothing to hook it onto.

Frank Armes came along about then in his car, and he went up to the Staffords' place and got their haying cables, 120 feet long, so we could now reach solid ground. We dug out a fence post from the right-of-way fence and planted it as a deadman to hook onto. At last everything was ready for the big pull. Brownie's motor wouldn't start. Water had gotten into the distributor and we had to get it all dried out. He tried and tried and soon his battery went dead. We had to take a battery out of Geoff's truck to get Brownie's started. Ready at last. Brownie gave her the full power and got the winch going, and the deadman pulled out of the ground and went sailing into the mudhole. We had to dig a new hole for the deadman and set the cable lower on the post.

All of this was taking time and we found ourselves in the middle of the afternoon. We hadn't had anything to eat since breakfast at three-thirty in the morning. Fred Gaspard was with us as a passenger. He had spent his life as a cook and handyman on fishboats on the coast. I told him to see what he could find in the way of grub in the trucks. Fred was a scrounger of the first order and he soon had a good selection laid out on a piece of canvas by the side of the road.

"If I had something to boil some water in, I could cook some eggs," he said.

My eyes fell on the hubcaps the old International boasted on the front wheels, and two minutes later we were boiling eggs. They were a little greasy perhaps, but good!

After Fred's meal we got organized and got Brownie's truck through. From then on it was easy. We pulled the other two through with no trouble, except we broke the cable we had borrowed from Staffords when it was hooked onto my rig. I found myself in the middle of the mudhole with the mud up to the doors. The only way in and out of the cab was through the windows. We had been thirteen hours getting the three trucks through that one mudhole and there were more to come. We got to Dog Creek at midnight.

I was becoming more aware by the day that the trucking business was not my kettle of fish. It is a far tougher business than most people think. I have often said that I worked real hard for General Motors, Imperial Oil, Goodyear Rubber, and the government, but didn't get much for myself. I started looking for a different kind of business and I found one in Williams Lake. The Williams Lake Auto Court was up for sale and I went and talked to the owner, Garvin Dezell, about buying it. We were well on our way to making a deal when I went to the bank to see about financing. When I got there I was shown into the manager's office and received a shock. The manager told me that the bank was foreclosing on Mr. Drinkell and the Dog Creek store and that they wanted me to take over the business.

It was decision time again. Naturally there was pressure from the family to stay in Dog Creek and eventually that won out. I decided to buy the store from the bank and Mr. Drinkell. I made arrangements with my Dad to sell him my half share in the trucking business, and he gave me $1500 for it. What I didn't know was that he had sold the business to Geoff for $6000, so I was "take took" as my friend Bert Chevigney would say.

By September 1945 I was out of the trucking business and into the store business. The money I got for the trucking business went to pay for the first load of groceries, and I had $150 left for operating capital. At the time I thought I had done the right thing, but on looking back I think I would have been a lot better off to have bought the Auto Court and the acreage that was in the middle of Williams Lake.

I guess I am proud of what I did in the trucking business. I started with one truck upside down in the ditch and ended with two good trucks and all the rigging, bought and paid for, in three short years.

There was also the feeling of omnipotence that one gets at the wheel of a powerful vehicle and the knowledge that I was considered one of the best bad-road drivers in the country.

It wasn't all hardship and hard work. There were the comical incidents too, like the time I was hauling grain one spring for the Diamond "S" Ranch. I had a seven-and-a-half-ton load on the old KS5 International, which was supposed to be a one-and-a-half-ton truck. The road was a glare of ice with a little gloss of water on it, the most treacherous driving surface there is. I was coming down Dog Creek Mountain and as I got to the most dangerous part, a steep pitch with an outside turn sloped to the outside edge, I wasn't sure that I would make it around the corner. There is no touching brakes in these circumstances. What you do is gear down as smoothly as possible and let the engine take the braking action. If you start to slide, you give the engine a little gas to catch the wheels up to the slide and then let the engine start braking again. That is what I was doing approaching the corner, but I had been slipping a bit and giving gas and was going faster than I would have liked. I had Drinkell with me as a passenger and he was slightly deaf. The engine was roaring and the transmission was howling when I leaned over to him and hollered, "If I say jump, you better jump and run clear 'cause we might be going over the bank."

All he heard was "jump" and he was gone. He hit that icy road and slipped and cartwheeled, hat flying off, and over the edge he went, out of sight. I made it around the corner and got stopped to see what happened to Drinkell. He came up onto the road spitting sparks and mad as hell, covered with mud and bits of sagebrush and cactus.

At the time it struck me as funny.

When I think about it now, in the comfort of my home in Vancouver, I wonder how the hell I did it!

CHAPTER 16

RANCHERS RETAIL

I was certainly happy to be getting into a business that would be easier on my back. It turned out to be a lot harder on my head.

Our first dilemma involved finding a name for the store that would make it easily identifiable. Drinkell called it Dog Creek Trading Company, but we wanted a new name because the credit rating under the old one wasn't any good. Rita and I searched our brains until we came up with Ranchers Retail, which fit the store perfectly.

Ranchers Retail was a country general store, open seven days a week and, theoretically, 24 hours a day. This was thanks to Drinkell, who was a bachelor while he ran the business. His doors weren't open all the time, but he was on call, and if anyone needed supplies, day or night, Drinkell accommodated them. The store carried everything our customers might need, including food staples, hardware, clothing, and household items.

Placing our first grocery order with the wholesaler, Kelly Douglas & Co., was certainly a learning experience. The salesman, Frank, arrived and we settled in to get things done. We were on even footing; he'd never taken an order before and I'd never given one. Neither of us had a clue what we were doing. Fortunately Drinkell had left all his invoices and records in the store, so we studied those and put together a list that was similar to what he'd done before.

After several orders I was much more comfortable with the process and began making decisions about what was best for us to carry. For example, we couldn't afford to carry two or three grades of an item, so we chose to stock only the best quality and that was all. Competition wasn't of great concern; the major problem was ensuring we had an adequate supply of everything in the store. Rita and I felt badly if someone rode twenty miles to our store for some #3 horseshoes and we didn't have any.

Rita and I started running Ranchers Retail in 1945 and had a wonderful time with it until 1960. You can see from the above photo that it was a real old general store with a bit of everything.

This led to another problem: balancing the orders against the amount of money we had. Sometimes we couldn't afford to stock everything we wanted to. Of course there were times when luck was on our side. That first autumn a salesman from Storey and Campbell, a dry goods wholesaler, called at the store and we ordered coats, heavy shirts, socks, and longjohns until we reached our budget limit. In due course the goods arrived and all was well. The next mail day, however, an identical shipment appeared. I contacted the company and told them what had happened. Instead of asking us to return the duplicate shipment, they said to keep the additional goods and pay for them after they sold. Well the items sold right away and we felt as though we'd been given a gift of gold.

Our customers consisted of about ten families of white people, the crews on three ranches, and around a hundred Indians. This wasn't much of a base to build the business on, but we did it. We countered the small size of the market by optimizing what we could provide each of our customers. We promoted a Christmas tree business and brought in a display of Christmas gifts. We bought fur, first for the Hudson's Bay Company and later on our own account, mainly squirrels and muskrats, and occasionally beaver, ermine, coyote, and mink. Fancy cowboy wear, saddles, and bridles were in demand around Dog Creek and we made sure we had a good selection of all of it. Ranchers Retail even provided groceries on credit for the Indians so they could contract haying and fencing jobs with the local ranchers. Rita and I recognized that anything that brought more trade to the store or money into our customers' pockets would eventually benefit us.

I had known most of our customers all my life and they knew me. The store was a meeting place for everyone, particularly the Indian people. They were always welcome at Ranchers Retail and we shared a comfortable rapport. It was not unusual to have 20 or 30 Indians in the store, waiting for the mail on a cold winter's day. While they visited I sometimes left them in the store and ran home for a quick bite of lunch. When I returned, several of them would sidle up to the counter and say they owed me for a chocolate bar or something else they'd eaten while I was away. Nothing was ever stolen—except once.

On that one occasion my old friend Sam Sault John stayed at the store after the others had gone. Sam told me Johnnie Mack took a flashlight when I was gone and then left the store without saying anything. I knew Johnnie well. He was Mack Duncan's oldest boy. (Johnnie took his father's first name as his last name, an Indian custom.) Mack was known as Crazy Mack, although I didn't know why; he was actually sharp as a tack, very sensible, and conservative.

Johnnie had never gone to school a day in his life. As a teenager he used to accompany his parents to the store occasionally, usually riding some half-broke skinny horse, reeling around and trying to show off. That boy grew into a big man, at least six feet tall and barrel-chested. He was drafted into the army and hauled overseas where they handed him a gun and told him to start shooting people. We all knew back home that Johnnie was an excellent shot and had shot thousands of squirrels in the head as they jumped around in the fir trees. Johnnie survived the war and landed home in one piece, only to now stand accused by Sam of being a thief. I thanked Sam for the information and assured him I wouldn't use his name when I spoke to Johnnie.

A few days later, Johnnie returned to Ranchers Retail. We were alone, so I seized the opportunity.

"Johnnie," I began, "if you needed a flashlight and you didn't have the money to buy one, why didn't you tell me and I'd give you one."

His small eyes darted nervously around the room as I continued. "You have earned your good name both here at home and during the war. I consider you a good friend and if you ever need something, come and see me and I'll do my best to get it for you." I looked up at him to see a tear rolling down his round, puffy cheek. "I want you to promise me that you will never steal anything from anybody again. You are too good a man for that."

Johnnie solemnly looked me in the eye as we shook hands on it. The incident was behind us.

Rita and I also operated the post office in conjunction with the store. I acted as the assistant postmaster under Drinkell, who wanted to retain the distinction of being one of the longest-serving postmasters in Canada. Running the post office was one of the biggest nuisances possible, especially considering our pay for the job was the munificent sum of $8.32 every three months. One major hassle was the fact we were a non-accounting post office, which meant we were not authorized to issue money orders. As a result, all COD orders from Simpson's, Eaton's, and our other suppliers had to be paid in cash, with the money sent in a special brown registered envelope. This also meant that we had to keep a large supply of cash on hand to cover these bills. This crazy system took all our cash each week as we sent payments to Winnipeg and Regina.

To add insult to injury, every once in a while we'd get a notice from a supplier's head office claiming our remittance was short by 50 cents or a dollar. Rita and I devised a plan of carefully counting and checking the COD slips and the money several times each in order to avoid any further notices. Despite our best efforts, another notice arrived a short time later. I wrote the post office inspectors department and said the shortage had to be from someone stealing at their end and I refused to pay another cent.

Sure enough, I soon learned it was indeed the work of two dishonest employees. Apparently about ten workers sorted the mail, with five people on each side of the table. One day employees 1 and 6 were opposite each other. The next day it'd be 1 and 7, and so on each day with a different partner. Two of the workers got together, and each time they were paired up they robbed the system of about $500. This "missing" money was made up by us poor non-accounting post offices when we were billed for supposed shortages in our remittances. I'm happy to say the skunks got ten years in the slammer, although Drinkell ended up taking the credit for catching the crooks because he was postmaster. He even received a nice letter, thanking him for the job Rita and I had actually done.

We carried on with our postal duties at the store until one day a car drove up and an official-looking fellow jumped out. He strode into the store and introduced himself as the post office inspector. "Could I see the post office please?" It was more of a demand than a question, so Rita and I showed him.

He took one look and declared that it would never do. "You have some of your store invoices in here with the post office goods. We simply cannot have that."

Just then Mother came out on the porch and said that if the gentleman wanted lunch, it was being served immediately. I relayed the message to the inspector and he went to the house for a meal.

When he came back, he realized something wasn't right and hurried into the post office.

"Where did you put all the documents and equipment?" He looked around, appearing quite bewildered.

"Oh! It's all right outside there in a cardboard box by the gas pump. You see, it was all mixed up with our invoices and things, and we simply can't have that!"

"You can't do that!" he sputtered in disbelief.

"I just did!"

End of the conversation.

Drinkell ended up moving back down from the airport where he'd been running a catering service. He took over operating the post office out of a little building we'd used as a powerhouse several years before. The old guy was happy to have it back; it made him feel rather important again. And he probably got a little better pay than we did.

We had many moments at the store that were unusual, both funny and tragic events that I'll never forget. Yet I also remember the ordinary activities, days that followed the usual routine, with the same people I knew so well. People like Fleasa Harry, for instance. Her real name was Placida, but Indians had difficulty pronouncing that so it came out as Fleasa. She was in the store one morning, consulting a piece of paper before she made her purchases. I knew Fleasa couldn't read or write, so I was curious to see what she had on the paper. I had to tease it away from her and she finally gave it to me with a shy giggle. It was a shopping list made up of little pictures of the items she wanted—a saltshaker for salt, a matchbox for matches, and so on. It was as effective as a written list as far as I could see.

As a young girl, Fleasa had been infatuated with a young man named Francis Camille, a cowboy of considerable skill. He also came from Indian aristocracy. His grandfather, father, and several other family members had all been hereditary chiefs. Determined to have children by this man, Fleasa managed to waylay Francis somewhere along the line and succeeded in becoming pregnant by him not once, but twice. She had two daughters with Francis; the first she named Angelique and the second, Angela.

Shortly after the arrival of her first child, Fleasa attended Dog Creek school for one day. When the school bell rang she joined the children filing into the room and took a seat at the back of the class. Her baby sat in a basket on her lap while she took in the lessons. At the end of the day she left and walked the three miles back to the reserve. From that time on, if anyone asked if she'd ever gone to school she replied, "Yes, I have gone to school." And indeed she had, for one whole day!

Alfie Edwards, one of Fleasa's brothers, was an interesting cuss himself. He got drunk one day and the Indians sent a message down to us that he was threatening to shoot somebody. They were quite concerned that he would carry out his threat, so Dad and I hopped into the old farm truck and headed off to the reservation. As we rounded the last curve we saw Alfie standing

Susan Edwards at Ranchers Retail.

in the middle of the road with a gun in his hand. Dad pulled up short, realizing we were staring down the business end of Alfie's weapon. He took one look at us and let go a shot that did more damage to the moon than it did to us, but that was all Dad needed. I didn't think he could move so fast, wheeling that old truck out of there in no time flat. We watched Alfie from down the road a piece until he decided to lie down for a sleep on top of the hay in the barn. Once we were sure he was fast asleep, Dad and I quietly went in and disarmed him. He didn't move a muscle and we left him there to sleep it off.

Of course Alfie wasn't always that crazy. In fact, he proved to be much smarter than most people realized. A family of beavers moved into the creek and dammed it up, flooding our meadow. Dad got some dynamite and tried blowing up the dams, but that didn't get rid of the beavers. That's when Dad had the bright idea of hiring Alfie to trap them out. Alfie did the job and returned again the following year at Dad's request to kill some more. It took another year or two before Dad got wise to the fact that Alfie was smart enough to leave a pair each time so that he'd always have something to trap the next year.

No, there wasn't much wrong with Alfie's head when it came to looking after himself. Minding others, however, was another story. Alfie's old mother, Susan, was doing her shopping at the store one day when it was full of people. Among her purchases was a 49-pound sack of flour. She was struggling with this heavy sack when I noticed her and I hollered at Alfie, "For heaven's sake, Alfie, help your mother with that sack of flour!"

He looked surprised by my request, but obliged anyway. "Oh, sure," he said, and lifted the sack up, placing it on his mother's back!

Alfie's younger brother, Joe, didn't have such an easy time of life. An injury at birth crippled Joe and left him retarded. He was called Joe Camp, most likely because he always hung around the camp, staying close to the warm fire. If any of the men appeared in a new pair of shoes or pants or any other new clothing, Joe immediately asked for the old ones. Everything was a "pair" to Joe, regardless of what it was. When one of the boys had a new shirt on, Joe would seize the opportunity, sidling over to him and asking, "You got an old pair of shirt?" Like everyone else, Joe knew how to fend for himself.

Willie Harry was another of our regulars. "How you tis moanni, Rita?" was his way of greeting Rita at the counter in the store. Always cheerful and pleasant, he was one of our most faithful customers. I'd describe his features, but I don't believe that's necessary for anyone who has seen a picture of Cro-Magnon man. Willie and Cro-Magnon man were basically dead ringers for one another. Well, perhaps Willie was a mite small for the designation, but other than that he was a perfect walking replica of his prehistoric antecedent.

My fondest memory of him dates from one Christmas. The children had just returned from the mission school for the Christmas holidays. Eager fathers and mothers had waited hours for their arrival. At last the bus came and stopped in front of the store and everyone rushed out to greet the kids. I stood by the door watching as the families were reunited, children running wildly into their parents' arms. Suddenly I heard Willie hollering at me.

It seemed there were always cows to be moved in the Cariboo. They would graze over one area and the cowboys would round them up and move them on to a fresh piece. It was slow and easy, not the wild stampedes and whooping and hollering you see in western movies.

"Hilary! Hilary! Look here! See this fellow...it's Norman!" Willie's son Norman had grown so much he could hardly believe it. Tears streamed down his face as he went around to each family, his face full of pride. "See this fellow? It's Norman. It's Norman!" and his voice would break with emotion.

Willie was such a likeable guy and kind to everyone, and seeing him so happy brought a tear to my own eye.

Frank Armes also thought highly of Willie, particularly after a certain episode one winter. He often told me of the time he was moving a herd of cattle from Gustafsen Lake up to the Holden meadow. Frank had sent in two brothers along with the wife of one of the brothers. They had to bulldoze a road in, clear the yard, and put out two loads of hay for the cattle to feed on when they arrived. The next day, Frank had Willie put a crew together and they rode out with the cattle. All went well on the drive and they arrived at Holden meadow after dark, around six o'clock, eager for a hot meal and a chance to warm up from the minus-25-degree temperatures.

There was no supper ready for the crew, however, and the hay hadn't even been put out for the cattle yet. Willie and his crew set to work right away and got the feed out for the animals. While they were hard at work, one of the brothers took Frank aside and told him they were not going to have any Indians sleeping in the same cabin with them. Overhearing the conversation, Willie called Frank over and assured him in his limited English that he didn't want to cause any trouble and they'd leave right away. With that, Willie and his crew saddled up and started out on a 35-mile ride back to their homes in Dog Creek.

We rarely had any problems with people's behaviour at the store. Rita always says she was treated with nothing but respect by all of our customers, whites and Indians. The same goes for me, except for one minor incident that happened one Sunday. It was particularly busy that afternoon, and the store was full of customers. Walter Gaspard, who was working for Dad at the River Ranch (Dad had traded the D4 to Victor Spencer for the River Ranch—the best deal my Dad ever made) staggered into the store around three that afternoon. He was obviously drunk and he started mouthing off and using foul language.

I would not tolerate that in the store and gave him the sign to shut up. He wasn't very happy with this, yelling at me and swearing even louder. I yelled back at him to shut up and get out. He wasn't backing down.

"I'll be waiting for you, you S.O.B., when the store closes." And out he went.

By the late 1940s our family had grown again and we'd moved into an apartment over the store. Here Rita is holding Martin and I've got Adrian.

The Cariboo was still an isolated place in the 1950s. This suspension bridge over the Chilcotin River is a long way from a garage if you have a breakdown.

Well, Walter hung around out there, muttering and cursing for about two hours. I shook my head as I watched him occasionally. The grandson of Gaspar de Versepeuch, Walter was a big strong kid and I normally liked him a lot. Right now, however, I had no idea what was going to happen at closing time. There was only one way to find out.

We closed our doors at five o'clock and I waited until Walter turned his back to the door. Then I burst out behind him.

"Walter!" I yelled, "What the hell do you think you're trying to do?" This startled him, and before he could get his temper up, he stuck out his hand.

"I'm sorry, Hilary. Let's be friends."

Boy, was I ever glad to hear that. I shook his hand and all was well again at the store.

Our second son, Martin Halstead Place, was born on January 14, 1947, and that year Rita and I moved into an apartment over the store. Around the same time I decided to build an unloading dock at the end of the building. This meant clearing out the old oil shed where we kept the barrels of kerosene. While I was doing this I found four cases of old dynamite, two boxes of caps, and a roll of fuse. The dynamite had been there God knows how long and it was all sticky and oozing out of the waxed paper wrapping—very dangerous. I knew nothing about explosives so I called on Ed Hillman, who'd hung his shingle out as something of a blasting man, for advice on how to handle the situation.

He came over to the store and surveyed the situation. "You have got to get rid of this stuff, brother!"

I heartily agreed and we set to work. We put the cases of powder in the back of the car and drove up the mountain to the first flat area, where there were some old Indian keequilly holes. These were the remains of ancient winter homes, which were several feet deep and covered with poles, branches, moss, and earth to provide warm winter quarters. The land all around the Dog Creek area was pockmarked with them.

Ed's plan was to unload the boxes in the bottom of the hole and blow the whole works up. Once the explosives were stashed in the keequilly hole we put a cap on the end of three feet of fuse line and stuck it into one of the sticks of dynamite at the bottom of the box. Ed got out his matches and tried his best to light the fuse, but it didn't seem to want to burn. Finally Ed thought it was lit, although I couldn't see any signs that it had ignited. After a few minutes I suggested we go sit in the car and wait awhile. With that I walked away, but Ed stayed at the bottom of the hole a few minutes longer before he returned to the car. Just as he was closing the passenger's door, an enormous boom shook the world around us. The hind end of the car must have gone two feet in the air.

Ed turned to me with a grin from ear to ear and said, "Your worries are over. She's gone!"

Only after I started the car and headed for home did I realize we had been no more than ten seconds away from blowing ourselves up. We went back to the hole the next day. A chunk four feet deep and six feet across had been blown out of the frozen ground. A little too close for comfort.

Fortunately, not every episode with Ed was life threatening—to humans, at least. One day while Dad was out somewhere, Ed decided

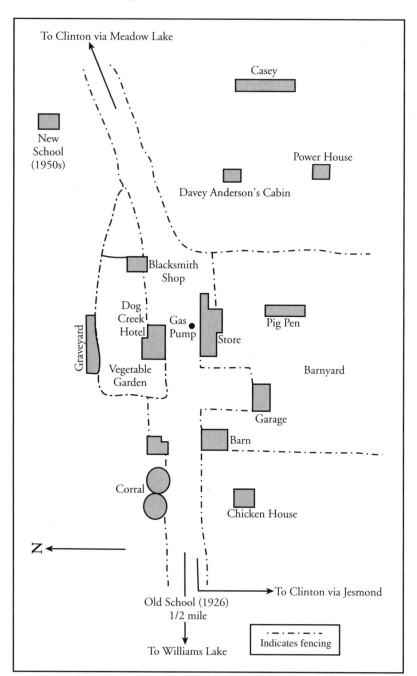

Dog Creek in 1950

that it was time to kill a pig for the upcoming winter months. Down by the pigpen we had a special place all fixed up for doing the job. It consisted of a fire pit under an old oil drum, and a trestle over the drum with a pulley for lowering and retrieving the pig. The idea was to lower the pig into the water boiling in the oil drum, then pull it out, scalded, so that the hair could be easily scraped off.

Ed got the fire going early that morning, and when the water started boiling he stuck the pig. Once it was dead he dragged the 250-pound carcass over to the scalding platform. As he quickly learned, getting the animal into the boiling water was just the beginning of his problems. Now he couldn't get the thing out again. If he didn't do something fast, he was going to have a couple hundred pounds of cooked pork with the hair still on sitting in that barrel. That's when he came running in to me at the store.

"For God's sake, brother, come and help me get this damned pig out of the barrel!"

I rushed down with him to the pigpen and we finally managed to get the corpse out and onto the scraping platform. By this time the hair was thoroughly cooked on and we had a devil of a time trying to get it off. We ended up more or less shaving the darned thing and it took us all afternoon to do a halfway decent job. At least we got a good laugh out of the whole ordeal!

A few years later, in 1949, I was dumb enough to buy the trucking business back from my brother, who had decided to go into the school bus end of things. By owning the trucking outfit I was at least assured control over my freight costs. The deal included an International KB7 truck and equipment, along with the mail contract. I had a Plymouth station wagon that I used as a passenger vehicle, and I hired Ronnie Evans, who was a good driver as well as a really nice man, to drive the truck. We ran scheduled trips from Dog Creek to Williams Lake and back on Tuesdays and Fridays.

On one of those trips Ronnie was bringing the freight and mail from Williams Lake. After reaching the airport he learned that the road to Dog Creek was washed out. Ronnie phoned and I told him to leave the locked sack of letter mail at the Mountain Ranch. I'd get it from there by saddle horse.

Willie Harry was in the store when Ronnie phoned, so I immediately arranged to rent one of his saddle horses for the following morning.

The next day I was rushing around the store, getting the outbound mail ready and selling the odd thing to customers. I paid no attention to the number of boys sitting along the fence and hitching rail in front of the store. Willie had the horse out by the gas pump, waiting until I was finally ready to go. Wheeling out of the store, I threw the outbound-letter bag on behind the saddle and fastened it down. It occurred to me then that the stirrups would be too short since Willie was a lot smaller than I was. Without untying the bridle reins from the saddle horn, I jumped on to test the stirrup length. Big mistake.

Suddenly I found out why everyone was sitting on the fence. All of the boys knew that the horse Willie rented me was one that liked to buck first thing in the morning. They were waiting patiently for the fun to begin and it started right away. The damned thing immediately doubled up and took to the air as soon as my rear end hit the saddle. Fortunately I'd got a pretty good seat when I hit the leather, so I stayed on top while the old horse did everything it could to buck me off. My biggest trouble was the bridle reins, which I couldn't get off the saddle horn in order to pull the darned horse's head up. I did manage to pull its head to one side, and it turned down toward Dad's garage where it came up short in front of the doors.

Seizing the opportunity, I jumped off, set the stirrups, undid the reins, and piled back on. I let out a big holler as I turned the horse around and gave it the whip. The horse responded, taking off like a jackrabbit. Around the corner of the fence we came, and all the Indian men were whooping and cheering as we flew by, hell-bent for election. I pounded the old horse on the ass halfway up the mountain, and it sure took the buck out of him in short order! My audience went home happy with the entertainment, and I was just happy I wasn't bucked off.

There was never a dull day at the store.

CHAPTER 17

WAS IT MURDER?

Friday was always a busy day for Rita. Come to think of it, every day was a busy day for Rita. What with two young boys to look after and all the housework to do, she was also the storekeeper for two days a week when I was away on the Dog Creek Stage run to Williams Lake. Stocking shelves, sweeping floors, stoking the wood stoves, pricing, and looking after customers as well as the post office kept her on the go all the time. She didn't mind most of the work, but she hated having to go outside and attend to the gas pump. It was one of those old ones with the glass bowl at the top that you had to pump by hand. The nozzle always leaked a bit and you ended up smelling of gasoline no matter how carefully you went about it.

Usually Rita would get her housework done in the morning, keeping an eye out for customers so she could get downstairs to greet them. Quite often it wouldn't get busy until late afternoon. This particular Friday in May 1949 was one of those occasions, a nice dreamy afternoon in early summer. The store was a welcome place to be, cool and quiet, while outside the sun was shining, shimmering off the rocks and as hot as blazes. The breeze kicked up little whirlwinds of dust and the air was alive with the sounds of summer. Rita was enjoying a respite from the heat and the work; the boys were out the back of the store playing.

The store door opened and jarred Rita out of her reverie. She was in the office so she got up and went into the store to see Simon Seymour.

Simon (everybody called him Si, with the long "i" sound like when the name is used in full) was a shy young man, just over the age of majority. He was five feet nine inches tall and although he was not very big, he was quite muscular and well built. He was so shy that he always seemed awkward in his movements. He would sidle around trying to be inconspicuous but accomplishing the opposite. Exactly who his parents were I do not know, but one thing was obvious; even though his family was Indian and dark skinned, Si was not all Indian. He was fair skinned with brown hair, a sharp-featured and good-looking young man by anyone's standards.

Si was raised on the Canoe Creek reserve, which was not an easy life for anybody. Ironically, although the dirty thirties were depression times for everybody, they did not affect the Indian population as much as they did the whites. The Indians had traditionally lived off the land, so during the Depression they were able to maintain their living standard at the same level as they had been used to. I suppose that there was less opportunity for work and less money around, but these things were not as essential to the Indian way of life as they were to the white man. The Seymour home was probably better off financially than most of the other homes on the reservation because Louie Seymour, Si's adoptive father, was an excellent cowboy who held down a steady job at Henry Koster's Canoe Creek Ranch.

There were two things in Si's life as a young boy that had great influence on him in later years. One was the fact that he looked like a white man. This was cause for considerable ridicule and derision from his peers, especially whenever he tried to dress up or act a bit more "civilized" than those around him. One of the peculiarities of this situation was that though most young Indian girls of that era would give their eyeteeth to get a white man and have a baby from him, the half-breed child was often ridiculed and scorned when it arrived. This was not a vicious thing, but it was there nevertheless and was more pronounced when the child resembled the white side rather than the Indian side.

The other big influence in Si's life was the fact that he had little education. Somehow he missed out on the usual years at the St. Joseph Mission school that all the rest of the kids had to endure.

As soon as Si was old enough to work he left home and got a job. He must have been twelve years old when he became the derrick boy at the Gang Ranch. This was a job that fell to the youngest and least experienced member of the haying crew. As they say nowadays, the job description was simple—drive the team that pulled the hay up to the top of the stack—but it was not an easy job. I can attest to that, having spent a few summers myself doing exactly what Si did. Most of the kids that tried it would last a few days or a week, but Si stayed with it all summer and that caught the foreman's eye. Old McIntyre liked the kid and gave him a job as choreboy for the winter. Si was never without work again. The choreboy was the butt of derision and jokes, but Si was used to being laughed at so it didn't bother him too much.

Si stayed at the Gang Ranch from then on, gradually working himself up through various jobs until he was a full-fledged cowboy. He improved himself. He learned to look after his personal appearance, took pride in his possessions, bought a good horse and saddle, and taught himself to read and write well enough to get by.

Over the years at the Gang Ranch he worked mostly with white boys and he emulated them more and more as he grew older. He came to think of himself as a white man more than an Indian, and when he came of age he had himself removed form the Indian list and became enfranchised. Si was proud of this status, maybe because of the teasing and derision he had received as a child. At any rate, he found a haven in his standing.

As so often happens when one moves from one strata of society to another, Si found himself not completely accepted in either. When working he was completely at home with, and equal to, his white companions, but when he was out socially with whites he felt ill at ease, inadequate, and uncomfortable. Similarly, when he was with Indians socially he was happy and comfortable, but their lacksadaisical, happy-go-lucky attitude to work bothered him.

Si gained little in a material way by becoming enfranchised and being taken off the Indian list. He got the right to vote. Indians at that time were denied that privilege. He got the right to buy liquor, another privilege the Indians didn't have. These were both of doubtful value to Si, as I am quite sure he knew absolutely nothing about politics. His vote would have been a complete mystery to him. His ability to buy liquor was just a nuisance, for he was not a great drinker himself. It only made him the envy of all the Indian boys who couldn't buy liquor. If he shared his liquor with any of his Indian friends he was a bootlegger in the eyes of the law, and if he didn't share his whisky his Indian friends saw him as the high-toned imitation of a white man.

This was the young man Rita greeted at the store door.

"Hello Si. What brings you over from the Gang Ranch on a hot day like this?" she asked.

Si went into his awkward act, leaning up against the store door and looking up and down the road and shuffling his feet. "I came over for my parcel," he said.

Rita remembered there was a parcel for Si from the liquor store and went into the warehouse to get it for him. Si paid the freight charges and laboriously signed the waybill. While he was signing, the store door opened and Susan Seymour came in. She seemed surprised to see Si.

Susan was married to Si's brother, Gilbert. Gilbert was a half brother to Si. He was all Indian, and just as Si was ambitious, Gilbert was not. In fact he was a bit on the lazy side. Gilbert was anything but handsome. He was smaller than Si, and skinny. His face was heavily pockmarked and pimply, and most of the time he looked like he hadn't had a bath for a month. He seldom worked and consequently he had poor clothes and poor rigging, and alongside Si he looked poverty stricken and uninviting. His marriage to Susan was an arranged one, a custom that was practised by the old Indians.

Susan was the chief's daughter, one of the two daughters of Edward and Lucy Billy. The Billys were good people. Edward, who went by the name of Stobie, was a quiet man who smiled a lot and said little. He held his wife in high regard and his daughters were the pride of his life. He was not a dynamic man, his performance as chief was not spectacular, but he was a good man, honest and straight in his dealings and truthful in all he said.

Lucy was the real boss in the family. She never learned to speak one word of English, but she never stopped talking in Shuswap. Her hands were badly crippled with arthritis and yet she made some of the best buckskin gloves and fine beadwork. It was always quite funny when she would come to the store to sell me some of her gloves.

Lucy would sit on the floor close to the store door while the chief took the parcel of gloves and brought it over for me to see. I would look them over and name a price—"I'll give you three dollars a pair."

Stobie would turn around to Lucy and tell her in Shuswap what I had said. This would set her off. She would harangue poor old Stobie for ten minutes with a cascade of Shuswap, her voice rising and falling and alternately fixing me with a baleful stare and going on and on. Old Stobie would stand there with his feet together like a schoolboy getting a lecture, with not a flicker of expression on his face. I would be thinking maybe I didn't offer enough and I was too cheap and that I was getting a good going over from old Lucy in the language I didn't understand. All we could do was wait.

Finally she was finished. Stobie's face would light up like a Christmas tree and he would say, "She says that's good!"

Susan had been to the mission school and had graduated with a Grade 8 education. She had been married to Gilbert for three years—ever since she left school. She was a particularly good horsewoman and rode not only with authority and courage, but also with style. She was a pretty girl, quick in her movements but quiet and respectful. She dressed in the more modern manner, in slacks rather than the long Mother Hubbard dresses most Indian girls wore at that time, and was always spotless. She was a sensible girl.

Susan bought a few articles from Rita that she wrapped in a gunnysack ready to tie on her horse. She said a few words to Si in Shuswap and they left the store together.

The next morning the Canoe Creek reserve was stirring at dawn. The chickens were cackling and the people were moving around, getting ready to go to work. Old Victor Lewis was preparing to go out after some saddle horses, and his wife Maudie was making him a lunch. Victor and Maudie were reliable people and quite sophisticated. In his youth, Victor had been a saddle bronc roughrider in a Wild West show that travelled all over the United States. He had even travelled to Australia on one occasion. Maudie had not travelled like her husband but was a smart and reliable person who knew which way was up.

She was taking Victor's lunch over to the barn for him when she noticed three horses coming down the road from Dog Creek. She stopped to see who it was and immediately recognized Gilbert and Si Seymour. Gilbert was leading the horse in between them, and although there was a saddle on it there was no one riding it. It looked like the boys had shot a deer and had it draped over the saddle. As they got closer, Maudie could see that something was wrong. That was no deer draped over the horse but a human body. She could see that Gilbert and Si were covered with mud and their appearance led Maudie to believe that they had been drinking. She wondered who it was that was drunk and laid out over the horse. She was about to call out to them and ask, but when they got close enough for her to see their faces she held her tongue.

"Maudie, help us," Gilbert said. "This is Susan. She was dragged by her horse and killed."

Maudie called out to Victor to come and ran over to the horse to look after Susan. They got her off the horse and over to the nearest cabin. Susan was in terrible condition. She was covered in mud from head to toe. Her face was scratched and her hair was matted with mud and blood. Maudie checked right away to see if there was a heartbeat and found none. Susan was dead all right and had been dead for some little time.

Victor went right over to Henry Koster's house at the ranch and phoned the police in Clinton to tell them of the accident. They cautioned Victor not to disturb the body and assured him that they would be out as soon as possible.

It took the police nearly three hours to get out to Canoe Creek; in the meantime, Stobie and Lucy had been notified of their daughter's death and had arrived at Canoe Creek from their home on Dog Creek Mountain.

The constable greeted Stobie with this remark: "I see you bunch have been boozing it up again. Who got killed this time?"

Stobie answered, "It was my daughter. She got dragged by her horse. She is in Maudie's house."

The policeman was a bit sorry that he had spoken so gruffly, but he pretended he didn't care and said, "Okay. Doc the stiff is in there."

The doctor from Clinton had accompanied the policeman so that he could issue a death certificate. By doing it this way they would not have to take the body back to Clinton for examination, then bring it all the way back to Canoe Creek for burial.

The doctor went into the cabin and took a fast look at the body. The girl had obviously been dragged by her horse. He could see where the one foot had been caught up in the stirrup from the marks on her boot. She must have turned over during the course of the dragging because she was scraped on both her back and front. He felt there was no use prolonging the examination. Death was caused by multiple contusions and concussion as a result of being dragged by a runaway horse. He completed the report and gave it to the police officer.

The officer gave a death certificate to Stobie and told him to tell his people to smarten up and lay off the booze or soon they would all be dead. The officer could hear Lucy wailing over the body of her dead daughter and he looked at Stobie, standing there with his feet together and his expressionless face, and he wondered how many more times he would have to go through this awful charade on one of these damned Indian reserves.

"Come on Doc, let's get to hell out of here. These places are starting to give me the creeps." They got in the car and drove back to Clinton.

Stobie turned away from the dust left by the police car and went over and sat down on a rock beside Maudie Lewis's cabin. Lucy Billy was wailing and her other daughter, Mary Jane, was crying. Gilbert and Si were sleeping it off in their uncle's cabin. Stobie couldn't cry like the women. All he could do was sit there and kick the dust and wish that this day had never come. His heart was broken.

Maudie got Lucy and Mary Jane out of the cabin and organized the other women into a crew to get Susan ready for burial. These women had worked on dead bodies before. It was an awful job but they handled it. Susan was covered with mud and they had to strip her clothes off and wash the blood and the mud off her body. Her hair was matted and it was a terrible job getting it clean. While washing her hair they noticed a small hole above the hairline by her temple. They examined it and knew immediately what it was. They had all seen bullet holes in animals all their lives, so they knew at once that Susan had been shot. She had not died as the result of being dragged by a horse at all.

Maudie called Stobie and showed him what the women had found. Everybody was talking at once. Some said it was murder. Some said accident. Some said suicide. They all agreed that they should get Gilbert and Si and confront them with their findings and see what they had to say about it. They were awakened and brought over to the cabin. They both denied that there had been a shooting and they stuck to their story. Susan had been dragged by her horse as far as they were concerned and that was it.

Stobie, as the chief, had to make a decision. He wanted to believe that his daughter had died accidentally rather than by murder or suicide, and he wanted to believe what Gilbert and Si had said. He decided to have Susan buried and accept the story that she had died accidentally by being dragged by her horse. Lucy didn't want to do it that way, but she was too upset and exhausted to stop it. The funeral was held two days later.

It did not stop the talk. Everybody was worried about the bullet hole. Everybody was treating Gilbert and Si strangely. Talk and innuendo continued throughout the next few weeks, a few whispers here and a few remarks there.

One day Si got up early and rode off into the mountains. Gilbert said that Si was an outlaw and maybe he would be dangerous.

For the next week or so Si did not show up anywhere. The Indians were getting nervous and scared so they asked Stobie to call the police. Stobie came over to Dog Creek to see about it. He arrived at our store first thing when we opened in the morning. He stood around there all day until closing time. Finally when we were alone he asked me to call the police and tell them what had happened.

It was the first I had heard of the bullet hole in Susan's head and I was shocked at the slipshod job the coroner had done when he examined the body. I phoned the police in Williams Lake and told them the story that Stobie had told me. They said that someone would be out to see about it.

The next day was a stage day, so Rita was left alone in the store while I went into Williams Lake for the mail and supplies. In the early afternoon a police car arrived at the store and an officer, an RCMP detective-inspector, got out and came into the store. There were quite a few Indian customers in the store at the time. The officer went over to Rita and in a loud and insulting manner asked her a bunch of questions about the liquor she gave to Si Seymour. Rita showed him the waybill Si had signed but he ignored it and said, "If you and your husband would stop giving liquor to the Indians we wouldn't have all this trouble." Then he stomped out of the store.

This remark really hurt Rita. We had never supplied liquor to Indians in our lives. For one thing it was illegal and for another we did not believe that it was good business. When I got home from town that evening, Rita told me all that had happened. She was so upset by it that she started to cry. I saw red. I found out that the policeman was up at the Circle "S" Ranch, so I phoned there and got the man on the phone. I told him that what he had said to my wife was a damned lie and that if he did not come down to the store and apologize to her immediately I would take action and see that he was properly dealt with in a court of law.

That was not what he had expected. He came down immediately and said that he wanted to discuss it privately outside in his car, but I insisted that we talk, as he had done earlier, in front of all the Indian boys in the store. I repeated all the things he had said to Rita earlier and I made him retract his statements about supplying liquor to Indians and made him apologize to Rita for the way he had treated her earlier. It was quite a scene.

I said that I believed he was trying to shut us up and to protect the doctor and the policeman who had botched up their job of examining the body and issuing a death certificate. I also said that if there was any further trouble as a result of this lack of professionalism I would hold him personally responsible for it.

He said the whole story of a bullet hole in the head was a lot of rot and that I would serve my community better if I learned to uphold the officials who knew what they were doing and took no notice of the Indians and their lies and wild stories.

I reached into my cash register and took out all the money in there, about a thousand dollars, and said, "I will bet you every cent that is here that if you dig that poor girl up you will find a bullet hole in her head." He shook his head, turned, walked out the door, and drove away.

Si stayed out in the hills. It must have been a month or more. All the Indians were upset and worried about him. They were afraid that he was acting so crazy he might hurt someone else. Several of the older Indians asked me what could be done about him, but there wasn't anything we could do. It was no use to call the police. Their attitude was that there was no crime committed and that we were a bunch of fools for thinking there was.

The Indians said that there would be more violence and more bloodshed if Si was left on the loose.

On a Sunday morning, three or four weeks after our confrontation with the police officer, there was a knock on the kitchen door of our apartment over the store. I got up, fully expecting to see one of the local cowboys wanting gas or something and quite prepared to chastize him for getting me up on Sunday morning. I was shocked to see it was Si.

He was shaking with emotion and he looked pitiful. His clothes were dirty and he was dishevelled. His hair had grown long and he needed a shave. All he had with him was a 30-30 rifle and his knuckles were white where he held it by the barrel.

"Hello Si," I said. "Come on in. I'm just going to make a cup of coffee." He sidled in and stood by the door.

"I want you to call the police and tell them I want to give myself up. I killed her you know, and I want to do what is right."

It was all he could do to talk, he was so nervous. I told him I would call them right away. He seemed to relax then, and I gave him some coffee and sat at the table with him for a few minutes. After two or three tries I got through to the police. I couldn't restrain myself and gave them a dig.

"I have Si Seymour here with me and he wants to give himself up for the murder of Susan Seymour, which you fellows say didn't happen."

The officer said he would be right out.

At that time, with roads as they were, it was a two-and-a-half-hour drive out from Williams Lake. I sat there with Si for the longest two-and-a-half hours I have ever put in. Si was in terrible shape. He seemed to hang on to me as if I were his last resort. I stayed right with him. If I had left him I'm sure he would have taken off again. I told him he did not have to go through with giving himself up. "The police don't even want you," I told him. "You can walk away from here and be a free man. As far as the police are concerned there was no murder and you are not even under suspicion." But when he asked me if I thought he was doing the right thing, he seemed to take comfort when I told him I thought he was.

"It was all my fault," he said and sat there and waited.

Finally we heard a car coming up the road. Si stiffened and grew pale, but he got up and came downstairs to meet the policeman. It was a different policeman, not the jerk who was out before.

He said that he wanted to take a statement from Si, so we went into the office in the store where Si made his statement and I witnessed it. The statement consisted of five lines containing Si's name and a declaration that he had shot Susan. When it was complete and they were ready to go, Si came over and shook my hand and thanked me for my help. I could feel him shaking when we touched. He got in the police car and they drove away.

I felt drained of all my strength and sad too. I kept thinking of Si all day and wondering what would happen to him. I found myself admiring the way he had handled himself. It had taken a lot of resolve and strength for Si to do what he had done that day. I hoped the law would take that into consideration when it dealt with him. He was a courageous young man and he was willing to pay the price for his "crime."

Early the next morning the phone rang. It was the police office in Williams Lake. The officer asked me if I would inform Chief Stobie Billy that Si Seymour had hanged himself in his jail cell during the night. It seems that he had to use his belt and had accomplished the deed by holding his feet up from the floor.

I have thought about Si many times during the years. Somehow I can't see him as a murderer. All I can see is a frightened young man who adopted a code and lived by it and died by it.

Susan lies in the graveyard at Canoe Creek. The police say that she was dragged by her horse and killed; the Indians say that she was shot and the bullet hole in her head is evidence of murder or suicide.

I believe the Indians.

CHAPTER 18

BARNEY

Barney arrived at the Gang Ranch about 1935. He was living in a dugout cabin up on Churn Creek, the river that was the southern boundary of the ranch. He presented a picture that was hard to believe, and for those who were not so stout-hearted he engendered a feeling of pure terror. I will try to describe him as he was when I first met him and for the duration of our friendship. He was a little over six feet two inches tall. A great brute of a man, barrel-chested and strong as an ox, he had a shock of grey hair that he cut once a year whether it needed it or not, and at times it hung to his shoulders. He never wore a hat, summer or winter. His complexion was ruddy, his features sharp and craggy. He had lost one eye in World War I and never wore a glass eye. He swore up and down that his eye fell out one day when he was lying on his belly having a drink of spring water, and it looked so good lying at the bottom of the spring looking back at him that he just left it there. According to Barney, he got exclusive rights to the spring after that as no Indian, thirsty or otherwise, would go near it. His eye wasn't the only thing missing, for he had parted with all his front teeth except the two eyeteeth that hung down in a passable imitation of Dracula. All in all he wasn't the handsomest thing on God's green earth.

Then there was his way of dressing. He liked a wool lumberjack shirt and heavy wool pants held up with the "police suspenders" that all the old-timers wore. He had worked in the bush for some time during his chequered career and had adopted the custom of cutting his trousers off just below the knee as the old woodsmen did. The loggers did it so the pant legs wouldn't get in the way and trip them when they were jumping around 60 feet up a tree, but Barney did it because he liked it that way. His footwear was twelve-inch-top loggers boots laced only to the ankle, with the laces wound around and tied there. The tops flopped around loose.

Barney

Churn Creek marked the southern boundary of the Gang Ranch. It ran through rugged, isolated country. My friends and I used to slide our horses down the gravel side of Table Mountain to Churn Creek—an exercise not suited for the faint-hearted.

I first met Barney before the war, in '37 or '38, when he was living on Churn Creek, but I didn't get to know him until we bought the store in 1945. Barney had a falling out with the storekeeper at the Gang Ranch about then, so he decided to come over to Dog Creek and give us a try. One day he came up the road from the Gang just as I have described him, leading two horses. He tied them up to the hitching rail alongside the store and came inside. Rita took one look at him and headed for the warehouse.

He had his want list with him and we were able to supply him with everything he wanted, at a better price than he had been getting at the Gang. He was quite pleased with that and soon he was a regular customer. He got a pension cheque from the government every month for the munificent sum of $40, and it just about kept him going. He worked on one of the local ranches during the summer, usually irrigating, and augmented this government largesse with a few extra bucks. We grew to like Barney and even Rita got used to this wild-looking individual and felt comfortable around him.

One summer he worked at the Empire Valley Ranch, which was owned at the time by Henry Koster Jr. Henry had two college girls working there for the summer. They came from down Revelstoke way. Barney took a shine to these girls and that fall, when the summer hands were let go, the girls headed back to Revelstoke with Barney in tow. Barney had a little stake of money saved up, and the girls had their eyes on that. I don't know what Barney had his eye on, but whatever it was, I doubt that he got any.

Just before Christmas the stage pulled into Dog Creek and who should get off but Barney. It was 30 below zero and he didn't have a coat or a shirt or even a pair of shoes, just his socks, some heavy wool Stanfields underwear, and some heavy, dark-coloured wool pants held up with police bracers. We did our usual mail-day routine, and when the last customer had been served, there was old Barney standing by the stove in his socks and Stanfields and jacked-off pants, giving me a baleful stare with his one big watery blue eye.

"I'm in a hell of a fix," he said. "I haven't got a damned cent. I wonder if you can help me out."

We were quite happy to outfit the guy with all the necessaries for his clothing, and then he asked if he could bunk out in the basement of the store until spring. It wasn't much of a basement. It had a dirt floor, the ceiling was only six feet high, and it was where I stored the wood for the homemade furnace I had down there. But it was 30 below outside, so what could we do? We found an old camp cot and fixed it up as best we could in the basement. He got a few supplies such as cheese and onions, and we found him some dishes, so he was set for the winter. He wanted to pay us for the accommodation but we refused to take anything. All I said was it would be a great help to Rita if he could stoke the stoves in the building the days I was away. "Just make sure that Rita stays warm," I said.

It was the warmest winter Rita ever had. As soon as the stove cooled off slightly, Barney threw open the door, smoke billowed out, and he stepped back and sized up the situation to see if it would hold another block of wood, in which case he went out and brought in another log. The pieces were four feet long and quite heavy. He would jam the new piece in, sit back, and enjoy the heat. At the end of the winter we had burned up a two-year supply of wood, but Rita was never cold the whole time.

We got to know old Barney pretty well that winter and found him to be a most remarkable man. He came from a well-to-do family in New Zealand. As a boy he was raised in a palatial home. He told

Victor Spencer's daughter Barbara once, when Barbara was putting on the rich girl airs, "I don't know what kind of a home you come from, but my mother had 30 people—maids, butlers, cooks, and the like—on her staff." He had received a good education from a private tutor who had had an extensive knowledge of the classics, and Barney was fluent in French and could get by in German. All this was coupled with a healthy disdain for any snobbery. One of his most memorable distinguishing traits was his laugh. He would throw back his head and out would come a booming cackle from between his two eyeteeth while the tears flowed from his one good eye.

As well, he was almost a mathematical genius. I remember one time wanting to know the cube root of a number for some reason or other. I was damned if I could remember how to do it, so when the local schoolteacher came into the store I asked him. He was no better than I was so we were stuck. About then old Barney came along and I asked him, "How do you get the cube root of 19,683?"

Barney rolled back his one good eye and said, "It is 27." He had done it in his head.

We had got so modern in the store that we had an adding machine that we used for adding up the sales slips, but Rita found it was easier to call out the numbers to Barney. As soon as she reached the bottom of the column of figures, Barney would sing out the total. Never a mistake. By stoking the stoves and being the store adding machine he enjoyed his stay in the basement and we enjoyed his company.

Barney loved to eat those big Spanish onions and Ontario cheddar cheese. The cheese used to come in great 30-pound rounds, like a barrel, all wrapped in cheesecloth and dipped in candle wax. When we were busy we often made a lunch out of cheddar cheese and raisins, which is quite delightful and nourishing when chewed together. Barney would munch on those big onions and our son Adrian would join in when he came home from school. The customers used to stare in astonishment at Adrian eating the onion like an apple, but he enjoyed it and Barney would chortle away.

When he was a young man, just before he reached the age of majority, Barney fell in love with a girl. His parents did not approve of the match. Barney wanted to marry her, but the strict regulations of the country prevented this without his parents' consent. They refused, so Barney jumped on the first boat to Australia and lost himself in the crowd. He was soon 21 and able to do as he wanted. He rousted about on the waterfront for awhile and as a result of his activities around the local ladies managed to get himself into quite a few fistfights. He generally won these battles hands down, but occasionally he met an adversary who held his own. On one occasion Barney was knocked flat on his rear end without ever landing a blow. His opponent proceeded to help him up and offered to buy him a beer to assuage the damage done. Barney knew that he was outclassed, but he didn't know that his adversary was Peter Jackson, the champion boxer of the country, until they had toasted one another.

From this association Barney got to know the boxing fraternity. He later joined Joe Choynski's boxing stable and became one of Choynski's sparring partners. Choynski was contracted to fight James J. Corbett on a barge in San Francisco harbour. It turned out to be one of the greatest fights of all time, and although Choynski didn't win, he was always respected afterwards as one of the greats of the sport. Barney fought a few fights himself along the way.

When World War I broke out, Barney didn't want to be in the American army so he travelled to Canada and joined up here. He was soon overseas and in the thick of the fighting. He lost his eye to a German sniper shortly before the war ended. The loss of the eye was a big blow, but the thing that did him the most damage was the morphine that he got for the pain. He was soon a drug addict.

After the war he tried working in the bush. He couldn't get a job because of his eye, so he ended up in Prince Rupert with no job and not much money. He was drunk half the time and scratching around looking for morphine the rest of the time. He had some money due him in the form of government help for veterans, so he bought a house, which he rented out. It was in a poor part of town, and the next thing he knew he was the proud owner of a house full of prostitutes. He made so much money he bought another one and so was the proud owner of two. One day he sobered up enough to realize what he was doing. Without any further ado he gave the two houses to the girls who were working in the places and decided he was going to kick the drinking and the dope. He looked around for a place remote enough that he could live there without backsliding into trouble again. This

The Big Bar ferry across the Fraser River. There was a ferry just like it at Churn Creek until 1912. The operator was Bill Wright, and American Civil War veteran with only one leg. He used to shout at people waiting for the ferry on the other side of the river, "Go around!"

place turned out to be five miles up Churn Creek in a dugout cabin.

For those unfamiliar with this form of architecture, dugout cabins were common habitations during the 1930s when the Fraser River was being mined for gold and a man equipped with a shovel and a half horse-power motor and pump could make about five dollars a day. The miners would stay in tents in the summertime, but if they stayed over the winter they required better, warmer housing. That is where the dugout cabin came in. The miner would find a suitable clay bank— and there are many along the Fraser—then he would dig into the bank six feet or so and excavate seven feet high and ten feet wide. He would scavenge enough lumber that had floated down the river to put a front with a door and windows on this edifice. The windows were glass if it could be found or the skins of animals if it could not. The most interesting part of the whole thing was the fireplace. The shape of a fireplace was excavated out of the rear clay wall, and a hole was dug out the top of the clay hill to act as a chimney. It was odd to see the smoke from the fireplace coming out the top of the hill.

The clay that was excavated out of the hill to make the rear of the cabin was piled up around the wooden walls of the front part for added insulation and security.

These little homes were remarkably comfortable, warm in the winter, cool in the summer, and fuel efficient, and there were many of them on the riverfront during the hungry thirties, with some fine and interesting residents. I know of one individual who stayed in a dugout cabin for several winters and then went on to become vice president of a major forestry company and, in later life, a great retriever-dog enthusiast. He sold a dog for $40,000 at one time and created quite a fuss by doing so. It was certainly a long way from his dugout cabin days on the banks of the Fraser.

Anyway, it was in one of these cabins on Churn Creek that Barney went through the terrors of drug and alcohol addiction withdrawal by himself. God knows how he did it, but he did. He shook so badly from then on that he could hardly hold a cup of coffee without it jumping out of the cup. He lived in that little cabin for over ten years and never left until he followed the girls to Revelstoke. He used to come out once a month and get his cheque and spend it on supplies. We would see him coming up the road leading his two fat pack horses. He always had them with him, but he never put a pound on their backs. He would load all his supplies onto a packboard and swing it onto his own back, and the horses would trot along behind with nothing on their backs.

Barney stayed in our store basement all that winter. In the spring he moved into the old cabin known as Casey and got a job at the Circle "S," irrigating. (Victor Spencer had sold his Diamond "S" Ranch to his daughter Barbara, and she changed the brand and the name to Circle "S.") One night after the stage had been in he joined us in our apartment over the store. He had bought a bottle of the best Scotch whisky and wanted to have a social drink with us. We settled down at the dining room table and started pouring a few fairly stiff drinks while we were shooting the breeze. This went on until about midnight, when Barney decided to go back to Casey. The booze hit him as he stood up and he almost fell down the stairs. Rita and I had all we could do to get him down the stairs without a major calamity. When we were finally at the bottom, we decided to load him in the car and drive him home instead of letting him try to walk. (It is only 100 yards from the store to Casey by the trail and 150 yards by the road.)

What we forgot was that the road had washed out a few weeks before. The next thing I knew we were stuck on some rocks halfway to our destination. There was nothing for it but to leave the car sitting there and walk Old Barney the rest of the way (50 yards) home. He stepped out of the car and immediately fell down. Rita got on one side of him and me on the other. We pulled and tugged and struggled as best we could, but we couldn't move him. He was lying there, laughing his head off so hard he couldn't tell us that his foot was caught between two rocks. We eventually got him loose, and by this time all three of us were laughing our fool heads off.

With Rita on one side and me on the other, all three of us well under the influence, we finally got him home, and along with a few more laughs we headed home ourselves. We totally forgot about the car and headed off across the trail and went to bed and were soon oblivious to the world. We didn't even notice the car missing the next morning until my Dad came into the store and asked me what my car was doing up there in the washout. He got quite a laugh out of it when I told him what had been going on, and then he helped me get the car out of the washout. It wasn't easy. We had left the lights on and the battery was dead as a nit.

When Barney came into the store a few weeks later, I noticed a change in him that I didn't like to see. He was even more dishevelled than he normally was and he didn't act quite normal. A few weeks later he came again. I think it was a Sunday. The store was full of people visiting and shopping, and he called me over and asked if we could go into the office. When we got in there he looked at me and said, "I want you to take me in to see the M.O." (Medical Officer. Barney liked to use these old army designations.)

"Sure Barney," I replied. "When do you want to go?"

"Right now!" he said. "It's my mind that has gone."

My Dad had walked into the store and I signalled him to come into the office. He took one look at Barney and saw right away what the problem was. Barney repeated his wish to go at once and my Dad said that he would take him to Williams Lake right away. He went and got the car. While Dad was doing that, Barney solemnly shook hands with Rita and the boys and me. He got in the car and drove away. We never saw him again.

He died a year or so later. The government notified us. It seems he had listed us as his only known kin.

CHAPTER 19

ALEC KALELSE

Back when Mr. Armes was running the Dog Creek Ranch, he had a crew of local men working for him. Alfie Johnson, Noel Johnson, Moffat Jack, Nelson Chelsea, and Alfie Edwards were the names of some of them that come to mind. They were all Indian boys in their early twenties who loved to laugh and talk and joke with you and just have fun. There was another man on the crew who was older than the rest. His name was Alec Kalelse and he laughed the loudest and told the funniest stories out of all of them. Alec always had fun with me. I was very blond as a kid, the original platinum blonde. He used to get a kick out of mussing up my hair and calling me Shama, which is Shuswap for white man.

During the summer Alec stayed with his wife and family in a camp of tents set up by the ditch behind the blacksmith shop where he worked at several different tasks. Besides blacksmithing, he also made rawhide ropes, fixed saddles, and taught some of the younger men how to do things with the horses and cattle.

Alec's wife didn't speak any English, yet you felt she understood everything because she was always smiling and taking part in the goings-on. Their daughter Selena was also a very happy girl, despite the fact she was badly crippled by a congenital birth defect in her pelvis. Walking was difficult for her but she managed to waddle along as best she could, usually with a wide grin on her face. Robbie, their only son, was already an adult by this time and was much more quiet and reserved than the rest of his family, although equally pleasant.

When fall came, Alec and his family packed their things and returned to their own place between the Gang Ranch and Big Creek for the winter months. We missed Alec when he left, especially the good times and hospitality we enjoyed at his camp.

Alec Kalelse in a democrat, driving in front of the Dog Creek Hotel.

Over the next twenty years I saw little of Alec, although I did hear news of his family every now and then. I learned that poor Robbie had been killed by a wild horse. Some time later I also heard that Selena was living with a white man and had three children by him, that the flu had hit the family hard, and so on.

It was only after I was running Ranchers Retail that I started to see Alec more often. He'd come all the way over to shop at our store, and I found out later he did this because the Gang Ranch charged him high prices for his supplies and generally made life miserable for him. According to Alec, they were trying to get a hold of his little ranch, the only piece of privately owned property in the middle of their vast holdings. As a matter of fact, they finally did get it in the mid-1950s, so perhaps he was right. Anyhow, Alec became a regular once-a-month customer and visitor to our store.

Alec liked to come to Dog Creek, stay a few days, and visit as well as do his shopping. Being an enfranchised Indian he had the right to buy liquor, and he loved to get a bottle of whisky from Williams Lake on the stage and enjoy a few drinks with his friends.

On one occasion Rita and I were having drinks with Alec and his wife after we closed the store for the night. We were sitting by the old barrel heater in the store, and during the conversation I asked Alec if he knew anything about Rita's grandmother, Mrs. Augustine Boitanio. All we knew was that she had been raised on the Alkali Lake reserve, but we didn't know by whom or, for that matter, if she was really an Alkali Lake native. There was one story that she was actually from up around Prince George. According to this tale, the Indians in that area occasionally got into wars with one of the more northern tribes. If the battle was going against them, they'd load the women and children into canoes or rafts and set them afloat on the Fraser River in order to protect them from capture by the enemy. With luck they'd survive the rapids and live to be reclaimed by their relatives at some future date. Mrs. Augustine and her brother were supposed to be survivors of such an adventure who had ended up at Alkali Lake to be raised.

Mrs. Augustine Boitanio, who was born near Prince George but grew up at Alkali Lake.

During the course of telling all this long and complicated story to Alec, with him translating it to his wife, we had been pulling hard on a bottle of good rye whisky that Alec had supplied.

"Do you know anything about the truth of the story, Alec?" Lots of talk about that and a few more drinks....

"Was the family that raised her the Spahans or the Chelseas?" More discussion and more drinks....

"Did Mrs. Augustine and her brother look like the Alkalis?" Several more profound statements and yet another full glass to empty....

All the while Alec was becoming more and more convinced that somewhere in this tangle of relationships we were getting closer to him and his family. Finally, well after midnight, this whole business had to be summed up so we could get to bed. In one last burst of enlightenment, Alec threw his arms around me and exclaimed, "Oh hell! You might just as well say we are brothers!"

The old Indians had a custom of claiming you as a relative if they thought highly of you, and the more highly you were thought of, the closer was the relationship claimed. From that time on, Alec and his wife referred to Rita and me as their daughter and son. Outsiders who didn't understand the connotation were often taken aback when Alec called me "son." I remember one time when an American drove up to the gas pump. It was a hot day in midsummer and Alec and his wife were sitting in the shade at the front of the store. I was busy with a customer inside and noticed that Alec had jumped up and was chatting with the American. This was exactly what Alec had been waiting for...a new set of ears. It wasn't long before Alec was giving the fellow the shot—Alec's life history, all you ever wanted to know about horse-breaking or how to swim herds of cattle across a river, where to shoot moose, and so on and on. The American stood there fascinated, and I could tell Alec was enjoying himself to the fullest.

Among many other things, I heard Alec tell the man that his son owned the store and would fix him up with gas as soon as he was done with his other customer. I'll never forget the look on that man's face when I walked out to serve him. He took one look at my blond hair and fair complexion and then at Alec's, which was black as your hat, but he didn't say a word. Neither did I. I imagine he still has questions running around in his head!

Because Alec was such a talker and joker, most people took him lightly. The ranch hands at the Circle "S" laughed and called him "Anyhow" because it was one of his favourite words. Others referred to him as "The big wind from across the river." Actually, he was a man of considerable intellect and eloquence. We only heard him in his second language and consequently we judged him on his understanding of our tongue. That is a mistake we so often make with people who are not too fluent in our own language.

I realized this fact one day when we attended the funeral for a young orphan boy on the Dog Creek reserve. My wife's mother was with us and she translated what was said. It allowed us a glimpse into the mind and heart of a man that we were unable to get from our unilingual understanding.

The day of the funeral was beautiful, one of those spring days where the clouds drift across large spaces of bright blue sky. One minute it is dull, then bright as the brilliant sun shines through. There was still a bit of bite in the air, but with a promise of warm days to come. We walked down to the graveyard and joined the little knot of people there.

A freshly dug grave lay open; two shovels had been placed across the grave to receive the coffin, which six of the boys were carrying from the house where the wake was held. They were dressed in blue jeans and jackets, the workclothes they usually wore. The coffin was home-built out of green lumber, with a piece of rope for the handles. A light wind ruffled the black, unruly hair of the men as they carried the coffin over and placed it on the shovels. It was silent as they stood back and waited.

Alec stepped up on a mound of earth by the graves and began to speak in Shuswap. The wind tousled his grey hair, and the ever-present laughter was gone from his eyes.

"My friends, we are here today to bury Freddie. This poor boy was an orphan; he had no father and no mother. They died from tuberculosis right after he was born. Freddie never had a family except for all of us. He wasn't lucky like the rest of us. The boy had the same terrible disease that killed his mother and father. He was sick all his short life, his body covered with sores. And yet he was cheerful and laughed and made fun and everybody liked him. We should remember that..." Alec paused briefly before continuing, "He was no better and no worse than the rest of us. But he was one of us. He was our brother and we loved him."

Alec leaned down and picked up a handful of earth, throwing it on the coffin as the boys lowered it into the grave. The Indian women started to sing one of their hymns in that high nasal manner that is so distinctive. Grabbing the shovels, the two lead pallbearers started to fill the grave as rapidly as they could. As soon as they were winded, the next pair took over, and so on until the grave was filled and heaped up.

With his head bowed, Alec stood silently until the final shovelful was in place. Then he put on his old cowboy hat and slowly walked away.

CHAPTER 20

CHANGING TIMES

By the 1950s, things were changing around Dog Creek and people were moving on. Ed Hillman, who'd been with my family since the thirties, moved to Mission where his son Eric lived with his family. Our old friend returned only twice to see us at Dog Creek. His first trip back was a short visit around the time logging began at Dog Creek. I took him with me while I made a delivery to the crew working at the Gang Ranch bridge. He was only a shell of the robust old Ed, but as we rode along he revealed that fine classic mind and quick turn of phrase I knew so well. Strangely, however, it was the first time I realized how strong his Swedish accent was. I guess having been raised with it, I had never noticed it before.

Ed took great delight in seeing the hills where he'd spent most of his life. Returning to Dog Creek brought back many memories of his younger days, and he shared a couple of anecdotes about the old days with me during our ride together. Seeing the Gang Ranch again reminded Ed of a local man named Wycotte, who was known at the Gang as an incorrigible thief.

The manager there back at that time had been Mr. Stobart, known to everyone as Stobie. Apparently Stobie had invested in a new harness for the ranch. He knew that the wily old Wycotte already had his eye on that harness, but there was no way Stobie was going to let that crook get his hands on it, no matter what. One Saturday night Wycotte turned up at the Gang, expressing a desire to join the weekly poker game in progress in the bunkhouse. He unhitched his team and hung his harness on the first peg in the barn. The new harness was hung up on the second peg. While the men continued their game, Stobie slipped out to the barn and quietly switched the two harnesses. Sure enough, when the game ended around midnight, Wycotte went out to the barn and, in the darkness, stole his own harness off the second peg.

Dog Creek in the 1950s. You can see the house, store, and corrals just to right of centre at the bottom of the photo. It was still a small, isolated place, but everything else seemed to be changing.

Stobie never tired of telling anyone of his classic win over old Wycotte, and Ed chuckled as he passed the tale on to me.

Another story Ed delighted in telling was about a certain lady of somewhat easy virtue who was consorting with a gentleman in the ram pasture up the stairs from the old bar room in the Dog Creek Hotel. (The ram pasture was a large room where all the unmarried working men slept.) It seems that Stobie was enjoying a few drinks with my Grandfather Place at a table in the bar room when all of a sudden there was the damnedest racket and the lady of ill repute landed at the foot of the stairs alongside the table. The fall left the woman in the unfortunate position of being upside down on the floor without any underwear. Stobie took a good look at the situation, then turned to my Grandfather and said, "Now where have I seen that face before?"

It was the type of story that Ed enjoyed telling the most, and he laughed as loudly as his audience when he finished.

Ed's last journey to Dog Creek was for my Dad's funeral. Dad passed away February 29, 1956. The weather was extremely cold at that time, and there had been a big snowfall, with the snowdrifts across Springhouse prairie measuring seven and eight feet deep. Sam McRae and Davey Anderson helped me dig the grave at the family plot in the old graveyard at Dog Creek. This was no easy task. The hole was full of great big rocks and we had to blast them to get them broken up and dug out. Sam was the powder man and I remember him warming the dynamite up in the campfire so that it would fire off properly. I guess Sam knew what he was doing because we didn't get blown to kingdom come.

After a memorial service for Dad in Williams Lake, Sam Sault John brought his team and sleigh to the front door of the house in

Ada Halstead-Netherwood Place, "Mumsie."

Dog Creek. We put the coffin on it and Mother sat up beside Sam on the sleigh for the journey to the graveyard behind the old ranch house. Dr. Stan Wood, a veterinarian and good friend of Dad's, read the service. Alice Belleau led the Indian women in singing old Indian hymns in that high nasal style that breaks your heart. I stood quietly with Ed.

It was a sad day for Dog Creek. My Dad had lived his entire life in the Dog Creek Valley, experiencing all his triumphs and defeats there. He had been a strong and courageous man, a good neighbour, and a fine friend. With his passing, an era at Dog Creek was coming to an end.

Mother tried to carry on with the ranch after Dad died. She convinced Geoff to return to Dog Creek and take over running it. Geoff had different ideas than my Dad, but as sole heir to Dad's estate, Mother had final say in everything. She preferred taking Drinkell's advice on matters, even though it was obvious that he had advised my Grandfather into bankruptcy and went broke twice himself in the store business, once taking Dad down with him. Drinkell always got the last word and Mother always believed him.

My brother and I got together and presented her with a proposition. Geoff would buy the River Ranch and take all the cattle, while I would take the home ranch. We would survey off the old home and garden space for her to keep and would each pay her $250 a month. She turned us down flat. Seeing that things were going down-hill fast, Geoff made the difficult decision to leave Dog Creek.

Ada Place dressed up for "tea" every day of her life. She was a remarkable woman— not easy to live with, but still remarkable.

I came to the same decision in 1959. For fifteen years I had tried to buy the store building that I rented from Mother and Dad. Finding herself short of cash, Mother indicated that she might be willing to finally make a deal with me on the property. I hired surveyors to survey the area I wanted, which was the store building and access to the creek so that I'd have enough room to maintain a water system. My next stop was my old friend J.H. McIntyre, the Gang Ranch foreman, where I secured a loan of $10,000 in order to avoid any delays. When I had the cash and documents ready, I went to Mother to finalize the deal. She turned me down again.

Since my boys were growing up and high school was beginning to be a problem, not to mention my difficulty in convincing my mother to sell me any of her property, we decided it was time to move on. We settled in Williams Lake in 1960 and I became the owner of a music store.

Mother hung on to the ranch until 1961, when she sold it to George Deming. She came to live with Rita and me in Williams Lake until Geoff had a small apartment finished for her in his house. One day she began having difficulty talking and walking, and it was several days before it passed. We had a doctor in to check her and he believed Mother had had a small stroke. The apartment at Geoff's was ready at this time and she moved in. Shortly after that she had another stroke, a much more severe one that left her in bad shape.

It occurred to me then that even though she had entertained nearly all of Williams Lake at some time or other at the ranch, she had few visitors now and she became quite lonesome. One of the few people to see her was Arthur Rosette, also known as Wahoo. That wild young man, who had no formal education and would do almost anything on a dare, dressed up in a white shirt and came all the way from the Gang just to visit Mother. I think it was because he liked her and she had been nice to him when he worked for her after my Dad died. I admired him for this show of respect and affection for my Mother.

Mother battled back for over a year, learning to talk and walk again as she struggled to get better. Just when things started to look promising, she suffered a third stroke that ended her life. That was the day the Cariboo lost one of its great characters. She had asked us not to bury her at Dog Creek and not to mark her grave until long after she was gone. Mother was truly one of a kind.

CHAPTER 21

BRIAN HIGGINS

Our neighbours in Williams Lake were Brian and Anna Higgins. I first got to know Brian when he was the bartender at the Maple Leaf Hotel in Williams Lake during the war. Although I didn't talk to him much, I knew him by sight. He was five foot ten or thereabouts and always seemed to wear khaki pants that were a little too big for him, along with some nondescript flannel shirt open at the neck. One thing I did know about him at that point was that he never got too excited about things, instead preferring to see the funny side of life. Brian worked on various ranches around the Cariboo, and his easy nature gained him many friends along the way.

He often fed cattle during the winters of the Depression. This was a tough job and one that required dedication and responsibility. The people who did it were often sent out to meadows to live in cabins by themselves, with the chore of feeding and caring for 300 or 400 head of cattle. Supplies were limited and, as Brian often said, consisted of 50 pounds of flour and 5 pounds of lard.

One winter in the late 1940s, Brian got a job feeding cattle for the Alkali Lake Ranch at one of its holdings known as the old Moore Ranch. It was located three miles down the road from the main ranch, toward Dog Creek. There wasn't much at the ranch: a barn and some corrals on one side of the road, and the old Moore home on the other, where Brian was batching. He had a good-sized herd to tend to and he stayed busy every day, chopping water holes in the ice, feeding the stock, looking after his team, and cooking his own meals. Of course animals don't keep Sundays, so this was a seven-days-a-week job. I'd stop with the stage truck and deliver Brian's mail and groceries, chatting with him for a few minutes each time.

One day I was driving back from Williams Lake with the big truck, bringing Rita's mother, Cecilia, who was coming out for a visit.

Brian Higgins

There was nothing to deliver to Brian that trip, so I didn't stop, but when I was a hundred yards or so past the old Moore house I happened to look in my rearview mirror and saw smoke pouring out of the building, with Brian standing up on the roof.

I slammed on the brakes and backed up to the front of the house, then jumped out and ran around back to see if I could help. Cecilia was right behind me. We saw Brian frantically throwing snow on the fire in an effort to stop the blaze. Positioning myself halfway up his rickety old ladder, I started passing up the full buckets of snow that my mother-in-law was quickly filling. It was a pretty hectic half hour but somehow, believe it or not, we managed to put the flames out. When the smoke cleared Brian came down from the roof, thanking us for the help. "You just saved me and forty thousand bedbugs from being homeless!" he laughed.

We hit it off after that, becoming good friends, and I learned a great deal about his life. Brian came from an interesting family. His real name was O'Higgins, and for any student of South American or Irish history, the name will ring a bell. It seems that one of Brian's ancestors, Bernardo O'Higgins, was a hero in Chile and Peru back in the early 1800s. In fact he was the military governor of Chile for a number of years. His authority was challenged in later years, and rather than risk a civil war O'Higgins retired and moved to Peru, where he was given an estate to live on. Eventually his honours were returned to him in Chile, and he died revered by both countries as a hero. Brian spent some time in South America as a young man and found his name was still magic some hundred years after Bernardo's death.

Bernardo wasn't the only relation of Brian's who was famous, however. Kevin O'Higgins was an important figure in Irish history during the 1920s. Apparently Kevin had some disagreements with the Irish government of DeValera. As a result of his activities against the government, Kevin was shot and killed on his way to church one day. Brian and the rest of his family were persona non grata in Ireland until after the end of World War II.

Since he was not allowed to enter Ireland, Brian took to roaming the world as a young man. He spent a lot of time in Argentina, working on the ranches there, and he loved to tell me about the exploits of the gauchos and their expertise as horsemen. Another of his expeditions was to Australia to take a job as a line fence maintenance man. It was about as far away from the violence in Ireland as he could get.

Upon arrival in Australia he set out for the ranch he'd be working at, which was located in the centre of the country. After a long, tedious train journey across the desert-like plains, Brian arrived at his new posting. The ranch headquarters were a collection of corrugated iron shacks surrounding the only green tree Brian had seen in two days. It was the middle of January and hotter than hell.

Brian was taught the rudiments of fence mending and equipped to head out to his station. It took several days of preparation before he was ready to leave. His outfit consisted of three camels, one for riding and two for packing. The enormous loads that each camel carried amazed Brian. There was all the food he'd eat for the next three months, all his clothes, bedding, camp gear, and tools that he'd need, not to mention the water he required for the trek and even some books to read. In addition was some wire to replace what the Aborigines stole. He found it strange that even with several hundred pounds on their backs, the camels made absolutely no sound when they walked.

Finally he set off, leading the two pack camels, with absolutely no idea of where he was going. All they told him at the ranch was to head north and after eight days of travel he should hit the fence that he'd be patrolling. So Brian just kept an eye on his compass as he rode. The first few days he was alert and watched what was going on around him while they passed over the desolate land, crossing a small coulee every once in a while, but he soon found it intensely boring. He dug into his library for something to read, and from then on he'd check his compass every so often to make sure he was still headed north, then get back to his book.

A cup of tea suddenly seemed like a great idea, so Brian stopped. When he turned to look at the pack animals, all he saw was miles and miles of flat land with not a camel in sight. He started thinking about what he had with him to survive. It was a terribly short list: bedding, his tent, a half-full water bottle, and his book. He decided to backtrack, hoping he'd find the animals. Sure enough, they were waiting for him in the first coulee he came to. This little exercise scared the hell out of Brian, and needless to say he was a lot more careful afterwards.

Paying close attention to the detailed directions (head north until you hit the fence), he finally arrived at his destination. By referring to his map and the numbered fence posts, Brian figured out where he was and found his campsite, a spot distinguished by three pipes with taps sticking out of the ground. One tap dispensed clear cold water, the second hot water, and the third salty water, which intrigued Brian no end. (He later learned this variety was accomplished by drilling down to different levels.) He never ceased to marvel at his ability to turn on the tap and make a boiling cup of tea at any moment. It was great for entertaining guests. The only problem was there were no guests. Brian's nearest neighbour was the next lineman, stationed a hundred miles down the fence. There was no means of communication, and he was alone most of the time.

Once a month he did get to see the other fence rider when they both arrived at the end of their respective fence lines. And he was occasionally visited by some of the Aborigines. Brian got to like them and admired their uncommon abilities. Sitting alone by the fire at night, he'd suddenly feel something brush up against him. It would be an Aborigine. A surprise like that might make most people want to get up and run, but Brian found them to be peaceful and always ready to help. Some of them could speak a little English, and Brian was able to understand them a bit. One of the men told Brian that he was proud that day because his wife had borne him a son.

"Well," Brian thought, "how the hell would you know? You've been here with me working for the last week."

It turns out the man did know and he was right.

This wasn't the only time Brian witnessed the uncanny powers of the Aborigines' instinct. During the roundup and cattle drive at the end of one season, all hands were working to bring in the livestock for the fall sale. Brian had several Aborigine men working under his direction. They were funny looking little guys, black as coal, and since they were approaching town the men were all newly fitted out with a pair of pants and a shirt. Normally they were stark naked, but this didn't go over so well in the towns. The Aborigines tended to be the butt of many jokes, particularly when they did things like trading off some of their clothes to other tribe members. What made this so strange was that half the time one guy would be wearing only a shirt while the next had only a pair of pants.

When the men on the cattle drive got to the town, they found it was in turmoil. A little girl was missing from her home and everyone was searching for her. The cowboys were asked to help, and Brian explained the situation to an Aborigine who was part of the cattle drive. Once he understood the problem, the Aborigine simply replied, "I find."

With that he took off running, stooping occasionally as if running on all fours. He ran through the little town, turning this way and that around buildings and down alleys until he reached a culvert a quarter of a mile out of town. The Aborigine reached into it and pulled out the missing girl. No one could believe what they'd seen. They'd spent two long, agonizing days of searching without any success, and this man just walked in and solved the mystery in mere minutes. His sixth sense became the talk of the town and nobody was making fun of him this time.

Brian held a great deal of respect for the Aborigines, particularly after witnessing such events. The feeling was obviously mutual, and the men he worked with gave him a kangaroo-hide belt that Brian wore daily for the next 40 years.

When he decided to return to Canada after one of his trips to Australia or South America, Brian would head for his little property in Williams Lake, which he rented out while he was away. On one occasion, after being in Australia for a year, Brian returned to Vancouver, quite happy to be back home. The immigration people were not so happy. They took one look at Brian's papers and without any further ado slapped the handcuffs on him, claiming he was entering illegally. Brian was led away, loudly protesting his innocence. His accent, as Irish as Paddy's pig, certainly wasn't helping him at that point. He later told me you can't imagine how lonesome you feel when those cuffs snap onto your wrists and you realize that these guys are playing for real.

Brian spent the night in the custody of the immigration people and was hauled up in front of the official in charge the following morning. Once again, Brian explained how he owned property in Williams Lake and that he was coming home. The official noted this all down on a piece of paper, then Brian was hauled back to the pokey. Confirmation of this data was requested from Williams Lake by mail. The mail system wasn't especially efficient, so Brian cooled his heels in the slammer for a week until the investigation was complete. They eventually turned him loose and he solemnly vowed he'd never leave Canada again.

Of course this didn't apply later on when Brian, now in his sixties, learned he could finally return to Ireland for a visit. While he was there he met his childhood sweetheart, Anna, and they got married. They returned to Canada and sought work. With Anna's qualifications as an accountant and Brian's knowledge of ranching, the couple soon ended up as bookkeeper and storekeeper at the Alkali Lake Ranch during the 1950s and moved into an old log house directly across the road from the store.

Mario Reidemann, an ardent Catholic with firm convictions, owned the Alkali Lake Ranch at the time. He was fond of bird shooting and introduced Chinese pheasants to the ranch. Strict "no hunting or shooting" rules were instituted by Mr. Reidemann, and everybody respected them—until the day Brian decided to go and do some grouse hunting down by the lake.

Mr. and Mrs. Reidemann of Alkali Lake Ranch.

Brian knew that blue grouse frequented a series of small gulches along the lakeside and he was dead set on getting a feed for himself and Anna. He cranked up his little old Austin car and set off down the road. Sure enough, he saw some grouse run over the hill and into the next gulch. It was at this point in his story that Brian's knowledge of grouse became suspect. As far as I know, blue grouse do not run anywhere; they fly, unbelievably fast, downhill, and away from their tormentor. Details aside, I'll get on with this tale.

He sneaked up over the hill and saw the birds in the bottom of the ravine. With one lucky shot, Brian killed two grouse. After retrieving them he started back to his car, feeling pretty happy about his good fortune and, of course, his hunting abilities. Brian was surprised to meet a gentleman walking toward him. He introduced himself first, and then the other man gave his name and line of business. Turns out he was the provincial game warden.

According to Brian, it was then that he found out he had broken the law for shooting blue grouse out of season. However, the situation became much more serious when Brian showed the warden his catch. The game warden took one look at them and told him they weren't blue grouse...they were hen pheasants. Brian knew he was in deep trouble if he didn't act quickly. Being Irish, he was somehow able to convince the warden to keep the whole matter secret and he'd quietly pay the fine. Luckily for my friend, Mr. Reidemann never knew a thing about it.

I was not so fortunate when it came to staying in Mr. Reidemann's good graces. For some reason that I never fully understood, he took a dislike to me. When I bought the trucking business back from Geoff in 1949, this dislike caused a problem. Geoff had borrowed some money from Reidemann against the trucking business, but Mr. Reidemann refused to transfer this loan to me. He said he needed the money—about $5000—to operate his ranch, which was worth well over a million dollars. It was a small setback until I got the money from my old benefactor J.H. McIntyre at the Gang Ranch. The trouble certainly didn't stop there.

On my first trip as owner of the stage line again, Mr. Reidemann waited for me at the post office in Alkali Lake to inform me that he'd made arrangements with Buster Henke to haul all his fuel. In addition, he'd be sending his own truck into Williams Lake once a week for his own freight. The Alkali truck left ahead of me each time, giving free rides to passengers that I should have been picking up for a fee. It became pretty rough going to make the stage business work, but I kept plugging away. I finally took the big truck off the road and replaced it with a one-ton panel that I modified by putting in a backseat for passengers. This switch paid off and I began making more money than I had with the big truck.

There was a schedule of arrival times that we were required to post at each stop and that we tried to stick to as close as possible. With the roads that we had it was nearly impossible to arrive and depart on time, especially in winter. I learned from Brian that Mr. Reidemann reported me to the head office of the post office every time I was late. What Reidemann didn't know was that his letter would be sent back to the postmaster at Alkali Lake (Brian) for confirmation. Brian showed me several of these letters. He always wrote back to headquarters telling them that the mail had been delivered without undue delay despite the unfavourable roads.

There were also times when I had the satisfaction of showing Mr. Reidemann how misguided his opinions of me were. One of these occasions happened during that same winter, while Reidemann kept up his relentless campaign against me.

It was a tough winter with lots of snow and wind, and the roads were in terrible shape. I was hauling the mail in from Dog Creek using a Plymouth station wagon with highboy wheels. Buster Isnardy, the ranch foreman at Alkali Lake who had plenty of experience with Cariboo roads, had started out to the Moore Ranch, three miles down the valley toward Dog Creek, in a horse-drawn sleigh. Somehow he got off the road and was stuck in a snowdrift. He had a hell of a time getting the horses out of the drift but eventually got them turned around and went back to the Alkali Lake store. The store was full of cowboys and Indians watching Mr. Reidemann as he paced around the room, slapping his riding crop against his leg and complaining about me. "He'll never make it today...Too bad we don't have a better mail contractor...I don't think he will even try to get through today."

In the middle of all this talk the door opened and in I walked.

"How is the road?" Brian asked me.

Alkalki Lake Ranch in 1959. The barn in this photo was built in 1900 and the house in 1861. According to Irene Stangoe in her book Cariboo-Chilcotin: Pioneer People and Places, *this may have been the first ranch established in B.C. She writes that it was pre-empted by Herman Otto Bowe (pronounced "Boo-ee") in 1861. In 1910 Charles Wynn-Johnson purchased it, and he in turn sold it to Mario Reidemann in 1940. The Reidemann family owned it until 1975.*

"Not too bad," I replied, "except where somebody got stuck and rooted the whole thing up."

It was my hour of glory!

Several years passed until one day Mr. Reidemann's attitude changed completely. I have no idea why it happened, but now it seemed I could do no wrong. For instance, one time I was coming out of Williams Lake with a full load. There was a whole bunch of bread in 25-loaf cartons piled on the roof along with some express parcels forwarded from the railway. When I got to Alkali Lake we began checking off the parcels and realized one was missing. We phoned back to the Pacific Great Eastern Railway (PGE) in case I hadn't picked it up to begin with. They didn't have it so we knew it must have got lost along the way. There was nothing I could do but go on to Dog Creek and hope it turned up eventually.

Just as I got home the phone rang. It was Brian. He thought he should let me know that the lost parcel contained Mrs. Reidemann's mink coat, valued at $25,000. My liability insurance was only for $10,000.

I didn't sleep too well that Tuesday night. Wednesday night was no better. On Thursday Brian called again to tell me that the coat had turned up. It was found along the roadside by one of the local Indians and he brought it in to the Alkali Lake store. The man wouldn't accept any reward for his actions; he was happy to do it. Mr. Reidemann never said one word about the whole deal—no letters, no acrimony, no nothing. He was just pleased that there was no harm done. Like I said, I have no idea what changed his mind, but I was certainly relieved by his new outlook.

I wasn't the only one to push his luck with Reidemann. During one episode, Brian found himself in deep trouble and dragged me into the middle of it with him. When that day began I believed it was a great winter morning. There was a skiff of snow on the ground but it wasn't creating any problems on the road, and for once I managed to arrive on time at the Alkali post office on my way into town.

Unfortunately, Brian wasn't having such a great time of it. He was jumping around in a haze of smoke in front of the old barrel heater.

"What the heck are you doing?"

"I'm putting out the fire!" he yelled, then pointed to a small flame burning on the floor. "Here! Jump on that one over there."

I quickly put it out with my foot and looked around. That seemed to be the last of it. "What the heck is going on, Brian?"

"I just burned up the money for the store."

I looked down at the ashes and sure enough, there were half-burned parts of ones, twos, fives, and tens all over the floor. "How in the world did you manage to burn up the money?"

Brian quickly explained that there was no safe in the store. Rather than leave the money unattended overnight, Brian and Anna always put the cash in a paper bag and took it home after closing each day. He'd been running late that morning and was in a hurry to get the mail ready for me when I arrived. In a rush he ran over from his house and set the bag of money on the counter while he started the fires. The evening before had been busy, and Brian found some chocolate

Williams Lake's railway station in the 1940s, one of the regular stopping places on my freight pickup route. The Pacific Great Eastern railway reached Williams Lake in 1919, connecting the Cariboo with southern B.C.

bar wrappers that the cowboys and Indians must have thrown on the floor. He grabbed them and threw them into the fire along with other bits of waste, then slammed the great iron door shut. Standing back, Brian waited for the warmth to hit him.

It suddenly struck him that something was wrong, but he didn't know what. Then it dawned on him that the bag of money wasn't on the counter anymore. Terror seized him as he remembered picking up the bag and absentmindedly tossing it into the stove along with the garbage. He grabbed the poker and was trying to pull the burning bundle out of the stove as I walked in.

"Oh my God! What am I going to tell Reidemann?" Brian lamented. "You have to come up with me to see him. I can't go there alone!"

Next thing I knew we were in the stage and I was driving toward Reidemann's massive house up behind the store. We arrived at the entrance, located at the back of the building, and Brian told the girl at the door that there was big trouble and he had to see the boss at once. She ran off and returned a few minutes later to tell us that Mr.

Reidemann would see us. We followed her to his bedroom, where he sat in bed, still in his pyjamas. Brian and I stood at the foot of his bed like two schoolboys caught with their hands in the cookie jar. Finally Brian got courage up to tell Mr. Reidemann the whole sorry tale. I held my breath and waited for the yelling to start.

"My, that's too bad, Brian. Is there any of the money left?"

It turned out most of the money wasn't burned since it had been secured in the middle of the bundle by a rubber band. There were lots of centres of bills with the ends burned off. I took the whole bunch into the bank for Brian and he later told me they only lost $40 altogether. Eventually we all had a good laugh about it, although at the time there didn't seem to be a funny thing about it. Looking back afterwards, though, I only wish that Norman Rockwell could have drawn a picture of Brian and me at the foot of Reidemann's bed...it would have been a classic!

For a time we both lived in Williams Lake where we both owned rental houses on First Avenue North. Brian gave his the name "Graveyard House" because of its proximity to the cemetery and advertised it as such when he wanted to rent it. Brian got a great kick out of Carmen, our youngest boy, born in 1956. One day while we were talking he chuckled as he told me about my son's busy afternoon. "I've been watching Carmen. So far today he's played out six kids and two dogs, running around in the field across the road!"

We remained close friends even after he and Anna decided to return to Ireland in the 1960s, where she suddenly passed away. Brian lived on by himself in the same little village. His neighbours dropped in often to visit with him and undoubtedly heard some of Brian's great stories. It was one of those neighbours who became suspicious when she saw Brian sitting in the same position in front of the television one day as she went to and from the market. She called the police and they went in to find that Brian was dead.

He was a good and staunch friend of mine, a true gentleman at all times, and a man I admired a lot. He loved to laugh and was one of the few men who could find humour in almost any situation, and over the years of our friendship there were certainly plenty of times that brought forth gales of laughter.

CHAPTER 22

PARSONS
AND PREACHERS

There were no parsons or preachers living near Dog Creek while I was growing up, but Mother read us stories about the life of Christ and quoted the Bible every chance she got. As I've mentioned, she was well versed in religious studies and had been raised as a Methodist in Victorian England, although she wasn't a devout follower. Dad, despite growing up in a strict Anglican household, never took a serious interest in religion, so our family simply had no formal church affiliation.

We had our share of clergymen who travelled through even the most remote areas in order to spread their gospels. One of these men, Father Thomas, had to be one of the greatest old characters in the Cariboo's religious world. The old French priest travelled the north country for over 50 years, ministering mostly to the Indian population as well as the Catholics in the region. Regardless of differences in faith, however, Father Thomas was always welcome to stay at my parents' hotel and travel with the Dog Creek Stage free of charge, a tradition begun years earlier when J.S. owned the businesses.

There were many times I watched him alight from the horse-drawn sleigh in midwinter for another visit, noticing the contrast of his short, sturdy shadow of black clothing against the stark white snow. He ambled along in his heavy workboots to our front door, where Mother greeted him warmly before teasing him mercilessly about whatever came to mind. Listening to her banter made him laugh out loud, his large yellow teeth revealed through the tangle of his straggly, white beard. After stepping out of his boots, Father Thomas immediately headed for the stove where he held the long tails of his black overcoat out in order to warm his rear end.

Father Thomas, wearing the big black coat that I remember.

That coat seemed to have pockets hidden everywhere; each time he reached into one of them, he brought out something different. Sometimes his worn Bible, his handkerchief, or a tin of snuff was revealed, or he'd pull out his famous silver toothpick, which he flourished after every meal. Beneath the coat the priest was always dressed head to toe in black, from the black wool trousers held up by heavy suspenders to his black waistcoat with a silver watch chain draped across his chest.

He was deeply devoted to his religion. Records of baptisms, deaths, and marriages were kept meticulously and he watched over his flock with great interest. Father Thomas was something of a martinet when anyone stepped out of line, and he strongly believed in punishments for any transgressions.

Of course he wasn't always fire and brimstone. The man had a great sense of humour, which was rather essential in certain situations. On one occasion he was baptizing an Indian child. The young mother was so nervous she shook uncontrollably while she held onto her baby. As part of the ceremony, Father Thomas asked her the name of the child's father. Swallowing hard, the girl cleared her throat and replied in a timid voice, "Father Thomas."

It didn't take long for this response to circulate through town, and everyone roared with laughter upon hearing about it. Appreciating the humour in the situation, Father Thomas chuckled over the incident himself.

Father Thomas was the first representative of organized religion that I knew, and I guess he became the yardstick by which I measured all subsequent clergymen. A lot fell short, but some exceeded. Reverend Basil Resker, who espoused the Anglican faith, was one of those men I respected. He, too, had a wonderful sense of humour and was a welcome visitor in our home. The reverend held services in our music room each time he came to Dog Creek. His sermons were not particularly enjoyable, especially when I couldn't understand much of what he was saying, but my attention was always focussed on his little dog, Carrots. Mother often said that Carrots would get up and walk out as soon as Reverend Resker started to preach. The reverend insisted that his dog only left when Mother played the hymns and sang. This colourful debate certainly made the services a lot more interesting for me as a kid, and I watched the little spaniel closely to see who was right. It seemed that most of the time Carrots sided with no one, sleeping through the entire proceedings, much to my disappointment.

Even though we often had priests and reverends in for sermons and prayers at Dog Creek, we never attended an actual church service. Instead, Mother continued to provide the education she felt was necessary to teach Geoff and me right from wrong. And although my early opinion of organized religion wasn't for or against it, I seemed to get into conflict with the church more and more in my adult life. Perhaps the lack of formal church exposure influenced my hearty disregard for church dogma and my healthy respect for the teachings of Jesus Christ. The older I became, the more I learned that they could be two very different things.

Reverend Basil Resker was minister of the Anglican Church in Williams Lake from 1926 until 1938. In Looking Back at the Cariboo-Chilcotin, *Irene Stangoe writes, "At that time the Williams Lake-Chilcotin Mission was the second largest in Canada, so he had an immense territory to cover. He didn't know how to drive, but quickly taught himself on the vacant flats where Safeway is today." The early clergy had to be pretty innovative and self-reliant.*

My distaste for some of the establishment's practices grew stronger after I purchased the Dog Creek store. The business brought me into close contact with the Indian people, who made up the majority of my customers, and I got to view things from their perspective.

One of their greatest concerns was always the Cariboo Indian school. Established in the 1800s, it was originally intended to provide education to both white and Native children. It began as a well-respected institution, but the character of the place changed for the worse over the years.

During the 1920s and 1930s many small communities started their own one-room schools, as we did in Dog Creek. I don't know if there were laws forbidding Indian children from attending, but it was plain to see that the only pupils in the area schools were white. The Catholics who ran the St. Joseph Mission school became more insistent that they should educate the Indian children.

I can only imagine what these poor kids went through, being taken away from their parents and subjected to harsh rules and regulations in a most unforgiving place. The children were denied the comfort and love of their families, then made to feel shame for their culture and heritage. It's no wonder that men like Sam Sault John tried to fight the system and take care of his grandchildren the way he saw fit.

*The opening and blessing of the Catholic Church
on Dog Creek reserve, 1948.*

While I was working at the store one September morning, I watched as a cattle truck drove past on its way to pick up the kids and transport them to the mission school. I remembered that they had made the same journey the previous year, with devastating results. As that truck was crossing Springhouse prairie, a flash hailstorm bombarded the children, who huddled together with no protection from the freezing rain. One of the children developed pneumonia upon arrival at the school and died. There was no way I could let the school do that to another group of kids.

I watched as the truck came back down the mountain with some children from the reserve and continued on to the valley to pick up the rest. This was my chance. They had to return the same way, past my store, to get back to the mission school. Running out the door, I blocked the road off with a log to prevent them from passing by.

When the truck returned, filled with children, it was forced to stop. Father Price jumped out of the vehicle and demanded to know what was going on. I was ready for him.

"That load you have in your truck is not a bunch of cattle. They are human beings. And if you move the truck one inch more while those kids are in it, I'll lay a charge against you and your church under the Motor Carrier Act!" I went on, quoting some specific parts of the Act that he was in violation of. It stopped him and his driver dead in their tracks.

The truck driver, one of the Felkers, worked on the mission ranch and also happened to be a devout Catholic. He looked at me as if he expected the Almighty to strike me down at any moment for talking this way to a priest. And he appeared to be disappointed when it didn't happen.

Father Price was growing more and more agitated with every infraction I rattled off. We stood near my old-fashioned gas pump, one of those with the glass bowl at the top. He became so infuriated that he took a swing at the pump and left a big dent in it. This didn't change my mind though, and I stuck to my guns. Left with no other alternative, Father Price returned the children to the reserve and headed back to the mission school with no new students.

The next day he drove into Dog Creek with a real school bus, and the children were taken to the school. It was a small victory, but definitely a worthwhile one.

A week later I was at Alkali Lake, unloading the mail, when who should appear but Father Price and Mr. Reidemann. Brian came over to let me know that the two men wished to speak to me. I figured I was about to lose all my business at Alkali Lake, since the Alkali Lake Ranch was solid Catholic from Reidemann down to the lowliest employee. Not only that, but I had also learned that Father Price was a boxing champion in his youth—where was that gas pump when I needed it? I grew more apprehensive about the conversation as I walked toward them.

Father Price was the first to speak. "I want to talk to you about what happened the other day at Dog Creek."

Boy! I'm going to get it now, I thought.

"I want to tell you," he continued, "that you were right and to thank you for making me see what we were doing was wrong."

I nearly fell over. The meeting ended with handshakes all around. To my knowledge, that ended the use of a cattle truck to transport any other children.

During the 1950s while my boys were in school, I spent six years on the board of School District No. 27, Williams Lake. I happened to be chairman when I had yet another brush with the Catholic Church over the Indian school.

We had reached a point in the district where we needed a new high school in Williams Lake. At one of our board meetings I suggested we explore the possibility of including pupils of high-school age from the mission school. The other board members supported the idea, not so much out of idealism as from the fact it would probably get us a substantial federal government grant. The board agreed to pursue the matter and we received all sorts of favourable response. Even the local press supported the idea, which was most unusual. Everything seemed to be going fine. Then the whole process stopped dead.

What was wrong? was the question on everyone's mind. As luck would have it, we were able to get an answer. Allan MacEachen, the cabinet minister responsible for federal funding in Ottawa, had been the wartime commanding officer of our local superintendent of education, Bill Mouat. A personal phone call revealed the problem...the Catholic Church was blocking our efforts.

I could not understand the motivation behind the church's roadblock. The whole idea of including the Indian children was such a good one, not only from a financial standpoint, but also from the point of view that their emancipation would help the children evaluate themselves and their relationship to the dominant society. This was an issue I would not let die without a fight. Correspondence ensued in which I pushed the church for an answer that could be quoted by the press. I was informed that Archbishop Duke, the head of B.C.'s Catholic church, would be coming up to the Cariboo shortly. At that time he would meet with the school board to discuss the matter.

Finally the day arrived and we met in the school board office—the Archbishop, Mr. Mouat, the Secretary-Treasurer Chuck McQueen, and myself. We began a friendly discussion of the matter, and then I asked the Archbishop why he opposed the deal.

"Well, Mr. Place," he said, "I am sure that your idea would turn out a more capable and competent citizen. However, from my point of view I am interested and concerned not with capability and competence, but with Catholics."

That remained the position of the Catholic Church until Pope John Paul allowed the winds of change to finally open up the church.

My disgust for all the wrong that was done to those defenseless Indian children has not subsided. In fact, it grows each time I hear another story of the abuse and poor treatment they were forced to endure. Of all the things the church did, this must be its single worst crime. And the fact that it was done "in the name of the Lord" makes it that much worse.

It is often said that it's easy to find fault and difficult to forgive, and so it is. But in this case we all must shoulder part of the blame. Nobody spoke up, neither Catholic nor Protestant nor anyone else, to defend the helpless and innocent. If anything is to be learned from this dark period in our history, it is that covering up or ignoring such abuse can never be accepted again. It's a lesson learned the hardest way.

CHAPTER 23

A LIFE OF MUSIC

One constant that has greatly influenced my life is music. Wherever I go, whatever I do, I go with music—tunes and melodies play endlessly in my head. Sometimes when I've told people this they look at me as if I'm not far from the nuthatch, and maybe they are right.

"Doesn't it bother you?" they ask, with that funny look in their eyes.

"No," I respond, "it doesn't bother me one little bit."

You see, I've enjoyed the concerts in my head all my life. It's like having a particularly catchy tune repeating itself over and over and being able to orchestrate it to my own liking, a little more bass here or some violins there, not too loud with the drums. It is a blessing to be able to do this, although I think people who possess this ability should keep it quiet so they won't be sent off to the funny farm.

Mother came from a very musical family. Her cousins were accomplished musicians in both the classical and popular field. One cousin, Haydn Halstead, was equally successful with both types. As a youngster conducting small pit orchestras for the vaudeville music halls, he once wrote a song for a performer and sold it to him for three shillings. Years later, when Haydn retired as the conductor of the Edinburgh Symphony, the city hosted a banquet honouring his years in music. The old music hall performer he'd sold the song to was also there and gave the original copy back to Haydn as a keepsake. The performer was Will Fyfe and the song was "I Belong to Glasgow."

This musical talent was shared by Mother, who learned to play the piano by herself during the long days of loneliness at the D4. She had no grounding in music at all, and she often said all she knew was that that note on the music sheet was this note on the piano. Despite this inadequate formal education, Mother could read to beat the band and got so that she could play some passable Chopin from her well-worn book of popular classics. She often had my brother and me sing while she played. Geoff had a good voice but he tended to stray off tune or go flat, so most sessions ended up with a family row, especially when I showed how I could carry the tune, much to Geoff's and Mother's disgust.

When our first teacher arrived in Dog Creek, she brought a ukulele along with her schoolbooks. She boarded with us and would often sit with the instrument, counting out the bars of "Ain't She Sweet" until she finally got her fingers on the right strings and started strumming. I studied this manoeuvre intently and one day when nobody was around I picked up the uke sitting by the piano and strummed out a tune. Mother heard me, and the roof dropped in. She gave me a good bawling out and told me never to touch the teacher's uke again. I never did, but I still watched Miss Price play, knowing that I could play that thing too if only I was allowed to. Obviously my teacher knew how fascinated I was by the instrument because when she left the following June, she gave me her ukulele. I was overjoyed and immediately began to chord along just fine. I quickly learned to follow the uke chord diagrams that were printed on most piano music in those days.

When I was ten, Eric Hillman got a guitar from Eaton's. He soon found he couldn't learn it, so Geoff bought the guitar from him for two dollars. My brother didn't have much luck playing it either, so it wasn't long before I got my hands on it. Right away I found the uke chord diagrams were the same for the top four strings of the guitar. I was off and running. Unfortunately, Mrs. Keeble was staying in the house that winter and she simply couldn't stand to have me making noise on the guitar, so I wasn't allowed to play it. Sometimes she went out for a walk and I quickly got out the old guitar and gave it a couple of plunks, but it was mostly verboten.

At the age of twelve, I could hardly believe my eyes Christmas morning when I got a violin from Mother and Dad. It wasn't much of a fiddle, five dollars from Eaton's with a bow, a piece of rosin, a set of steel strings, and a five-cent book, *How to Play the Violin*, but I was ecstatic even though I had no idea how to hold the instrument or the bow. I found pictures of people playing violins in the papers and followed them as near as I could, but I held my hand all wrong and

Musicians? These were taken the year after I got the violin for Christmas, after I'd figured out how to hold it and play it. Geoff would often fool around with the squeeze box.

experienced all kinds of difficulty getting my little finger to work. Still I made headway. All of my spare time was devoted to getting a tune out of the thing, which I did almost at once. After a while I could play a few tunes, mostly classics like "Clair de Lune," with my mother playing the piano. Dad enjoyed listening to the old fiddle tunes, and he always wanted to try playing, but he wasn't musically inclined. Work was his big thing.

It was around this time that I got sick, and it was a few years before I could play again. I missed it a lot, but as I've said, the music continued going around in my head even if it wasn't being played on an instrument.

I was seventeen when I was reintroduced to music. A logging crew came up from Williams Lake to cut Christmas trees in the valley, and it turned out they all played in the local dance orchestra. Bodie Webb, one of the players, was an excellent musician who could play just about any instrument around. He was particularly good on the trombone, although he was no slouch on the piano, fiddle, and sax either. Archie Pinchbeck played the sax and fiddle, and Wally Naef played the piano well. In the evenings these men gathered around Mother's old piano and went at it until bedtime. I tried to join in as

I picked up the sax after my illness, though fiddle and accordion were my main instruments. Another of the musicians I played with was Jim Worthington (right), with the sax. He was a real fine young man with a great sense of humour. In World War II he went overseas and was killed.

much as possible and picked up fast on what they were doing. They were all chord men and I got the hang of that approach to music.

Archie Pinchbeck and Julian Gordon were big influences on me musically. Archie was a member of the old Pinchbeck family. His grandfather, along with his partner Lynes, owned all the valley where Williams Lake now stands. Archie's mother was an Isnardy, and both the Pinchbecks and the Isnardys were musical families. Archie played the sax and a bit of the piano and fiddle and was fond of progressive jazz. A strong player, he had been playing mostly by ear when I met him, although he was beginning to understand the chord system more and more. The two of us puzzled out the chords and eventually we figured out what a minor or a seventh or a ninth was and how to construct them. It was a time of great rejoicing when we found out what a diminished chord was and how it fit into the scheme of things.

Archie and I played a lot of dance jobs together, sometimes with a couple of others in a four-piece outfit for the bigger dances or just the

The Cariboo Symphony, a group of musicians that played around the Cariboo about 1890 or 1900. Archie Pinchbeck's uncle was a member and so were a couple of Rita's uncles.

two of us if the venue was a small schoolhouse. We used to sit up there on the stage honking away on our instruments (I was playing a bit of sax and accordion myself by then), and between tunes we made caustic remarks about the dancers. Our music wasn't very good at first, but we improved as we went along and got some passable arrangements of the popular tunes of the day.

One time Archie and I were to play for a Springhouse school dance at the same time we were working for the Christmas tree outfit, and we ended up arriving late. A local guy named Boland Tressierra had been sawing away on his fiddle until we got there, so we thanked him for his efforts and asked if he'd like to play a tune along with us. He was a great big, six-foot-two, rawboned man with hard-worked hands the same size as the fiddle. Although he couldn't play very well, we managed to struggle through "Red Wing" with him and got ready to carry on with something else.

Suddenly he struck up "Red Wing" again, so we joined in again. We decided to play a waltz next for a change. Then Boland started the same tune for a third time. This was too much for me. Reaching over,

I grabbed the fiddle out of his hands and bonked him on the head with it. I didn't bargain on the darned fiddle completely exploding into God knows how many pieces. I stood there transfixed while Boland got down on his hands and knees and started picking up the pieces of his fiddle and putting them in his case. Once all the pieces had been gathered up he closed his case and quietly walked out of the schoolhouse and went home.

Archie and I went on into Williams Lake after the dance shut down at six that morning. I told him how bad I felt about Tressierra's fiddle and I wanted to do something about it. We looked around town and darned if Mr. Gosman, the second-hand man, didn't have a fiddle in his store. I paid him two dollars for it and on our way back to Dog Creek we stopped in at Springhouse to give it to Tressierra. His little log house was off the road and there were eight kids running around all over the place like wild animals. It was easy to see that they were dirt poor. The chickens seemed as at home on the kitchen table as anywhere, and the hound dogs wandered in and out. I had my little speech thought out in my head as I approached the house.

"I'm sorry, Boland, for the way I treated you at the dance last night and I wonder if you would be good enough to excuse my bad manners and accept this fiddle as a gift to replace yours."

"Well, by golly, that's damned decent of you." He looked down at the new fiddle. "This one is a lot better than the one I had. I don't know how to thank you."

It is at times like these that I wonder about mankind. One thing I know for sure, I wouldn't be so forgiving and nice to anyone who smashed my fiddle over my head!

When I was playing at dances in Williams Lake during the late 1930s, I had to find a way to get to them since I didn't have a car. Sometimes I hitched a ride right into town, but other times I walked quite a bit of the way carrying my instruments. Fortunately I was playing the accordion and fiddle, so the load wasn't too heavy.

I remember one trip I made from Dog Creek to one of the big dances in Williams Lake with my accordion slung over my back with two ropes and my fiddle in my hand. A Circle "S" cattle truck gave me a ride to Frizzi's, where I got off and walked the five miles to Springhouse. From there I caught a ride to Frost Creek, walked three

The Lakeview (you couldn't see a bit of the lake from anywhere in the building) Hotel was a frame building from Williams Lake's early years. By the 1930s the original building had been moved back on the lot and a new part built on the front. The result was that there were two classes of rooms. Rooms at the front, in the new part, were four or five dollars per night, while the rooms at the back were 50 cents per night. My friend Jack Lepinski had one of these 50-cent rooms rented by the month, and I often used the floor in his room for a bed when I was first playing for dances and didn't have the price for one of my own. Jack Chow, the owner-manager of the building, was a very fine gentleman.

miles to Pinchbecks, then got another ride to Williams Lake. We played from nine o'clock at night until six o'clock the next morning. The band made five dollars at these big dances and two dollars for the smaller ones. It sounds like a ridiculous amount of money, but in those days five dollars was a lot more money than it is today. Men worked on the ranches for five dollars a month and board. I played the dances mostly for the satisfaction I got out of performing. It was also the only way I could afford to get to any kind of entertainment and to get out of Dog Creek. Music was my ticket to freedom.

Julian Gordon came to Williams Lake around 1940. It was funny how we met. I had a job taking census, covering some of the Cariboo Road, so I had a room in the back of the Lakeview Hotel in Williams Lake. Heading back to my room after work one evening to wash up before supper, I heard accordion music coming from one of the rooms. I immediately went to the room and knocked on the door.

A voice called out, "Come in!"

I went in, stuck my hand out to the tall, gangly man still holding his accordion, and said, "Anybody who can play an accordion like that has got to be a friend of mine!"

We hit it off right away and I invited him to join me for supper at the restaurant. I learned that he was from Bella Coola and needed to find some work right away since he was flat broke. The local stampede was on, so I rustled him up some work playing both on the street and with our group at the dances. Not only was he an excellent player, Julian was also a great guy to be around. He loved a good laugh and always got a kick out of the antics Archie and I dreamed up.

Julian was the type of player who did it right. If there was a bass run in the piece, he practised until he got it just right. Each chord was given its hearing and each nuance of the piece was brought out. Playing with him made me a better musician and taught me something of self-discipline in music. I just wish I'd been able to learn his fine technique.

One time Bert Roberts threw a rodeo out at Riske Creek and hired Julian and me to play for the dances. There was nothing at Riske Creek but an enormous old hotel that had been built back during World War I by a Mr. Becher. It looked totally incongruous in that shallow little valley in the great Chilcotin plains. A more likely setting would have been on the main street of Kamloops.

I had made arrangements to meet Rita out there since she was going to Riske Creek for the weekend to stay with her friend Mary Jasper. Mary's brother Gordon and I were sharing a room at the Riske Creek hotel. Gordon was working the chutes at the rodeo during the day and I was playing the dances at night, so one of us could sleep while the other was working. Great efficiency!

The dance was held in the old hotel's dining room. It was a great big room with a twelve-foot ceiling that was lined with the embossed tin that was so popular at the time. Julian and I were both playing accordions and we worked hard all that night. Fred Mellish ran a hot-dog stand in a tent next to the grounds and he fixed me up with a breakfast of bacon and eggs; then I hit the sack, absolutely bushed.

I woke up later in the day, still half asleep, and lay there with my eyes closed wondering why there was so much racket coming from the next room. There were gales of laughter and loud voices. Finally I opened my eyes and, to my horror, realized I was staring right into the face of Alfred Bowe. I immediately rolled over and, lo and behold, there was Alfred's wife Minnie. Both of them were enjoying a real good sleep on top of the bed on either side of me. By this time I was sitting up and fully awake.

That is when I understood why the noise was so loud. Down by the foot of my bed was the Alkali Lake cowboy detachment, involved in a poker game. Every time somebody won a pot there were great gales of laughter from the Twan brothers, who were noted for their enjoyment of life. At that moment I was not sharing their joy. "How the hell did you guys get in here anyway?"

"Shut up and go back to sleep!" somebody yelled, followed by more loud guffaws. It was no use. I crawled out of bed and got dressed, leaving Alfred and Minnie to continue their comfortable sleep.

The second night of playing seemed like it was two days long. About three o'clock in the morning I had to get a few minutes rest, so I started to take the accordion off. Just then a cowboy seven feet tall and three axehandles across the back bellowed at me, "Play that damned thing!"

"Yes sir!" was all I could say, and we played on.

Rita and I left right after the dance to drive back to Williams Lake, 30 miles away. It is one of the most beautiful bits of country in B.C., from Bechers Prairie down the Sheep Creek Hill to the Fraser River, then up over to the Chimney Creek Valley and over the mountain to Williams Lake, each vista different and more beautiful than the last.

We were chugging along through the rain in my old car with its big disc wheels, and when we were almost to the top of the hill going into Williams Lake, we blew a tire. The tire was wrecked but I decided to go easy into town and worry about it there. It clicked every time the split rim came around and sounded like a small version of the PGE, but we didn't give a damn.

After that memorable weekend, Julian stayed around Williams Lake and Riske Creek for the summer, then came out to do the chores at the ranch that winter. He continued practising on his accordion and got a job playing on the radio in Kamloops, even getting billing

The Sheep Creek Bridge crossed the Fraser River, taking travellers from the Cariboo to the Chilcotin. It was built in the early 1900s and demolished in the 1960s. The stone pilings were built by a relative of Augustine Boitanio who came out from Italy to do the job, then returned to Italy and never came back again.

as Western Canada's best accordionist, which I truly believed he was. His success was short-lived. Disaster struck Julian when a pain in his back was diagnosed as TB and he was hospitalized. For nearly six years he was flat on his back on a board in the hospital until a cure was found. Not one to stay idle or give up, Julian learned accounting while he was laid up. After he was discharged he married his beloved nurse and raised a family. He has always been one of my heroes.

The war came on soon after that, and most of these fellows were called up or volunteered for service and shortly they were gone, including Archie. I was never able to get into the service so I stayed behind. A few older musicians were left in the area to play for the local dances, and I was often called in to join them when I wasn't working eighteen hours a day, seven days a week, in the trucking business. Once in a while Phil Temple, who was stationed at the airforce base in Dog Creek, played the banjo with me. Phil had some fingers missing on his left hand, but he was still a solid player and his banjo went well with my accordion.

Archie and I took one final kick at the can when he returned from the war. He booked us to play the Clinton Ball, one of the oldest dances in Western Canada, which started in the early 1860s. The gang was gathered up for the event: Dahl Junek on the piano, Doug Malette on drums, Archie on sax and fiddle, and me on sax, accordion, and fiddle. We hadn't played a note together for four years, so we were pushing our luck a bit.

There were two orchestras hired. One orchestra would play from nine until one, and the second (ours) would play from one until six in the morning. Rita and I set off for Clinton, taking the shortcut to the Gang Ranch only to find the road was half washed out. I had to drive down the mountain with two of the car wheels on a cattle trail, and Rita had the sorry task of running along ahead of the car to roll the big rocks off the road. It was too steep for me to put on the brakes or else I would have rolled over the bank. We pulled into Clinton at nine that night and met up with the others.

The Bluebirds orchestra from Kamloops was playing the first half. It was a good, sweet-style, Guy Lombardo type of band. The musicians were all paper men who read every note. Their sound was smooth and melodious, but a little bit dead. Our group sensed that the Clinton crowd was wanting something a bit more lively, so we fortified ourselves with a few drinks to get ready for the dance.

By midnight the place was packed and ready for action. Suddenly it was our turn. We dusted off some of our old favourites and hit it. I could hardly believe the reaction. The crowd came alive and started to hoot and holler, and away we went. Those few drinks had given us the courage to try anything, and we got away with it! We even had a three-set square dance at about four in the morning with the fiddles going full bore. The night was a great success and we thoroughly enjoyed ourselves.

After the dance we decided to have breakfast at one of the local restaurants, which was actually a little old house with four tables and a counter. A big kitchen stove sat at the back, with a huge bin of sawdust next to it to keep it lit. We were all deciding on what to eat when Doug got into a snit with the waitress. I think he was just played out, but even so he was being pretty nasty. Archie gave me a look and nodded to the sawdust bin. A moment later we both grabbed Doug and threw him into the bin, then shut and locked the door. You should have heard the hollering! We left him there and calmly ate our breakfast. The cook was scared to open the bin door when he needed more sawdust for the stove, so we let old Doug out. He emerged, covered in sawdust and madder than a wet hen. It worked, though; he was very nice to the waitress after that, but it took him an hour or two before he began speaking to us again!

I don't remember playing a dance again until some fifteen years later. Our oldest son, Adrian, was fifteen when he started to play the guitar. He'd been staying in the dormitory in Williams Lake, going to high school, and one of the girls in the dorm got him interested in music. We moved into town ourselves the next year, by which time Adrian was playing guitar with a group of his friends at parties. They soon formed a little band and played for dances. Every once in a while Adrian roped me into playing with his band if someone hadn't turned up. Next thing I knew we were playing fairly regularly around town, and I was also playing at the Elks lounge every Saturday with a couple of guys, one on steel guitar and one on drums.

By this time I had the music store, so it seemed like a natural to have a band. Bill Downie came into the store one day and I asked him if he'd be interested in joining Adrian and me. I had often heard he was a good player, but it seemed that I was always playing when he was, so I'd never been able to see him perform. He said yes and came to a practice at the house. It only took two toots on his sax before I knew he could play all right, and he was good on the banjo too. I got a hold of Jack McKay, who played drums with me at the Elks, and we had a band. We tossed around names for the group and settled on The Saddle-ites.

Bill became my right-hand man in the band. He was always dependable and on time—two features not found in abundance in musicians—and he was an excellent musician as well. Although he was self-taught and couldn't read music, he had a good ear and played

The first incarnation of "Hilary Place and The Saddle-ites." Left to right: me, Bill Downie, Jack McKay, and Adrian Place.

with ease in most any key, which is not easy to do on the sax. His banjo was a delight and complemented my old-time fiddle for a complete change of pace. Bill and his wife Martha ended up being our best friends, and if you looked forever it would be hard to find better ones.

We played in every hall in the Cariboo at some time or other, all the way from Lillooet to Wells including Lone Butte, Lac la Hache, 100 Mile House, Horsefly, Likely, McLeese Lake, Alexandria, the Cariboo Indian school, Alexis Creek, Puntzi Mountain USAF station, Kersley—along with every hall and club in Williams Lake. Our band played for regattas, stampedes, weddings, reunions, high-school proms, and even a moonlight dance at McLeese Lake, using the service station grease pit for the orchestra stand!

Our group became more proficient and modern as we went along. We got a PA system and nice red jackets, so not only did we sound pretty good but we also looked half-decent to boot, and we even had a good bunch of fans who followed us around wherever we played. We made a deal to play on a percentage with the community club at Alexandria. It was a nice small hall halfway between Williams Lake and Quesnel. The deal was we'd split the earnings with the club 70-30, with the 70 percent going to us.

The first month we played, we each made $5. Our second time brought in $30 each and the third split brought us each $90. The club couldn't stand to see us making so much money, so they cancelled the deal. This didn't slow us down at all; we just moved up the highway to Kersley, where we made a similar deal. That hall was right beside the highway and I remember on one occasion the crowd was so big that it blocked the road. The police were in a tizzy and the motorists were in a tizzy, but everyone else was having a great time.

Every so often the U.S. airforce station at Puntzi Mountain, 100 miles west of Williams Lake, hired us to play. Those were great dances, always well attended. The commanding officer would send a couple of buses into Williams Lake to bring out the local girls, who were given the royal treatment at the dances. Our band was also treated well, and the airforce provided good quarters for us to stay in. I remember that there were two MPs who policed these dances; one was Sergeant Black, who was white, and the other was Sergeant White, who was black. These were two tough customers, and the other men behaved themselves or else they were sent to the lockup.

One night at Puntzi Mountain we had Rodger Law playing with us. He had been raised not far from the station, and he knew some of the local Indians. On this particular night one of the older Indian women, dressed like the old-timers in a long Mother Hubbard dress and moccasins, with a big shawl around her broad shoulders and her black hair hanging over her face, had been sidling up toward Rodger all evening. He was getting a little tired of her constant attention. Suddenly he dropped his guitar and let out a yell you could hear all over. "That's my dad!"

Sure enough, it was. Hank Law had done himself up in the costume and had fooled everybody, including his son, for over two hours.

Another time after we finished playing at the airforce base we started back for Williams Lake. Bill and Adrian sat in the back and got into my bottle of vodka. It was a three-hour trip home, and by the time we got there the bottle was empty and Bill and Adrian were full. We saw a sign in the window of a Chinese restaurant that said, "Chinese Smorgasbord. All you can eat for $2.00 each," and decided to take them up on it. That sign was not only an international anomaly but also an invitation to disaster.

After stopping by the house to pick up my other sons, Martin and Carmen, we descended on that restaurant like a plague of locusts. The Chinese manager greeted us with smiles and bows, but his smiles quickly turned to frowns when the boys and Bill returned for thirds, then fourths.

The next day I drove by the place and there was a new sign out front. "Chinese smorgasbord discontinued."

One night we had a real good time playing at the Alkali Lake Indian reserve. They didn't have power then, so for electricity we used a rig I had that hooked up to the battery in my little panel truck. The power was on as long as the truck was parked up close to the back door with the engine running. After the dance the fellow playing guitar, Bob Reusch, was pooped out and nodded off to sleep in the back seat of the van while we put away the instruments. Margaret, one of the local Indian girls who knew Bill Downie well, was teasing Bill about being a good-looking guy, which was just what she was looking for. Bill told her he was too old, but Bob there in the backseat was just the right age for her. She let out a whoop and jumped in the van, right on top of poor old Bob. He let out a yell, and you would have sworn he thought he was going to be ravished right on the spot. Everybody howled with laughter as we watched Margaret keep Bob pinned down. The man was absolutely helpless! Margaret finally relented and let him up and we left for Williams Lake. We laughed all the way and teased Bob unmercifully. By the time we got home at five, the sun was already shining and it looked like a beautiful morning.

We ate bacon and eggs at our house, and then Bill decided to drive the rest of the way home. I asked him to stay and have a sleep, but he wanted to get back and get his chores done early. That decision nearly cost him his life. He fell asleep at the wheel and hit the ditch, his car going one way while he went the other. Bill was taken to the hospital at Williams Lake.

The hospital staff had an awful time keeping him in bed. He seemed to think he was going home and he fought the nurses, orderlies, and doctors. With no alternatives left, they asked a group of his friends to take turns sitting with him to try to keep him still. I was to watch him from midnight to six that morning. When I checked in, the nurse in charge said they were having a hell of a time with Bill; he wouldn't listen to anyone. I went into his room and sat by his bedside. He started to climb out of bed right away. "Bill! Get back in bed and stay there!" I hollered.

He froze for a moment, then crawled back under his sheets and didn't move again the rest of the night. The nurse shook her head in disbelief.

We were booked to play the Clinton Ball that year, but it was obvious that Bill would not be well enough to play. There was another band in town with some good players, so I made arrangements for two of them to play with us at Clinton, but Bill insisted on being there. He was white as a sheet and shaking, but he played all night long without missing a note. This was one more example of Bill's dedication to the band. The accident affected Bill for over a year, but he pulled through thanks to the understanding and love of his family.

There was always turnover in the band personnel. Adrian, who had been a steady, good musician (and an attraction for the girls) ever since the Saddle-ites got started, eventually married and moved away, and Bob Reusch filled his place for a while. Then along came my second son, Martin, who took up the drums and after a few lessons from Gordon Gibbons was doing all right. He got a set of Japanese drums that I had repossessed and he soon took his place in the band. Another new member was Rodger Law, an exceptional self-taught musician who could play anything on the guitar. He had the Chet Atkins finger style down pat and could play everything Chet had recorded, sounding exactly like the original. With the two new additions to the band I booked us to play a New Year's dance in Lillooet. It would be nice to get away from the home crowd, and we didn't have to drive since the train went straight there.

Both Rodger and Martin were excited about the trip. They had never been on a train before, and they had never played outside Williams Lake. We got on at Williams Lake, and Bill was going to join us at

The Williams Lake Stampede grounds in the 1950s. The grounds were originally used as a campground by the Indians who attended and competed. In the evenings they would all have their campfires burning and we would go down there and visit our friends.

Enterprise Station, which was only a half mile from his house. When we got there, Bill was nowhere in sight. Panic took over and none of us knew what to do. Searching the deserted highway across the valley, I suddenly spotted his car barrelling down the road at a hundred miles an hour. The train conductor was in our coach and I asked him to slow the train down so Bill could catch up. He did, and at the next station there was Bill, packing his sax and running for the train. Martha was left behind to shovel the car out of the snowbank where Bill had come to a lurching stop.

At Lillooet there were two cars waiting to take us to the hotel. The local drivers grabbed all our instruments and suitcases and gave us the royal treatment. Rodger and Martin thought they had hit the big time! The dance was a great success and the hall was packed with people. Ma Murray owned the Lillooet paper at the time, and I still have a copy of the write-up she gave us. She didn't get her facts right, which wasn't unusual, saying that Martin was Bill Downie's son, but it was a glowing report full of high praise for our group.

I was elected to the Williams Lake town council in 1963 and then appointed to the Stampede Association as the town's representative.

The old Squaw Hall being demolished in the 1960s.

Soon I was in charge of everything concerning the stampede except the actual rodeo. This meant I looked after the midway events, concession stands, the queen contest, and any dances held in conjunction with the stampede. This included "Squaw Hall," which had been operating for a few years by then but wasn't making any money.

Squaw Hall was originally set up because the Indians were not allowed in the white dances. (The Indians themselves came up with the name.) At first the "hall" was just a shiplap floor surrounded by fir saplings where the Indians could play some music for themselves and have a dance. By the time I got mixed up in the business, the area had evolved a bit. The floor was enlarged and a board wall about eight feet high replaced the saplings, but there was still no roof. Even the crowd had changed and was no longer exclusively Indian. The people at the white dances often headed down to Squaw Hall after their own dance closed. I had noted this and so was surprised to learn that the Stampede Association's largest take from Squaw Hall was only $150. When I brought this up at a meeting, other board members told me to take over the dance and see what I could do. The Association was in a desperate financial situation, with the bank threatening to foreclose if it could not make a substantial payment on the debt.

My plan was to have Squaw Hall operating from ten at night until six in the morning with nonstop music. In order to do this I hired a couple of extra musicians and arranged it so that between the six of us, four would be playing at all times. Rita and Martha took tickets. None of us could believe the crowds. Every night of the stampede was like a circus, always full of action. We policed the thing by getting on the public address system and talking to the crowd. For example, when somebody threw a bottle over the fence into the dance area, I grabbed the mike. "Hey you guys out there. Someone chucked a bottle in here. We don't want anybody to get hurt, so get that guy the hell out of here!"

With that they grabbed the poor guy and threw him over the fence that ran back of the hall. The only problem was they didn't know there had been some excavating done on the other side and it was a twenty-foot drop down. He ended up at the bottom with a broken leg. Tough for him, but it did stop the bottles from flying.

That Sunday we were to begin playing at one minute after midnight. A steady light rain was coming down and we figured no one would want to dance in it. We gathered at the house and decided to go down and set up anyway, play for half an hour, and see what happened. At least the orchestra stand had a roof over it so we wouldn't get too wet. When we switched on the lights to begin, we could hardly believe our eyes. There was a steady stream of car lights coming over the hill and the ticket takers were busy right away. Over 600 people paid admission to dance in a rainstorm. Not only that, they stayed right until six the next morning. One pretty young nurse from Vancouver who came up to the orchestra stand to make a request was absolutely drenched. Water was dripping off the hemline of her short red dress and her hair was plastered down like she'd been swimming. Yet she grinned up at us and said she had never enjoyed anything so much in her life.

When the show ended and the money was counted, we were in for a surprise at the post-show Stampede meeting. The reports on the rodeo revealed that it had only broken even, and the take from the concessions was just enough to meet the expenditures we had incurred to put on the Stampede. It appeared to be a grim situation, and the directors were a pretty downhearted group since it looked like there wasn't enough to make the $1500 minimum payment to the bank. The banker had obviously already figured this out, and he was not smiling. That's when I reported that Squaw Hall had made $1850.

"How much were the expenses?" the chairman asked.

"That's the net amount," I replied. "Everything is paid. This is the money for the mortgage."

Not many people know that Squaw Hall saved the stampede. It's a crying shame that over the years the organizers let the Squaw Hall dance deteriorate into a brawl until they finally cancelled it, losing a feature that helped make the Williams Lake Stampede unique. Playing for those dances was different and a whole lot of fun.

Of course playing for any audience gives me a kick, and being able to play with my own family is an even bigger kick. It's the only thing I've ever done with my boys. We haven't gone fishing or skiing or camping—we've always gone playing. After we moved to Vancouver in 1968, I didn't perform for a few years until we were hired to play the Clinton Ball in 1972 or '73. And now, 38 years after Adrian started the Saddle-ites with me, we're still playing. We've kept the name and we're proud of it, although we have been called other things along the way, everything from Saddle-sores to Saddle-itch...even as far as Saffle-nitch! But we've survived and the thing we like most about it is, we have done it together.

During all the time we played, one fan in particular always thought we were the best—Rita. She rarely missed a gig. Wherever they were, in drafty old bars, Legions, and dance halls all over the Interior and Vancouver, Rita was there to encourage and support us. When the band is introduced, she is always mentioned and receives her well-earned round of applause. Rita's love has done more to hold our band together than any one other thing, and we thank her for it.

I have never been a great player and I am certainly not a great musician, but I have thoroughly enjoyed my musical experiences and the associations they have brought me and my family. It has been my good fortune to have played with some excellent musicians over the years, especially my own sons.

There is hardly a day passes that I don't sit down at the piano and bang out some song or pick up the fiddle and squawk out an old fiddle tune. It's part of me and it probably will be until the end.

INDEX

Index

Index

PHOTO CREDITS

British Columbia Archives and Records Service (BCARS) 8758 (p. 9), A-02046 (p. 13 insert), A-3962 (p. 13), E-05599 (p. 15 top), C-08235 (p. 23), NA-04402 (p. 36), G-06383 (p. 54), H-07239 (p. 71), A-03942 (p. 101), I-50837 (p. 121), E-05558 (p. 127), I-29855 (p. 146), F-08645 (p. 160), I-51871 (p. 162), I-27096 (p., 176), E-04410 (p. 197), E-06886 (p. 218), G-03440 (p. 220), E-05233 (p. 236), E-09963 (p. 239).

"B.C. 1912" by H.J. Boam and A.G. Brown (p.19), Frank Armes (p. 30), Irene Stangoe (p. 39), *Vancouver Province* (p. 69), Dr. Sheila (Doherty) Watson collection (p. 37 and p. 82), John Roberts (p. 223), *Williams Lake Tribune* (p. 247), Gilbert A. Milne (p. 250).

All other photos are the author's.

THE COVER

June 28 '59

Dear Mrs. Place,

Under separate cover I am sending you a copy of "A Painters Country"-there is no charge so I am returning your cheque. Just a little remembrance of the happy time I had at Dog Creek fifteen years ago.

I am very sorry to hear that Charles has passed on and that you have to run the ranch alone, though I am sure that you do it very efficiently and that they all carry out your orders and adore you at the same time. I still keep working and wandering about the country. I moved here from Toronto over four years ago, to this village fifteen miles south of Ottawa. I still hear from Mrs. Cowan and Arnold Long of Williams Lake. The review of the book in Saturday Night was rather patronizing. The publishers wanted a narrative just as though I was speaking and were very pleased with it.

If I am out your way again I would love to visit you at Dog Creek.

With very best wishes to you and your family.

Sincerely,

Alex Jackson

A.Y. Jackson came to Dog Creek in 1944 or 1945. He was quite taken by the scenery in the area and enjoyed a week wandering the hills, sketching. He and my Dad would get in the old farm truck and head for the River Ranch at seven in the morning. My Dad would irrigate and do whatever needed doing; Jackson would sit on the hillside and paint. At five-thirty they would start home. Number of words spoken: about six for the day. He later sent my Mother the painting that graces the cover of this book.

THE AUTHOR

Born in England of Canadian parents in 1920, he had sense enough to leave the famed isle at six months of age and spent the rest of his life in Canada—forty years at Dog Creek, ten years at Williams Lake, and the remainder in Vancouver. He was the recipient of a somewhat doubtful primary education in a one-room schoolhouse and of an even more doubtful high-school education by correspondence. First employed by an American Christmas tree company, he soon ran the Dog Creek district for them. Along the way he owned and operated the Dog Creek Stage, Ranchers Retail, Place Music Co., Place Holdings (a real estate rental business), and several real estate ventures in Williams Lake and Vancouver. He helped organize and run the Dog Creek Community Club in Dog Creek. He was elected to School District No. 27 (Williams Lake) school board in 1950 and served for six years, the last two as chairman, and served four years on Williams Lake town council (1962-1966). During this period he was also chairman of the Court of Revision, a member of the Stampede Association, president of the Chamber of Commerce, and president of the Social Credit Party in Williams Lake.

One of the current incarnations of the Saddle-ites, playing at our 50th wedding anniversary in 1992. Carmen is at left, Adrian is in the middle, I'm on the keyboards, and Martin is the drummer.